Yo:
I was very Lucky To
have been your husband.

[pages 31-32 are a mess.
  The alphas on pages 37
  and 39 generate pure
  nonsense.]

     Hugh

Platonistic and Disenchanting Theories of Ethics

PETER LANG
New York • Washington, D.C./Baltimore • Bern
Frankfurt am Main • Berlin • Brussels • Vienna • Oxford

Hugh S. Chandler

Platonistic and Disenchanting Theories of Ethics

PETER LANG
New York • Washington, D.C./Baltimore • Bern
Frankfurt am Main • Berlin • Brussels • Vienna • Oxford

Library of Congress Cataloging-in-Publication Data

Chandler, Hugh S.
Platonistic and disenchanting theories of ethics / Hugh S. Chandler.
p. cm.
Includes bibliographical references.
1. Ethics. 2. Platonists. I. Title.
BJ1251.C472   170'.42—dc22   2006022709
ISBN 978-0-8204-8858-5

Bibliographic information published by **Die Deutsche Bibliothek**.
Die Deutsche Bibliothek lists this publication in the "Deutsche
Nationalbibliografie"; detailed bibliographic data is available
on the Internet at http://dnb.ddb.de/.

Cover design by Joshua Hanson

The paper in this book meets the guidelines for permanence and durability
of the Committee on Production Guidelines for Book Longevity
of the Council of Library Resources.

© 2007 Peter Lang Publishing, Inc., New York
29 Broadway, 18th floor, New York, NY 10006
www.peterlang.com

Printed in Germany

For Leslie, Angus,
Owen, and Elise

TABLE OF CONTENTS

• PART TWO •

PLATONISTIC AND REDUCTIVE REALISTS

ACKNOWLEDGMENTS

Vera Kauffman and Robert McKim read at least three drafts of this book and each time provided helpful comments and criticisms. Many of my students (mostly with names I have now forgotten) made important objections and suggestions. Frederick Schmitt, Timothy McCarthy, Arthur Melnick and Gary Ebbs have at various times chatted with me about some of the topics in the book. These discussions, and the encouragement these people have given me, have been invaluable.

CHAPTER ONE

Introduction

One of the tasks of a theory of ethics is to provide some sort of response to the question "How should I conduct my life?" Of course the theory need not offer an answer. After all, the question presupposes that there *is* some way we should conduct our lives. Perhaps there is no such way. That's a claim made by some ethical theorists.

Another kind of inquiry in regard to ethics takes the 'morality of common sense' as its subject matter.[1] The morality of common sense is the network of ethical beliefs and evaluations (both moral and prudential) generally accepted by the members of a given group at a given time—a 'folk-ethics'. A good theory of this sort is one that faithfully depicts the folk-ethics it undertakes to explore. If the folk-ethics has an underlying, unifying, structure, the theory should make this clear. The task is essentially descriptive and sociological (even if, as it happens, the investigator thoroughly accepts and endorses the folk ethics she is exploring).

Then, of course, there are studies of particular moral problems. Under what circumstances, if any, is abortion morally permissible? When, if ever, is it obligatory to lie, or to break one's promise? What is a 'just war'? And so on.

For the most part, this book deals with 'second order' problems, the metaphysics and epistemology of ethics, rather than with particular, down to earth, moral or ethical issues.[2] Of course the down to earth problems are important; but the larger issues are important too, and they sometimes underlie particular moral issues. One important metaethical question is whether or not there is anything to morality. Is it, perhaps, a kind of sham? What else could it be? Another such question is whether or not morality is 'reducible' (in at least some broad sense) to something other than morality. Is it reducible, or is it *sui generis?*

In one sense, it is obvious that morality is something real—our society, like most if not all others, has a folk-ethics. There is such an institution—such a practice. No one denies that. On the other hand, there are many people who regard morality as a sort of illusion. In this regard, they think, morality is something like witchcraft. Is there such a thing as witchcraft? Well, in a sense, of course there is. There have been, and still are, people who regard themselves as witches. Some people still hold the relevant beliefs and values. Groups of witches meet, and perform their rituals and ceremonies. This much is well known, and is not a matter of controversy. Nevertheless, many people think it's a kind of illusion, or sham. There are no *genuine* witches, they say, although there are people who *think* they are witches. Their gods and goddesses are, in fact, non-existent. Their 'spells' don't have paranormal effects. There is no *genuine* sorcery. Analogously, there are lots of people who hold that there is no such thing as *genuine* morality.

Reductionists hold that morality is reducible to something other than morality (for example, prudence, or the commands of God). Morality is real because it is thus reducible. *Disenchanters* (as I call them) by definition reject genuine morality.[3] They are flat-out *anti*-realists in regard to genuine morality. They think that believers in that kind of morality suffer from a peculiar illusion. I do not mean that they deny the existence of folk-ethics. But they do deny, for instance, that we have genuine moral obligations, that there are people who are in fact bad, and so on (if you see what I mean). On their view, there are no such properties, strictly speaking.

There are at least two importantly different kinds of Disenchanters, namely: '*thin rationalists*' and '*total* Disenchanters.'

Disenchanters

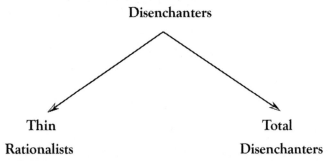

Thin

Rationalists

Total

Disenchanters

Thin rationalists typically hold that it is sometimes simply a mistake to do what so-called 'morality' requires.[4]

Suppose I am thrashing around in the sea after a disastrous shipwreck. It's stormy and dark. I think I'm about to drown. Then I spot someone clinging to a small plank. It's barely enough to keep him afloat. Surely it couldn't save both of us. The other man looks scrawny and weak. He could easily be induced to 'slip' off. No one will ever know. Should I do it? Or should I leave him alone—swim away, and almost certainly drown? Morality presumably tells me to swim away. But wouldn't that be stupid in these circumstances?[5]

Notice the assumption that behavior can be stupid (not make sense—be less than fully rational) even if it is required by so called 'morality'. A defining feature of thin rationalism is the idea that we have other standards by which to judge behavior, and that these other standards have real authority, whereas 'morality' per se has none.

When thin rationalists tell us what we should do, they are not using 'should' in a moral sense. Instead, their 'shoulds' are based on a theory about what sort of behavior makes good sense, or is smart. According to them, the basic components of ethics are to be found in areas we might not ordinarily think of as part of ethics at all. They try to work out the principles of good choice making, and use those principles in figuring out how we should behave. For thin rationalists, one might say, genuine ethics is something distinct from morality. On their view, the claims of morality (that is to say, of our local folk-ethics) are to be judged by the standards provided by the best available theory of good choice making. It may turn out that it is almost always a mistake to do what morality requires. Or we may find that the smart thing to do is practically always what morality recommends.[6] Or, as a third possibility, perhaps there are many times when it is wise to comply with morality (because of the rewards it offers), and many times when it isn't.

Thin rationalism is a disenchanting theory in that it denies the existence of genuine morality. Of course the existence of 'folk ethics' is admitted. But, as the thin rationalists see it, we may well have good reason to violate folk ethics. Thin rationalists offer a thin, instrumentalist, account of rationality, and claim that rationality in this sense ought to govern us.[7]

'Total disenchanters' hold the same general view of morality, but reject the idea that instrumental reason (or any other kind) has authority over us. For these people, the idea that we 'ought' to be rational in seeking pleasure or trying to fulfill our desires, or whatever, is as unacceptable as the idea that we have absolute moral obligations.

The principal theme of this book is the contrast between disenchanting theories and Platonistic realism in regard to full-scale more or less traditional morality. 'Realism' in regard to morality is a metaphysical doctrine. The idea is that there are objective, absolute, moral truths that are not made true by our conventions or practices, nor by our preferences, desires, decisions, commands, or acts of will.[8] In addition, many realists give top-level authority to morality. That is to say, they hold that no other considerations (prudential, aesthetic, or whatever) outrank moral considerations. Many of them also hold that the content of morality is fairly stringent—one can, they say, have a moral obligation to sacrifice one's own life or happiness. Realists who are 'Full Scale' moralists (as opposed to wishy-washy ones) hold both that morality is stringent, and that moral considerations *trump* all others.

One can coherently accept realism in regard to morality and yet hold, for instance, that it has less authority than prudence, or even than etiquette. One could hold this even though one took the content of morality to be very stringent. Could one also coherently hold that moral considerations trump all others, and yet be a nonrealist? I'm not sure about this. The claim itself may commit one to realism.

As I have said, thin rationalists offer a thin, instrumentalist, account of practical rationality—an account that disregards morality—and then they add that reason thus defined, and this alone, is the final arbiter of what ought to be done. It seems to me that moral realists in general can, and perhaps should, also accept a fairly thin account of practical rationality, with one important emendation. They should add that deliberate compliance with morality for its own sake is *not stupid*. Thus, for instance, in regard to the shipwreck case described above, realists might well insist that it is *not* foolish to refuse, on moral grounds, to drown the man clinging to that plank.

Realism in regard to morality has at least three different forms, namely Platonism, Naturalistic Realism, and Supernaturalistic Realism.

Platonists hold that at least one basic moral fact, or property, is 'irreducibly' moral. By definition, so to speak, they believe in genuine morality.

On the other hand, *Naturalistic* realists hold: (1) that there are objective moral facts, and properties, (2) that these facts and properties are, in some sense 'mind independent',[9] but, (3) that they are, or are constituted by, nothing more than various naturalistically acceptable facts and properties. I take this cluster of doctrines to characterize 'Cornell Realism.' The view is naturalistic, and (in a broad sense) reductive, hence not Platonism.

Divine Command theorists hold that moral facts and properties are, or are constituted by, facts about what God has commanded or forbidden—divine acts of will. This is a *Supernaturalistic* and reductive account of morality. Is it a form of realism? Clearly, on this view, moral facts are what they are only because of the acts of will by which God made them facts. This suggests nonrealism. On the other hand, according to this view, there are moral facts that are independent of all finite minds. This suggests realism. More or less arbitrarily, I call the Divine Command theory a form of realism.

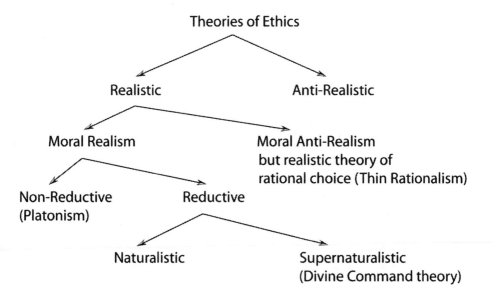

Total disenchanters are up there on the right. They are anti-realists in regard to both morality and the alleged norms of practical rationality.

Since about the beginning of the twentieth century, Platonism has generally been called 'non-naturalism' or 'anti-naturalism'.[10] This is admittedly misleading since the Divine Command theory is supernaturalistic (hence *non* and *anti* naturalistic) but is patently not a form of Platonism.

Perhaps I should add that the term 'Platonism" is almost equally misleading. By 'Platonism' I do not mean Plato's theory of ethics. Plato was a Platonist; but a good portion of Plato's ethics is rejected by at least some card-carrying Platonists. Thus, for example, Plato (and perhaps Socrates) held that no one ever knowingly does what is wrong—people only do bad things out of ignorance and confusion. Many Platonists (in my sense of the word) would deny this. They think that occasionally we are aware that we are about to do something we really shouldn't do. Or again, Plato held that we are born with certain moral ideas already implanted in us. Many Platonists would deny this.

Of course there are significant divisions among Platonists. In particular it may be useful to draw a distinction between 'intuitionists' and 'non-intuitionists.' I take David Ross to be the paradigmatic intuitionist of recent times. Ross was a Platonist. He believed that moral properties are real and not reducible to non-moral properties. In addition, he was a 'pluralist' in regard to the basic principles of ethics. That is to say, he held that there is more than one such principle. Lastly, he held that the basic principals of ethics are self-evident.[11] Let's assume that these three features define 'intuitionism.' We do not need a special term for the Platonists who aren't intuitionists.

Platonism was one of the central strands in western culture for something like twenty two hundred years. Augustine, Anselm, Aquinas, Butler, Price, Reid, Sidgwick, G. E. Moore, and Ross (to mention only a few) were Platonists. Its pedigree is impeccable; but in more recent times it has often been dismissed with something like contempt.[12]

It seems to me that Platonism is still in the running. On the other hand, as I have indicated, I am more than willing to admit that it is not the only account that deserves consideration.

Let me say a bit more about realistic accounts of moral truths, properties, relations, and so on, and those that are non-realistic. The distinction is less clear than one would like. As I have said, 'realism' in regard to morality is the view that at least some moral facts, properties, or whatever are 'mind-independent.' But what does that entail? Does it entail that if there were no minds there might still be moral facts, properties, and so on?[13]

Consider realism in regard to spoons. Can we defeat eating-utensil realists by claiming that spoons are 'mind *dependent*' in the sense that, if there had never been any minds there would be no spoons? I don't think so.

On the other hand, consider money. Money seems to be like spoons in that if there had never been any minds there would be no money. But money seems 'mind-dependent' in some stronger sense. Money is, in part, so to speak, *made to be* money by being thought of as money—by being believed to be money. Money seems more obviously a 'social construct' than spoons are.

(Note that anti-realism (e.g. idealism) in regard to money would not entail that there *is no money*.)

Let's say that moral realism is the view that (a) at least some moral properties, relations, or whatever, are 'mind independent' in the sense that they are not, even in part, *constituted by being thought of, or represented, in a certain way,*[14] and (b) that at least some moral truths are objective and are made true by states of affairs which are 'mind independent' in the same sense.

Before we move on, perhaps a few examples of (alleged) objective facts and 'facts' that are almost certainly *non-*objective would be helpful. If there are any objective facts at all, then, surely, one such fact is that elephants tend to be bigger than fleas; another is that moonlight is mostly reflected sunlight. On the other hand, we are inclined to think it is not an objective fact that anchovies taste awful ("That's just *your* opinion—I love 'em!!"), or that Woody Allan is funnier than Steve Martin.

Notice that the existence of objective truths in regard to a domain implies the existence of objective falsehoods too. It appears to be objectively false that fleas are bigger than full-grown elephants. (Perhaps it is neither objectively true nor objectively false that Steve Martin is at least as funny as Woody Allan.)

What is a reductive account of a domain? There are at least two distinct kinds of reduction. The first is the up-shot of a discovered *identity*. Typically the identification is discovered by scientific research. Water turns out to be H₂O. Heat in a gas turns out to be mean kinetic energy of the constitutive molecules. These discoveries were not the result of analyses of the meanings of the terms 'water' and 'heat', or of these concepts.

On the other hand, traditional reductions were taken to be accounts of the meaning of problematic terms, or analyses of the associated concepts. Thus, for example, some people have said that claims of the form 'x is morally wrong' just *mean* 'x has been forbidden by God'. This sort of reduction is intended to be the product of meaning or concept analysis.

In addition, I take 'constitutivity' (in one sense of the term) to be a reductive relation (in a broad sense). The Cornell Realists seem to favor 'constitutivity' (in this sense). The suggestion is that all moral properties are 'constituted' by natural properties. This theory is discussed in Chapter Sixteen.

'Ethics', in my sense, is a more inclusive term than 'morality.' Both realists in regard to morality and thin rationalists offer positive theories of ethics. To put it crudely, the realists think we should be moral and, probably, that we should be rational too. Thin rationalists think we should be rational, period.[15]

It would seem that terms of art—technical terms deliberately designed to serve a specific purpose—would, or at least should, have clear and unambiguous meanings. Nevertheless, it often happens that such terms are ambiguous and vague. And sometimes, surely, this is a good thing. Discussions of problems not yet well formulated sometimes require the (cautious) employment of sketchy language. Nevertheless, many of the key terms used in this book are much less clear and more ambiguous than they ought to be.

'Naturalism' is a good example. In one sense, 'naturalism' is just reductionism in regard to morals. As I have already suggested, there are at least two possible forms of 'reduction'. In its traditional form the theory would be that the characteristic terms of morality (or the only such terms we need to worry about) can be fully analyzed in non-moral terms. In its more up-to-date form, the claim would be that each genuine moral property or relation is one and the same thing as, or is constituted by, some non-moral property or relation. Platonists reject both old the fashioned and the newfangled forms of reductionism. That is to say, they hold that there is at least one moral property, or relation, that is neither identical with, nor constituted by, a non-moral property or relation. It is *irreducibly* moral.[16]

There is another sense of 'naturalism' in which it designates the world-view according to which there are no genuine facts other than scientific facts. Naturalists in this sense, hold that science alone, and more specifically, the hard sciences (physics, chemistry, astronomy, and so on) delineate reality. Real things are, or are reducible to, or are constituted by, the individuals, properties, and relations, mentioned in the natural laws of these sciences. In a closely related sense, 'naturalism' is the view that the methodology appropriate to science should determine what we accept as genuine knowledge and what we reject as lacking that status. Platonists definitely reject the ontological restriction and tend to reject the methodological one as well.

During the last three centuries or so, naturalism (in some blend of these last two senses) has gained ascendancy at the expense of Platonism and supernaturalism. Quine's emerging preeminence among American philosophers during the last thirty years or so has signaled its triumph in this country. Serious, respectable, up-to-date, philosophy is naturalistic; or so it seems. (On the other hand, the most popular present day philosophy—philosophy particularly appealing to humanist non-philosophers—is anti-realist, anti-naturalistic, and linked to the romantic tradition.)

My principal tasks in this book are to provide (a) a rough sketch of anti-realist disenchanting ethics (and, in particular, of thin rationalism), and (b) a rough sketch of realism (and, in particular, Platonism). I hope to show that disenchanting theories and Platonism both deserve serious consideration. They belong among the contenders for our allegiance. Unfortunately, so far as I can see, we do not know, and perhaps can never know, which, if any, of the various contenders is true.

Chapter Three contains some fairly easy, and crude, arithmetic. Those who really dislike numbers, and 'mathematical' things in general, might well just skip this chapter. In fact, perhaps it would be a good idea to skip chapters Seven and Eight too. Obviously, you can always go back to these sections later if you find you need to know something that, apparently, was discussed in them, or, perhaps, you just become curious about what it was that you missed.

NOTES

1. The phrase is derived from the work of Henry Sidgwick. It occurs frequently in *The Methods of Ethics*, (1874).

2. David O. Brink writes, "Second-order, or metaethical, issues are issues about, rather than within, morality and typically take the form of metaphysical, epistemological, semantic, or psychological issues about morality and our moral claims. In what sense, if any, is morality objective? Are there such things as moral facts or truths? Can we justify moral judgments? In what sense, if any, do moral considerations guide conduct? Is it irrational to be indifferent to moral considerations? If there are moral facts, how are they related to the natural features of agents, policies, and actions that those moral facts concern? These questions raise second-order issues...", *Moral Realism and the Foundations of Ethics*, Cambridge University Press, Cambridge, 1989, p. 1.

3. My use of the term 'disenchanters' was inspired, in part, by John McDowell's employment of it in *Mind and World*, Harvard university Press, Cambridge, Mass, 1994. For instance, "If we acquiesce in the disenchantment of nature..." etc. p. 72.

4. I do not mean to imply that only thin rationalists hold this. Most moralists would agree that it is sometimes a mistake to do what *folk-ethics* requires. So, in that sense, they would admit that the thin rationalist is right.

5. The story comes from the skeptical philosopher Carneades (c. 213–129 BC) *via* Cicero and Lactantius. Carneades famously argued both for and against 'justice.' Here he is arguing that 'justice' is often unnatural and absurd. See Lactantius, *The Divine Institutes*, translated by sister Mary F. McDonald, *The Fathers of the Church*, Vol. 49, The Catholic University of America Press, 1964. pp. 367–368. Lactantius is repeating material from Cicero's account of Carneades in *De Re Publica*. (There are a lot of gaps in the text. Lactantius supplies some of the missing pieces.) John Locke attacks Carneades' line of thought in his *Essays on the Law of Nature*, Essay eight. (Edited by W. von Leyden, Oxford, at the Clarendon Press, 1954, pp. 205–215).

6. Any actual folk-ethics (e.g. ours) is likely to contain many incompatible elements and contradictory demands. Hence, *complete* compliance with what thin rationalists admit exists (i.e. folk ethics) is likely to be logically impossible.

7. Technically, one could hold the thin theory of rationality and also be enthusiastic about genuine, full-scale, morality. Such a person would not be a disenchanter, hence not a 'thin rationalist' in my sense of the phrase. I find this combination of ideas so implausible that I simply disregard it. David Gauthier might appear to be an embarrassing counter-example to my dismissal. One might think he accepts the thin account of rationality, and uses it to justify a fairly robust kind of morality. But, in fact, his admittedly thinish rationalism is gerrymandered in such a way as to provide the alleged justification. (See, Holly Smith's "Deriving morality from rationality", in *Contractarianism and Rational Choice*, edited by Peter Vallentyne, Cambridge University Press, 1991, pp. 229–253.) So, because of this, and his support of morality, I say he not a thin rationalist.

8. For fairly recent expositions of realism in ethics, see, for example, the Preface to *Essays on Moral Realism*, edited by Geoffrey Sayre-McCord, Cornell University Press, Ithaca, 1988,

and David O. Brink's, *Moral Realism and the Foundations of Ethics*, Cambridge University Press, Cambridge, 1989, chapter 2.

9. See Brink, ibid. pp. 14–23.

10. C.D. Broad used the term 'non-naturalism' in his *Five Types of Ethical Theory*, Routledge and Kegan Paul, London, 1930. This is Brink's term too. See e.g. op cit. p. 238. A. N. Prior defended 'anti-naturalism' in his *Logic and the Basis of Ethics*, Oxford: Clarendon Press 1949.

11. See Philip Stratton-Lake's introduction to David Ross's *The Right and the Good*, Clarendon Press, Oxford, 2002, p.xiii. In Chapter 15 of his *The Dawn of Analysis*, [Princeton University Press, 2003] Scott Soames provides a helpfull discussion of Ross's intuitionism.

12. See, for instance, S. L. Hurley, *Natural Reasons*, Oxford University Press, New York, 1989, pp. 14–15.

13. From here on, my sketch of moral realism and anti-realism is based upon Frederick Schmitt's general delineation of realism and anti-realism. Schmitt's account is the most sophisticated one I know of. Nevertheless, I have introduced some departures from his theory. (See his *Truth, a Primer*, Westview Press, Boulder, 1995, pp. 6–14.)

14. Schmitt speaks of "... constitution by the mind in virtue of being represented by it," e.g. ibid. p. 12.

15. Consider the claim that "One should act rationally." Is it a moral claim? If so, then thin rationalists accept at least one moral truth. However, as I see it, thin rationalists should deny that this is a moral truth. The 'should' here isn't a moral 'should.' Perhaps it's simply the hypothetical, advice-giving sort of 'should' used, for instance, in business. ("You should invest some of your money in IBM.")

16. C. D. Broad claims, not implausibly, that the issue as to whether or not there are irreducible moral 'characteristics' is "...the first and most fundamental problem of pure ethics." See his *Five Types of Ethical Theory*, LittleField, Adams & Co., Totowa, New Jersey, 1965, p. 257.

• Part One •

Disenchanted Ethics

CHAPTER TWO

Introduction to Disenchantment Theory

Thin rationalism might reasonably be expected to have at least the following components: First, it ought to tell us what sort of choices make sense—what rational decision-making is. And, second, like any theory of ethics, it should help us evaluate folk-ethics. To what extent, if any, does it make sense to comply with the commonly accepted moral principles of our tribe? Should we try to be 'good people'? In this book I say a bit about rational decision-making but very little about the relation between disenchantment theory and folk-ethics.

As I said in the general introduction, thin rationalists hold that the objective, and basic, part of ethics is to be found in a domain we might not ordinarily think of as part of ethics at all. Traditionally, the favored domain was prudence, wisdom in looking out for oneself, skill in avoiding injury, pain, or death, and gaining pleasure or satisfying our desires. Now the claim is more likely to be that the real stuff is to be found in decision-theory, and game theory, or in the results of computer simulations of rational agents and their interactions.

Thin rationalists do not regard work in the favored domain as merely preliminary to an eventual vindication of traditional morals. If such work yields proof that we should be cooperative in certain circumstances, or that we should be forgiving, that's interesting, and perhaps important; but the relevance of the work to ethics (in a broad sense) does not depend upon such positive results. Demonstration that we should be *un*cooperative, quick to retaliate, nasty, or whatever, would be equally interesting and important from the thin rationalist point of view. Thin rationalists would regard a demonstration that we should be nasty in such and such circumstances as *exactly that*. I mean, they would conclude that *they* should be nasty in those circumstances— even though such behavior would be 'unethical' and 'immoral' (i.e. contrary to the local folk-ethics).

There have been three main phases in the history of disenchanting views. In the 'classical' phase, there were materialists and egoistic hedonists like Democritus, Aristippus, and Epicurus. Epicurism was one of the important schools of thought in, say, the year one.

In the Seventeenth century, this approach, or something much like it, revived and subsequently flourished for at least two hundred years. Hobbes, De La Mettrie, and Helvetious, are examples of the resurgence. Mark Twain is a late specimen.[1]

At the present time, disenchantment theory, and, more specifically, thin rationalism, has close ties to economic theory, decision and game theory, computer simulations, and evolutionary theory. Robert Axelrod is, I think, representative of this new phase.[2]

The chapter immediately following this introduction is on utility theory. The approach is philosophical. And, of course, we are motivated by an interest in the role of 'utility' in ethics. Some present-day versions of thin rationalism are based on the claim that we ought to maximize our utility. In part, this means that our preferences ought to yield a coherent utility function. It is easy to loose sight of this basic feature, as we wander in the forest of disenchantment theory.

The fourth chapter is on pleasure and pain. This is relevant to our topic, in part, for strictly historical reasons. Traditional disenchantment theory was simply egoistic hedonism. I sketch several possible hedonistic principles for the governance of behavior. In addition, there is a bit more about 'utility.'

The fifth chapter introduces some absurdly simple creatures—for instance 'Hobbots' (not to be confused with *Hobbits*). We look at make-believe simplistic block-diagrams of their psychological anatomy. The point is to get some idea of what sort of arraignments in a creature could generate rational (and non-rational) decisions. What might the psychological anatomy of an absurdly simple egoistic hedonist look like? And how might such a creature's various needs, wants, and desires generate its choices?

In Chapter Six we begin our examination of the sort of choices our creatures should make and the strategies it would make sense for them to adopt. We also take a preliminary look at the 'Prisoner's Dilemma.' Does it refute thin rationalism by showing that in some circumstances we should constrain our desire to maximize our own long-term happiness?

Chapter Seven deals with 'one shot' versions of the Prisoner's Dilemma and the idea that a basis for morality can be found in a transformation of character that resolves the dilemma.

Chapter Eight outlines some of the results of recent work in the exploration of cooperation, and the breakdown of cooperation, among various kinds of (simple) choice-makers. We glance at the 'Genetic Algorithm,' and evolutionary game theory.

In the ninth chapter, I discuss the thin rationalist's view of rationality. We consider some old arguments that might be taken to show that Hobbots cannot be rational, or that their self-love is somehow absurd. There is also some discussion of Platonism in regard to practical rationality.

Our basic project in Part One is to gain an understanding of Hobbots—their capacities and limitations. The hope is that this will help us understand the disenchanters.

NOTES

1. I take Helvetius and Mark Twain to have been *total* Disenchanters in that they thought that everyone, or almost everyone, more or less automatically tries to act in conformity to self-interested rationality. Thus, as they see it, there is no point to the claim that we 'ought' to do what (thin) rationality requires of us. See Helvetius, *A Treatise on Man*, and Twain's *What is Man?*

2. See Robert Axelrod, *The Evolution of Cooperation*, Basic Books, New York, 1984, and *The Complexity of Cooperation*, Princeton University Press, Princeton, New Jersey, 1997.

Utility Theory

Section One: Daniel Bernoulli

Bernoulli (1700-1782) among others, developed the idea that the *value* of a thing, or a given amount of money, for a person, is not simply a matter of its price, or amount. Value is determined by *utility* (*emolumentum*: profit, gain, advantage). Bernoulli tried to work out a way of measuring it.

Let's begin with what was, in his day, the standard theory. Consider bets on the roll of a fair die. Suppose a player, Judy, is offered the following bet. She wins $3.00 if the die comes up 5, or 6; but she looses $1.00 if it comes up 1, 2, 3, or 4. Is this a good bet? How should we work it out?

There are six relevant possible outcomes, only one of which will be actualized. The (objective, *a priori*) probability of each outcome is the same—namely 1/6. Two of the outcomes would give Judy $3.00, and the other four would cost her $1.00.

Bernoulli's procedure for determining *actuarial value*[1] is to add up the payoffs multiplied by the number of ways they can occur, and then divide the result by the total number of possible outcomes:[2]

$$\frac{(2 * \$3.00) + (4 * \text{-}\$1.00)}{2 + 4} = \$0.33....$$

Does this represent the value the bet has for Judy? Is value simply actuarial value? This, in effect, was the standard hypothesis of the scientists of Bernoulli's day.[3]

The paper in which Bernoulli describes and defends his new approach to value begins with a brief description of the accepted view and then describes a case that may help us understand what's going on.[4]

The Poor Man and the Lottery Ticket

A poor man finds a lottery ticket which guarantees its possessor a 50/50 chance of winning $600,000 dollars or gaining nothing. What is this ticket's actuarial value? Let's do it Bernoulli's way:

$$\frac{(1 * \$600000) + (1 * 0)}{1 + 1} = \$300,000$$

The actuarial value is $300,000; but would the poor man be making a stupid mistake if he sold the ticket to a rich man for $270,000? Bernoulli thinks this might be a wise decision. (He also thinks it might make good sense for the rich man to buy the ticket at that price.)[5]

The idea is that the worth of the ticket to the poor man may well be something other than its actuarial value. What matters is the utility it has for him. In figuring out how we should proceed in games of chance, and in various other dealings, we should, Bernoulli thinks, aim at maximizing expected *utility*. (So far as I know, he was the originator of this important idea.)

It isn't always easy. The utility of given amount of money (or land, or whatever) at a given time, is different for different people. And different too, in some cases, for the same person at different times. In normal circumstances, the richer a person is, the less utility a given additional amount of money offers her. Unfortunately, as Bernoulli points out, even this general rule has its exceptions. Suppose, for example, that Smith's net worth is around $600,000.00; but she desperately needs that, plus another $600,000.00 to buy her way out of jail.[6]

(Bernoulli clearly allows deviations from his general procedure for measuring utility. Hence, he does not take his procedure to *define* 'utility.')

Leaving aside peculiar situations, Bernoulli says that every increase in wealth, that is to say every increase in the quantity of goods possessed—food, clothing, land, and so on—or in the means of acquiring such goods, yields some increase in utility, and also that the amount of increase depends upon the prior wealth of the person in question. The wealthier he or she is to start with, the smaller the increase in utility. That is to say, the utility of a monetary gain is inversely proportional to one's prior wealth.

It's fairly clear what he is doing. Once he had seen that monetary gains are not, in fact, generally evaluated simply by the amounts in question, he naturally wondered how the value function (i.e. utility) actually works. What kind of a function is it? By what factors is it determined?

He regards the utility of a gain in money or goods as something dependent upon one's prior fortune, and therefore, in a sense, a *relative* matter. But it is, he thinks, *strictly objective.* A given person's utility function, at a given time, could, for instance, be determined by a team of judges appointed by the government.[7] There's nothing subjective about it. It's not 'a matter of opinion.'

As we have seen, he is confident (1) that every increase in wealth yields an increase in utility, and (2) that the amount of the increase in utility depends upon prior wealth. The greater the wealth, the smaller the increase.

He also seems to assume that the utility scale goes down to zero. He definitely holds that there a level of wealth that goes with bare subsistence. The case he sketches is, in effect, that a beggar who is able to gain $300 a year by begging might well refuse to sell his future right to acquire money, or goods, for anything less than $3,000. Hence, apparently, the beggar values his present productive capacity—his ability to beg—at something close to that amount. (Note that this beggar whose 'fortune' is presumably at least $3,000 may well have no money at all, and no tangible property other than the clothes he is wearing.)

In addition, Bernoulli holds that there is some minimal unit of increment in utility—an 'infinitesimally small' gain.

These are intuitions about utility. They provide constraints on Bernoulli's hypothesis as to the nature of the utility function. Perhaps, he tried to find the simplest function that would satisfy those constraints. In any case, it's time to have a look at his formula.[8]

The Bernoulli Utility Formula

Amounts of money (or whatever) added to one's fortune, **fort**, yield increases in utility inversely proportional to **fort**. Somehow, this, or this together with other constraints, seems to Bernoulli to suggest the following formula:

$$d\,U = b\ \frac{d\,\textbf{fort}}{\textbf{fort}}$$

The 'd **fort**' represents an increase in one's fortune. And 'd U' represents the related increase in utility. b is a constant needed to make the formula work right.

Let x be **fort** plus the increase. The formula can then be re-written as:[9]

$$U = b\,\text{Log}\ \frac{x}{\textbf{fort}}$$

Bernoulli was wrong in thinking that utility is usually, or normally, governed by this formula. We will discuss this matter later. Our present task is to see how the theory is supposed to be applicable to rational risk-taking.

Bernoulli's procedure for determining *utility* departs in two ways from the standard method for determining *actuarial* value. First, Bernoulli works with the relevant *fortune-plus-possible-gains*, rather than just the possible gains. Thus, for example, if Smith has a 50/50 chance of winning a thousand dollars, or loosing two hundred, the standard procedure would have her multiply $1,000 and –$200 by 0.5, and add up the results. The Bernoulli procedure, on the other hand, requires Smith to take her prior fortune into account. Suppose she is 'worth' about one hundred thousand dollars. In that case, Bernoulli regards the possible outcomes of the bet as $101,000 and $99800. Those are the figures Smith should use.

Second, Bernoulli, in effect, counts up the number of relevant, equiprobable, possible outcomes, n, and finds the product of the n roots of the pay-offs given those outcomes. Thus, in the case just considered, he would have Smith multiply the square root of $101,000 by the square root of $99,800.

$$\sqrt{101000}\ *\sqrt{99800}\ = 317.805\ *\ 315.911 = 100398.21$$

She's not done yet. There is one more step. Remember, we have been working with fortunes-plus-pay-offs. In order to get the value (i.e. utility score) of the wager itself, Smith's fortune (the $100,000) must be subtracted from the result just obtained.

$$\$100,398.21 - \$100,000 = \$398.21$$

Let's try this procedure on some other wagers. (The trick is easy once one gets the hang of it.) Here is a case Bernoulli himself works through. Two men each have an initial fortune of one hundred ducats.[10] One of them has proposed the following game. Each will contribute fifty ducats to the pot. A fair coin will be tossed, winner take all. What is the expected utility?

If they decide to play, the situation will unfold as follows. Each player will put half his fortune on the table. At that point, they will each have fifty ducats. And each has a 50/50 chance of winning an additional one hundred ducats, or nothing. That is to say, he will end up with one hundred and fifty ducats or just fifty. So, when they put their money on the table, the expected value (i.e. utility) of the situation is:

$$\sqrt{50} \ * \sqrt{150} \ = 7.07 * 12.25 = 86.60$$

But the game hasn't started. There's no money in the pot. To arrive at the expected utility of entering the game, we have to subtract the player's initial wealth (100 ducats). Hence, the 'expected loss' (as Bernoulli calls it)[11] is:

$$86.60 - 100 = -13.40$$

The smaller proportion of one's total wealth one puts at risk in this way, the less imprudent one is. Suppose, for example, that one of the players in the game initially had a fortune of 200 ducats. In that case, his expected loss would be:

$$(\sqrt{150} \ * \sqrt{250} \ ) - 200 = -6.33$$

Both of these cases are taken from Bernoulli. Let's go a bit further. Pretend the wealthy player began with 500 ducats:

$$(\sqrt{450} \ * \sqrt{550} \ ) - 500 = -2.49$$

Imagine, on the other hand, that a relatively poor player entered the game with only 75 ducats:

$$(\sqrt{25} * \sqrt{125}) - 75 = -19.1$$

Suppose now that *three* people play the game—and only one can win. Now the pot is 150 ducats, and each player has just one chance in three of getting it. Let's say the initial fortunes are still 100 ducats each. Notice that there are now *three* equiprobable possible outcomes: A wins; but B and C lose. B wins; A and C lose, or C wins while A and B lose. Hence each player has one way of winning and two of loosing. Bernoulli would now have us multiply the *cube* roots of possible outcomes:

$$(\sqrt[3]{200} * \sqrt[3]{50} * \sqrt[3]{50}) - 100 = (5.848 * 3.684 * 3.684) - 100$$
$$= 79.37 - 100$$
$$= -20.63$$

Well, actually, he wouldn't do it quite this way. He prefers a more tidy procedure, namely, to raise each distinct amount of pay-off to the power of the number of ways it can be obtained, and then proceed as before. Thus he would multiply the cube root of 200 (to the power of one—i.e. leave it alone) by the cube root of 50 squared. It's just another way of doing the same thing, but nicer.

$$(\sqrt[3]{200^1} * \sqrt[3]{50^2}) - 100 = 79.37 - 100 = -20.63$$

Not too surprisingly, the expected loss in this game is worse than in the two person version.

Four players make it worse yet:

$$(\sqrt[4]{250^1} * \sqrt[4]{50^3}) - 100 = 74.77 - 100 = -25.23$$

Note that these bets are all perfectly *fair*. Consider this last game. Each player has one chance in three of winning 150 ducats, and two chances out of three of gaining nothing. So the actuarial value is:

$$(\frac{1}{3} * 150) + (\frac{2}{3} * 0) = 50 + 0 = 50$$

Or: doing it Bernoulli's way:

$$\frac{(1 * 150) + (2 * 0)}{1 + 2} = 50$$

Since each player pays, so to speak, 50 ducats to play, it all comes out even.

As Bernoulli points out, *all* wagers that are 'fair' in this 'it all comes out even' sense are bad bets, as measured by Bernoulli's utility function. People who accept such wagers 'act irrationally,' he says[12]

The St Petersburg Paradox

As I said at the start of the chapter, this is the problem that made Bernoulli think hard about the value of risky monetary gains, and led him to distinguish 'utility' from actuarial value. The problem was invented by Bernoulli's cousin, Nicolas Bernoulli—another mathematician.

Peter will flip a fair coin. If it lands heads, he will give Paul one ducat, and the game ends. If it lands tails, Peter will toss it again. And, again, if it lands heads, he will give Paul his winnings and the game ends. But, if this occurs on the second toss, Paul wins *two* ducats. On the other hand, if the coin lands tails on the second toss, Peter flips it a third time. And so on, the pay-off doubling for each additional toss in the sequence.[13]

The problem is that (a) the expected actuarial value of the game seems to be *infinite*. That is to say, it would seem we should be willing to pay any finite amount—all we have—to play. But (b), as Nicolas said, any halfway reasonable person would gladly sell his or her chance to play for just twenty ducats (say $600).

The probability of the coin landing heads on the first toss is 1/2. The probability of the coin landing tails on the first toss, and heads on the second is 1/4. And so on. Thus, the actuarial value of the game appears to be:

$$(\frac{1}{2} * 1) + (\frac{1}{4} * 2) + (\frac{1}{8} * 4) + (\frac{1}{16} * 8) + (\frac{1}{32} * 16) + \ldots\ldots\infty$$

One just goes on adding half-ducats forever.

Bernoulli's solution to the problem, as you may have guessed, is based upon the idea that the *utility* of the alleged possible pay-offs doesn't double with each additional toss.

Unfortunately, his way of dealing with probability led him into non-sense.[14] He thinks we are looking at an infinite number of cases, N, such that in half of them, $N/2$, the player wins one ducat, in one quarter, $N/4$, the player wins two ducats, and so on. But, of course, infinity cannot be halved, quartered, or whatever.

Here is a slightly different approach. Suppose some frivolous god, say Hermes, enjoys playing truncated versions of the St Petersburg game with mortals.[15] Sometimes it's a one-toss game. A fair coin is tossed. If it comes down heads, the mortal wins one ducat. If it comes down tails, she wins nothing.

On other occasions, Hermes offers someone a possible-two-toss game. If the coin lands tails on the first toss, it is tossed again, and this time the player either wins two ducats, or nothing. End of game. Or he offers a possible three toss game, or ... ; and so it goes for various finite numbers of possible tosses. Once in a while Hermes invites someone to play the full-scale St Petersburg game.

Consider the series of games: one toss, possibly two tosses, possibly three tosses, and so on. Pretend the mortals who play these games all have a prior fortune of exactly one hundred ducats. What is the expected Bernoulli-utility of the games? (The hypothesis is that as we work our way into this series, we narrow in on the worth of the full-scale game.)

The one-toss game has a familiar look. The mortal who plays it either ends up with her original fortune or with that plus one ducat. These two outcomes are equally likely. Hence we have:

$$(\sqrt{100} \, {}^* \sqrt{101} \,) - 100 = .499$$

The possible-two-toss game looks like this:

$$(\sqrt{101} \quad {}^* \sqrt[4]{102} \quad {}^* \sqrt[4]{100} \quad) - 100 = .998$$

Possible-three-toss:

$$(\sqrt{101} \quad {}^* \sqrt[4]{102} \quad {}^* \sqrt[8]{104} \quad {}^* \sqrt[8]{100} \,) - 100 = 1.494$$

As we go further into the series, the expected B-utility seems to climb endlessly towards something just a little above 4.38937 ducats. (Bernoulli says the value of the St Petersburg game for a person with a fortune of one hundred ducats is approximately four ducats.[16])

If a player begins with *no fortune at all*, the relevant scores approach two. (Bernoulli says the (B) value of the St Petersburg game for the no-fortune person would be precisely two ducats. I take it he has this exactly right—as a claim about B-value.)

For a person worth ten ducats, the series approaches something just over 3.04314. (Bernoulli says for such people the game is worth about three ducats.)

A fortune of a thousand ducats heads off towards somewhere not far above 5.97225. (Bernoulli says approximately six.)

Finally, for people with a million ducats (roughly thirty million dollars), the series seems to stretch towards something just above 10.9372. We are still a long, long, way from the *twenty* ducats Nicolas mentions.

Objections to Bernoulli's Utility Function

1. There are no end of functions that would satisfy the 'intuitive constraints' mentioned earlier in the chapter. Bernoulli himself provides a note from a mathematician named Gabriel Cramer who suggested one or two alternatives. Perhaps, for instance, 'moral value' is directly proportional to the *square root* of the 'mathematical quantities.'[17] Bernoulli says that he and Cramer hold the same 'basic principal,' namely that we should evaluate money by the utility it yields us. Thus it seems clear that he takes this to be the most important part of his theory—more important than the particular function he recommends.

2. Bernoulli himself points out that there are cases in which the utility of money for a person is not determined by his, or her, fortune. (Remember the case of the wealthy prisoner.) He thinks these exceptions are very rare; but even one exception would suffice to show that he has not yet discovered what determines utility.

   According to Bernoulli's calculations, *all* 'mathematically' fair wagers are imprudent. I take this to suggest that his calculations are, in many cases, off the mark. That is to say, cases in which it is perfectly reasonable to accept a fair risk seem common.

3. Bernoulli's utility function has no upper bound. Under these conditions it is possible to construct a revised version of the St Petersburg puzzle just as vexing as the first.[18] Consider, for instance, the version proposed by Jeffrey.[19] In this game, the payoff goes up by $2^{(2^n)}$ at each toss: $4 for heads on the first toss, $16 for heads on the second, $256 for heads on the third, and so on.

Given this system of pay-offs, the B utility of the games explodes. Here are the expected B utility scores for the first ten truncated Super St Petersburg games offered to someone with a fortune of $100:

-89.802, -66.5319, -30.2471, 39.5191, 179.038, 458.077, 1016.15, 2132.31, 4364.61, 8829.23

I take it that very few people would be willing to pay their entire fortune to play the Super St Petersburg game. (Remember: there's a 50/50 chance of winning just $4.00; one chance in four of winning $16.00; one chance in eight of winning $256.00, one chance in sixteen of winning $65,536.00 and so on.) Even in this super form, the game doesn't have *infinite* expected utility.

Bernoulli didn't resolve the basic puzzle.

What **Did** Bernoulli Get Right?

1. As he himself saw, the most important feature of his theory is the idea that the value of a 'game', a risky deal, or some object, to a person is not simply its price, or its actuarial value. The important thing is '*utility*.'
2. Bernoulli was plainly aware of the fact that money, and many other things, exhibit (or tend to exhibit) 'diminishing marginal utility.' Generally speaking, twice as much doesn't mean twice as good.
3. He also saw that people have *different* utility functions. (He thought this was because their fortunes differ.)

Section Two: Frank Ramsey

In just seven pages of an important paper written when he was twenty three, Ramsey (1903-1930) outlined a way of measuring utility.[20] (Ramsey was a disenchanter in regard to ethics.[21])

The paper ("Truth and Probability") develops a theory of 'partial belief,' or 'degrees of belief.' We would now call it 'subjective probability.' Part of his task is to show how to measure degrees of belief given various preferences. In order to do this, he needs an account of utility. Degrees of utility and degrees of belief are tightly linked in Ramsey's theory.

As I understand it, Ramsey thinks of the task of measuring utility as a two-part job. First he must work out a way of assigning a creature's 'values' precise positions in an order of magnitude.[22] Then he must show how these values can be correlated with real numbers.

He adopts a somewhat simplistic, partly fictional, psychological theory which, he says, is false. The theory is that our behavior is determined by our beliefs and desires. We do what we think is most likely to bring about the states of affairs we want brought about. It's an *approximate* truth in regard to *some* of our behavior.

(Why does he say the theory is false? Apparently he believes that some of our behavior is determined by subconscious factors. Perhaps he holds that we sometimes act in ways that seem designed to bring about situations we definitely *don't* want.)

Some of the things we want are wanted simply as means to other things. For instance, someone might want to go to Chicago, not as an end in itself, but in order to meet a friend, or go to a special concert. The things that are desired for themselves, and not just as means, Ramsey calls 'goods.' And the things we avoid, not as a way of dodging, or preventing, something else, but because of what they are in themselves, he calls 'bad.' It is important to keep in mind that he is *not* using these terms in their 'ethical' or 'moral' sense. Things are 'good,' or 'bad,' in Ramsey's usage *relative to a particular person* (and, I assume, a particular time). To say that x is 'good' (with respect to Jones, at the present time) is just to say she now desires x for its own sake.

He is not espousing egoistic hedonism. He holds that there are many different kinds of good things and bad—not just our own pleasures and pains, or our own anything. Smith may very much want *Jones* to be happy, and visa versa. And they may want these things, not as means to something else (e.g. their own satisfaction), but as ends in themselves. It isn't egoism, and it isn't hedonism. One tends to think: "Well, Smith and Jones want to have their own desires fulfilled, and *that's* egoistic;" but this is a mistake.

Here, then, is the crude, preliminary, version of Ramsey's simplistic, false, hypothesis: we desire various goods, and want to avoid various evils, and we always act in ways we believe likely to lead to those goods and not to those evils.

Round One

Pretend that goods and evils are additive and immediately measurable in some numerical way. And imagine a rational creature for whom there is nothing that seems likely or unlikely—a good bet or a bad one. All the creatures' opinions are held as flat-out certainties. Under these conditions, the simplistic theory says that the creature always does what it believes will in fact lead to the largest sum of good (relative to itself).[23]

Pretend that George is such a creature, and that he now faces a choice between (a) having three cups of coffee or (b) buying a new necktie for his son Gus. Here is how George sees the problem:

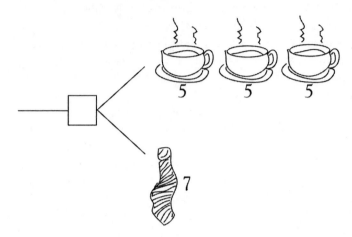

The square represents the 'place' where the decision must be made. Each cup scores 5 goodness points. Buying the necktie for Gus scores 7. Since 15 is more than 7, George drinks three cups of coffee.

Not counting the simplistic hypothesis itself, there are, in this fantasy, at least two other substantial departures from real life. Perhaps the most glaring is George's lack of probabilistic beliefs—the fact that there is no proposition, p, such that he half believes p, or thinks there's a good chance that p.

The other is the pretense that goods and evils are 'additive.' My impression is that Ramsey accepts G. E. Moore's notion of 'organic unity,' which is, in part, a *denial* of the claim that goods and evils are additive.[24] The issue is interesting, and sometimes crucial in thinking about ethics.

Take the pleasure of winning a tennis match. One might think of it as having several 'components.' (Moore tends to think of things this way.) There is, for instance, the publicly observable event: Jones wins; Smith leaps over the net and congratulates her. Then there is Jones' conscious experience of these events, and her pleasure. Suppose the 'goodness' score for the whole package is 100. (Never mind what this means.) Must the individual scores of the components add up to 100?

Imagine Jones reasoning as follows: "I find the whole package very desirable. But when I subtract the pleasure—when I imagine the rest, *without any pleasure*—the remainder seems to me worthless. So it must be the *pleasure* I value, not the rest." Is this good reasoning?[25]

For Moore, a whole is 'organic,' if, and only if, its intrinsic value is *not* the sum of the values of its parts.[26] He is an absolutist in these matters. The values under consideration are, on his view, objective and absolute. A given 'whole' either is, or is not, 'organic.'

This is not Ramsey's view. But I do take Ramsey to hold that sometimes the value of a whole to a person J, at time t, is greater than, or less than, the sum of the values of its parts; and that there need not be anything irrational in J's valuing things in this way. (Note that this set-up may be an *objective fact*. I mean, it may be an objective fact that W is 'organic,' in a relativised Moorian sense, to J at t.)

In this relativised form, the Moorian doctrine seems plausible. In fact, I think it's true. 'Subjective' goods and evils are *not*, by nature, additive. Moore's absolutist version of the doctrine is more controversial.

Round Two

In this round, we retain the assumptions that goods are additive and immediately measurable in some numerical way; but we give up (temporarily) the requirement that all of the creature's beliefs are 'certain.' In this round our creature has probabilistic beliefs.

Ramsey suggests, as a 'psychological law', that we always act in such a way as to *maximize expected good*. Here is George again, under the new assumptions. He now faces a choice between buying the necktie for Gus, or going to visit Gertrude. He thinks that if Gertrude is wide-awake, the visit will score 10; if not, just 4. George's degree of belief that she will be less than wide-awake is about 0.6. Hence:

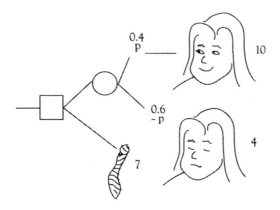

The square, again, represents the point at which George faces his options, and makes his choice. The circle represents a risky place to be—a point in time at which just one of two things may happen, and which one happens isn't up to George.

As a maximizer of expected good (relative to himself) George (perhaps subconsciously) multiplies 0.4 times 10, and 0.6 times 4, and sums the result. The expected good of going to see Gertrude is only 6.4. So George buys Gus the tie.

Round Three[27]

We now drop the assumption that goods and evils are additive and immediately mathematically measurable,[28] but re-adopt the supposition that our creature has 'certain' beliefs, not probabilistic ones. The project in this round is to work our way towards an ordinal utility scale given just the creature's preferences (or choices), and no 'risky' options.

Suppose an omnipotent being were to show a rational creature of the relevant sort all of the various 'possible worlds,' in pairs, and invite it to say which, if any, of each pair it would prefer.

The 'possible worlds' are different possible 'courses of the world,' 'totalities of events,' 'ultimate organic unities,' among which the creature must choose.[29] I have the impression that Ramsey is thinking, at least in part, of alternative futures branching from the present-day actual world.

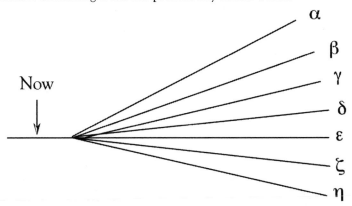

At the end of the experiment (?!), we, or the omnipotent being, or the creature itself, can work out an order of merit (ordinal ranking) for all the worlds as evaluated by the creature.[30]

Let's try it. Consider just four worlds: **α, β, γ, δ**. The possible pairings of these worlds are offered for the creature's appraisal:

$$\begin{array}{cc} \text{δ} & \text{δ} \\ \text{δ} & \text{δ} \\ \text{δ} & \text{δ} \\ \text{δ} & \text{δ} \\ \text{δ} & \text{δ} \\ \text{δ} & \text{δ} \end{array}$$

Take 'x > y ' to mean 'x is preferred to y', and 'x = y' to mean that the creature doesn't prefer x to y, and doesn't prefer y to x—doesn't, in fact, care which one is actualized.

Pretend the creatures pair-wise preferences are as follows:

$$\begin{array}{c} \text{δ} > \text{δ} \\ \text{δ} > \text{δ} \\ \text{δ} > \text{δ} \\ \text{δ} > \text{δ} \\ \text{δ} = \text{δ} \\ \text{δ} > \text{δ} \end{array}$$

Given this set of preferences, the creature itself, and anyone else who is interested and clever, can form the appropriate ordinal utility scale.

$$\gamma \quad (3)$$
$$\alpha \quad (2)$$
$$\beta, \delta \quad (1)$$

This scaling just says that δ is preferred to the other three worlds, that δ comes next, and that δ and δ tie for last place. It should *not* be taken to say, for instance, that δ is halfway between δ and δ in value.

Ramsey assumes that the creature's preferences are *rational*. Some sets of pair-wise preferences would not yield an ordinal scale of values.

Round Four

In this round, we allow our creature to have probabilistic beliefs. The general question is how can preferences be used to identify degrees of belief? More specifically, Ramsey suggests a way to use our creature's preferences to identify beliefs it holds to degree 0.5.

Loosely speaking, Ramsey's procedure is a refinement of the usual test: offer the believer various bets, and see what sort of odds he or she is willing to take. Suppose Smith thinks it will rain tomorrow. We offer him the following bet: We will give him $10 if it rains. He will give us $40 if it doesn't. Is he *that* certain it will rain?

Ramsey says the usual test is fundamentally sound, but inaccurate, and not general enough.[31] It is inaccurate because (a) money exhibits diminishing marginal utility, and (b) some people are pleasantly excited by betting, or dislike it. This affects their preferences.

Back to our creature. Suppose we want to test the degree of its belief that p. Ramsey recommends the following general procedure: Ask the creature whether it would prefer world α (whether or not p is true) or world α if p is true, and α if p is false.[32]

Suppose the creature is absolutely sure p is true. In that case, it can disregard the α world, and just consider whether it prefers α to α, or visa versa, or is indifferent between the two.

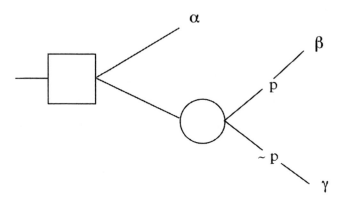

On the other hand, suppose the creature thinks p is just as likely to be false as true—it is equally prepared to bet either way. In that case, it will have to compare both α and α with α.

The general test procedure looks promising. But there is a problem in regard to p. The creature may have strong preferences in regard to p itself. This possibility makes the test unreliable.

To avoid this complication, Ramsey stipulates that p is to be an 'ethically neutral' proposition (with respect to the creature now). An 'atomic' proposition, p, is 'ethically neutral' if for every pair of possible worlds, differing only in that in one p is true and in the other p is false, both worlds are of equal value (to the creature now).

Molecular propositions (conjuncts, disjuncts, if-then statements, and the like) are ethically neutral if all their component propositions are ethically neutral.[33]

We are now ready to explain what it is to have 0.5 degrees of belief in an ethically neutral proposition—i.e. to give such a proposition a 50/50 chance of being right. A creature has 0.5 degrees of belief in ethically neutral proposition, p, if (a) the creature is indifferent between option 1 and option 2, and (b) the creature either prefers world α to $\overline{\alpha}$, or $\overline{\alpha}$ to α.

It's easy to see how this works. By hypothesis, the creature prefers α to $\overline{\alpha}$. If it thought p was more likely than not-p, it would prefer option 2. And, if it thought not-p was more likely than p, it would prefer option 1. But it is *indifferent* between option 1 and option 2. So it must take p and not-p to be equally good bets.

Let's try it. The proposition to be tested is: "Scott was the author of *Waverley*." First the omnipotent being checks our creature on all the pairs of possible worlds that differ only in regard to whether or not Scott wrote *Waverley* (and the things entailed by that difference). It turns out that the proposition is ethically neutral for the creature. Thus it can be used in the '0.5 degrees of belief' test. But, before we do that, we need a pair of worlds such that the creature prefers one to the other. Presumably, α and $\overline{\alpha}$ have this property. We run the '0.5' test using that pair. It turns out that the creature is indifferent between the options, and therefore can be said to have 0.5 degrees of belief in the *Waverley* proposition.

Note that we have derived a subjective probability from pure preferences. But, of course, we needed more than just preferences in regard to pairs of possible worlds; we needed a *lack of* preference between a pair of risky options. That was an essential feature of the trick.

Ramsey supposes (by an axiom) that if an ethically neutral proposition, p, passes the '0.5' test in regard to one of the creature's un-equal utility world-pairs, (e.g. α $\overline{\alpha}$) it would do so in regard to any such pair.[34]

We are now able to move beyond a merely ordinal ranking of the possible worlds. We do it by defining what it is for the difference in value between one pair of worlds ($\alpha\overline{\alpha}$) to be equal to the difference between another pair ($\overline{\alpha}\alpha$).

Let 'W' be a proposition which is ethically neutral for the creature and is believed to 0.5 degrees (e.g. 'Scott was the author of *Waverley*'). If the creature is indifferent with respect to options 1 and 2—doesn't prefer either one to the other—then the difference in value between α and $\overline{\alpha}$ must equal the difference between $\overline{\alpha}$ and α.

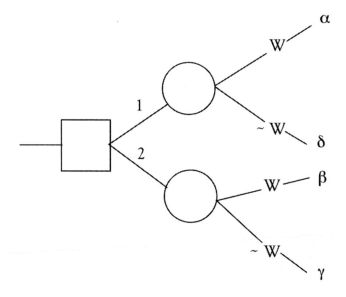

Each option offers the creature a chance of getting either the best of one pair, or the worst of the other.

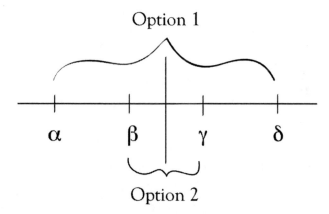

Hence, if the value 'distance' between the worlds in each of the pairs is the same, the medians of the test options (i.e. their expected values) will be the same too.

Otherwise not. For instance:

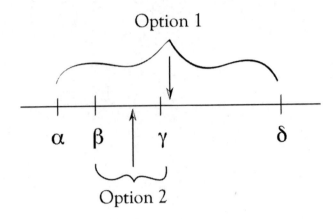

Ramsey defines a 'value' (for a creature at a time) as the set of worlds equally preferable to a given possible world. Thus, for example, taking α as our starting point (so to speak), we look for a world, w, which is preferred to α and such that the difference in value between it and α is the same as that between α and α. The set of such worlds (including α, of course) is a particular 'value.' Values are sets of possible worlds.

If any world in one of these sets, S_1, is preferable to a world in a different set, S_2, then, presumably, *any* world in S_1 is preferable to any world in S_2. Given that α is preferable to α, all the worlds of the same value as α are preferable to the worlds of the same value as α. This is expressed by saying that the value of world α is 'greater than' the value of α.

A set of axioms wraps the job up, and shows that the values can be correlated with real numbers. (See the next section of this chapter, item (3).)

Let me just sketch what I take to be Ramsey's way of measuring *degrees of belief*. Assume that we have a nice set of real numbers representing the creature's evaluation of the possible worlds. (I take it we are also to assume that α > α > α) And think, again, of this general set-up:

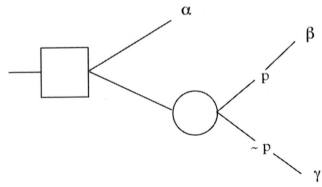

Suppose the creature is indifferent between these two options (i.e. between the omnipotent being making α the real world or making α the real world if p is true, and α the real world if p is false).[35] If the creature is thus indifferent, then the value of α (for the creature now) must be equal to the expected value of the risky option.

$$\alpha = \text{Deg}(p) * \alpha + (\text{Deg}(\neg p)) * \alpha$$

Via some algebra, this says, in effect, that we can use the ratio of α - α to α - α to measure the creature's degree of belief that p.

$$\text{Deg}(p) = \frac{\alpha - \alpha}{\alpha - \alpha}$$

Thus, for example, if α = 100, α = 50, and α = 0, and the creature is indifferent between α for certain and the risky option, then its degree of belief that p must be 0.5.

Or, to take another example, given that α = 85, α = 35, and α = 34, and the same indifference as before, the creature's degree of belief that p is roughly 0.196.

Conclusions and Left-Overs

(a)   Ramsey has, I think, shown that a creature's utility scale can be defined in terms of the creature's preferences. He has also shown that the degree to which the creature believes things is determined by its preferences. To put it in slogan form: *Preference determines utility and subjective probability.* (Alternative formulation: Utility and subjective probability supervene on preference.)

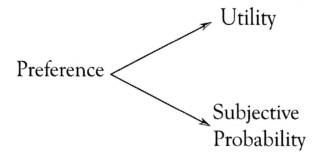

As a way of thinking about belief, desire, and the behavior of rational creatures, this picture has been beneficial. Behaviorists and logical positivists are especially likely to find it attractive.

On the other hand, here is another slogan: *Utility and subjective probability together determine preference.* (Preference supervenes on utility plus subjective probability.)

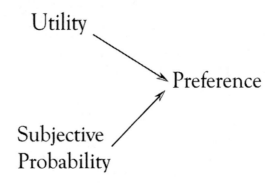

People who are trying to design good decision-makers, business people, and those attached to the 'first person' point of view, are likely to picture the relationship among the concepts this way.

So which is right? Which way better reveals the natures of these three inter-related things? The answer is that the determination (or supervenience) *goes both ways.* Neither relationship is more basic, or revealing, than the other.

(b) All *Platonists* in regard to morality hold that some possible worlds are better than others. Or, more accurately, all Platonists who can tolerate talk about 'possible worlds' do. For instance, many of them would say that pairs of worlds that differ only in that there is much less justice in one than in the other differ in value. But, of course, these Platonists do *not* think this is a matter of value *relative to them*, or relative to anyone else.

Suppose Ramsey were to ask Moore which of these worlds he preferred. It's a good bet that Moore would find the question puzzling. Is Ramsey inviting Moore to decide which world is (objectively, absolutely) *better?* Or is he being invited to say which one he, Moore, would like to see actualized? These need not be one and the same.

As I see it, utility theory is available to everyone. It is not the special property of thin rationalists. So it ought to be possible for Platonists—even mad-dog Platonists like Moore—to embrace it. Utility theory is, or ought to be, *neutral.*

Nevertheless, it seems clear that Platonists must be very cautious, and guarded, in their acceptance of it. From their point of view, the theory tends to blur some crucial distinctions.

(c) For those who are interested in such things, here (partly fleshed out and translated into prose) are Ramsey's eight axioms for a rational creature's values:

> (1) There is at least one ethically neutral proposition, p, which the creature believes to degree 0.5.
> (2) If p and q are propositions of this kind and the creature is indifferent between the options
>
>> (i) α if p, α if not-p, and
>> (ii) α if p, α if not-p,
>> then the creature is also indifferent between the options
>> (iii) α if q, α if not-q, and
>> (iv) α if q, α if not-q.
>
>> By definition: under these conditions, $\alpha\alpha = \alpha\alpha$

(3) If the creature is indifferent between option A and option B, and between option B and option C, then the creature is indifferent between option A and option C. (Indifference between options is transitive.)
(4) If $\alpha\alpha = \alpha\alpha$, and $\alpha\alpha = \alpha\alpha$, then $\alpha\alpha = \alpha\alpha$. (Equality of difference in value is transitive.)
(5) For every trio of possible worlds, α, α, α, there exists exactly one world, x, such that $\alpha x = \alpha\alpha$
(6) For every pair of worlds, α, α, there exists exactly one world, x, such that $\alpha x = x\alpha$.
(7) Axiom of continuity.
(8) Axiom of Archimedes. (Perhaps something like this: If the difference in value between one pair of worlds, $\alpha\alpha$, is greater than the difference between another pair, $\alpha\alpha$, then the surplus by which the one exceeds the other, is itself the difference in value between a pair of possible worlds. The point is that there are no *indivisible* differences in value.)

(d) It is far from obvious that these axioms provide the most accurate way of representing values. The values of some creatures seem much less precise.

Imagine a simple creature that has just two definite value categories for the possible worlds, 'good' (score: 1), 'bad' (score: 0). There are infinitely many worlds in each of the two classes.

When asked which of two good worlds it prefers, the creature expresses complete indifference, and, similarly, all bad worlds are equally bad.

In addition there are worlds that fall somewhere *in-between* good and bad. When confronted with these worlds, the creature hesitates, and waffles. Thus, for instance, when forced to make a decision, the creature classifies world μ as *good* (and thus preferable to any bad world) about 50% of the time, and as *bad* (and worse than any good world) the other 50%. In a case like this, we might say that the class of good worlds and the class of bad are 'fuzzy.' And we might take the percentage of times a world gets classified as good as showing the *degree*, so to speak, to which the world is a member of the fuzzy class.

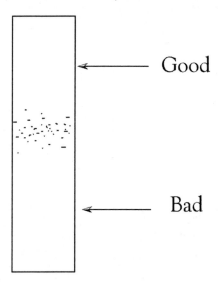

Imagine a 'smart' bulldozer that works in a gravel-pit. It is equipped with a devise—namely, a sieve—that enables it to distinguish 'good' pebbles from 'bad.' Of course there are pebbles that sometimes go through (in the course of the standard 10 second shaking) and sometimes don't.

Note that we have shifted to the 'engineering/first-person' point of view. We are considering how a creature assigns a value to a pebble (or a world) and thus decides whether it is better or worse than other pebbles (or worlds).

Is a world the creature tends to classify as good about 75% of the time *better* than one that gets that classification only about 73% of the time? That's not at all clear. Perhaps the world is just easier to classify.

Things can get more complex. Thus, for instance, there may be creatures that have three fuzzy evaluative classes.

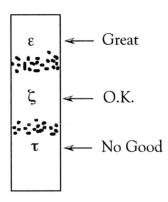

And so on.

(e) What is 'preference'? There are at least three theories:

(1) *The behaviorist theory.* 'Preference' is just a propensity, or disposition, to choose in a certain way—a habit of choosing in a particular way. Patrick Maher has produced two plausible counter-examples to this approach. Here is one of them: Suppose you know several days in advance that you are going to have a choice between option *f* and option *g*, but you are now, and will remain, indifferent between these options. Nevertheless, suppose you decide to choose option *g* (for no reason other than that you are going to have to make a choice here. You pick *g* at random.) Having done this, you have a disposition to choose *g* (because of your decision to do so); but, presumably, you are still indifferent between the two.[36]

(2) *The phenomenological theory.* Von Neumann and Morgenstern endorse the positivist principal that every measurability claim must be based on an immediate sensation, which requires no further analysis. Utility, they say, is based on the immediate sensation of preference.[37]

(3) Then, I guess, there are people who say that 'preference' is defined by its role in the theory we have been describing, and by such facts as that it entails a 'disposition to choose.'

Section (d) above, suggests the following question: Given that a person, say Jones, prefers x to y, must this fact be *immediately accessible* to Jones? Is it like pleasure and pain in this regard? Can Jones prefer x to y without knowing it?

To go at this from a different direction, is it possible for Jones to prefer x to y even though it is, for all practical purposes, impossible for Jones to discover this fact? (I am thinking of theories of preference which would force us to say, for instance, that Jones prefers possible world αto α even though there is no way he could come to know this. Axiom 5 may have this consequence.)

NOTES

1. Bernoulli doesn't use this phrase.

2. These days the procedure would be to multiply probabilities times pay-offs and sum the result. In the present case: $(2/6 * \$3.00) + (4/6 * -\$1.00)$.

3. Or so he claims; see Alfred Page (ed.) (1968) *Utility Theory: A Book of Readings*, 'Exposition of a New Theory on the Measurement of Risk', p. 204.

4. Ibid. pp. 199–214. The translation from the Latin original is by Louise Sommer.

5. I have changed the story a bit. Bernoulli says the lottery ticket gives one a 50/50 chance at *twenty thousand ducats* or nothing.

6. See ibid. p. 201 for Bernoulli's version of the story.

7. Ibid. p. 200.

8. See ibid. p. 204. See also George Stigler's paper "The development of utility theory," ibid. pp. 55–119.

9. This move is made in the sentence at the bottom of p. 204 of Bernoulli's paper.

10. In, say, 1732, a ducat would have been worth (ballpark figure) about $30.

11. In fact, Bernoulli does this last bit of the calculation the other way around. He subtracts the results of his computations from the initial fortune, and calls the (*positive*) remainder the 'expected loss'. Of course it doesn't make any difference which way we do it, so long as we are clear whether the expected value is a loss or a gain.

12. "Exposition ...", ibid. p. 206.

13. This is the original version of the game. See ibid. p. 209.

14 Karl Menger points this out in a footnote to Bernoulli's paper. See ibid. pp. 209–210, footnote 10.

15. I have made Peter a god in order to avoid the common complaint that no individual human, nor any company, nor any nation, is rich enough to pay 'Paul' the amount required when the sequence of tails stretches out to 50 or 60 in a row. See, for example, Richard Jeffrey, *The Logic of Decision*, 2nd Edition, University of Chicago Press, Chicago, 1983, pp. 150–155.

16. Op. cit. p. 210.

17. This objection, and number (3) below, are to be found in Stigler's paper, op. cit. p. 88, footnote p. 129.

18. Richard Jeffrey seems to say that this was one of *Bernoulli's* discoveries. I can't find it in Bernoulli's paper. And, so far as I can see, it constitutes a serious *objection* to his view of utility. (See Jeffrey, *The Logic of Decision*, p. 152.)

19. Ibid.

20. "Truth and Probability" has been printed several times. My source is Ramsey's, *Philosophical Papers*, Edited by D. H. Mellor, Cambridge University Press, Cambridge, 1990, pp. 52-94. The pages referred to are pp. 69-75.

21. The evidence is scattered, and not voluminous. But see, for instance, the half-serious paper, "Epilogue," written in 1925 for the Apostles (a conversation club of Cambridge intellectuals). [Especially, ibid. pp. 246-247.] See also, Ramsey's 'Introduction', in *Frank Plumpton Ramsey On Truth*, edited by Nicholas Rescher and Ulrich Majer, Kluwer Academic Publishers, Dordrecht, 1991, pp. 3-5, and pp. 82-83.

22. He says this in regard to *degrees of belief*; but I take it to apply to values as well. See his "Truth and Probability", op. cit. p. 64.

23. Ibid. p. 70.

24. Evidence for this impression is very sketchy. But note, for instance, Ramsey's remarks in the Postscript entitled "Probability and Partial Belief," about the man who thinks 1 good and 1 bad = 2 neutral, but takes 2 bads to be off the chart—totally unacceptable at any odds. Ibid. p. 96.

25. Moore accuses Sidgwick of reasoning in exactly this way. See Moore's *Principia Ethica*, chapter III, section 55.

26. Ibid. pp. 35-36.

27. Ramsey's sketch of 'Round Three' (not his phrase) is on pp. 72-73, ibid.

28. Ibid. p. 72. This, I think, is the first occurrence in the paper of the phrase 'immediately measurable.' Previously (p. 69), he had written 'numerically measurable.' I assume he intends both.

29. Ibid. pp. 72-73.

30. Michael Resnik's book, *Choices An Introduction to Decision Theory*, University of Minnesota Press, Minneapolis, 1987, contains some introductory remarks on the various kinds of scales relevant to decision theory. See, e.g. pp. 24-25.

31. Ibid. p. 68.

32. This is one of the things that suggest that Ramsey may be thinking of the relevant 'possible worlds' as (physically?) possible futures.

Ramsey mentions a problem about the names 'a' and 'b.' These names must be *referentially indeterminate* in that each of them is compatible with *p* being true *and* with *p* being false.

33. Ramsey: "...a non-atomic proposition *p* is called ethically neutral if all its atomic truth-arguments are ethically neutral." Ibid. p. 73 This sentence fragment has a footnote adding that, at this point, he is assuming Wittgenstein's (Tractarian) theory of propositions. (Ramsey (at 18) was the original translator of the *Tractatus* into English.)

34. Ibid. pp. 73-74.

35. Ibid. p. 75. Here again it looks as though Ramsey must be thinking of possible worlds that

branch off, now, or in the future, from the actual world. (This much is certain: The 'creature' already exists!)

36. See Patrick Maher, *Betting on Theories*, Cambridge University Press, 1993, p. 13.
37. See John Von Neumann, and Oskar Morgenstern, *Theory of Games and Economic Behavior*, Princeton University Press, Princeton, 1953, p. 16.

CHAPTER FOUR

Pleasure and Pain

According to the classical proto-type of disenchanting ethics, one's own pleasure is the thing one tries, or should try, to maximize, and one's own pain the thing one tries, or should try, to minimize. A rational creature goes, or should go, for pleasure and the avoidance of pain. This was the view held by Democritus, Aristippus and the Cyrenaics, Epicurus and the Epicurians, Helvetius, Bentham, and many others.[1]

The Cyreniacs, for instance, held that particular pleasures are the only things that are genuinely good, and particular pains the only things genuinely bad. Pleasures are smooth and gentle inner motions. Pains are violent.[2] I do not know whether the Cyrenaics would have said that pleasure is *absolutely* good, or only that it is good *relative to the person who enjoys it*. My view is that they should have been relativists in this regard. In any case, I take them to have been realists, or at least objectivists of some sort, in regard to ethics (but not morality). On their view, it is simply an objective, absolute, fact that each person should pursue his, or her, own immediate pleasure. This is the only way of living that makes sense. Thus they were, roughly, thin rationalists.

Creatures Without Pleasures

Some animals (for instance, amebas), apparently, feel neither pleasure nor pain. If there are such animals then, of course, their behavior is not governed by those feelings. In any case, there are various mechanical and electronic entities that go about their business without the benefit of pleasures and pains. Some of these entities are very 'smart,' and they are getting 'smarter' all the time. There are electronic devices that play chess at a grand-master level of expertise, without any pleasure in victory or misery in defeat. This gives rise to the following question. Is it possible for there to be rational creatures of this sort? I don't know the answer; but such creatures aren't obviously impossible. Perhaps rationality does not invariably urge the pursuit of pleasure and the avoidance of pain. There may be real, live, animals that have relatively simple pain-systems, but are incapable of feeling pleasure (e.g. snails?). Even if there are no such creatures now, it might, eventually, be possible to build them.[3]

Let's imagine, or pretend to imagine, a rational, non-accountable, creature that feels pain, but no pleasure. How should this creature evaluate its options? The relevant, quasi-cyrenaic answer seems obvious: *minimize pain!*

But how, exactly, is this to be done? Pain endures through time, and varies in intensity. Given a choice between three hours of mild pain and three hours of intense pain, our creature should, no doubt, choose the mild pain. Given a choice between a moderate pain that lasts ten hours and a moderate pain that lasts three minutes, it seems reasonable to prefer the three minutes. Both intensity and duration seem relevant in evaluating the options.

What should the creature do when confronted with a choice between a fairly mild pain that lasts quite a while and a moderate pain of shorter duration? At this point, we (and the creature) need more detail about the options. It might be helpful to construct a scale—say, from zero to ten—by which to measure the intensity of pain. The most terrible agony the creature can suffer scores 10 on the scale. Moderate pains score between 2.5 and 5, and so on.

The creature tries to minimize pain. With this aim in mind, it makes rough estimates of the 'amount' of pain associated with each option. Perhaps it thinks of the prospective *moderate* pain in some such way as this:

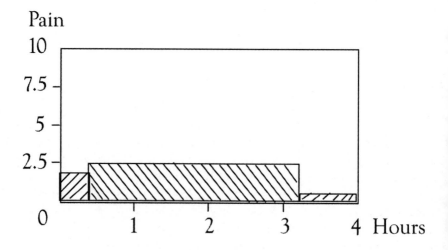

The experience is represented as composed of three blocks: 20 minutes of degree 2 pain, almost 3 hours of degree 2.5 pain, and then nearly an hour of 0.05 pain. The total score is roughly:

$(20 \times 2) + (170 \times 2.5) + (50 \times 0.05) = 468$ pain-minutes
$$= \text{about } 7.8 \text{ pain-hours}^4$$

Suppose our creature thinks the *mild* pain would score about 0.15 for about two and a half days (60 hours).

$(60 \times 0.15) = 9$ pain-hours

Given this analysis of its options, what should the creature do? The obvious suggestion is that it should choose the moderate pain. That is to say, it should choose the experience with lowest score in estimated pain-hours. More generally, the suggestion would be that it should go through life minimizing its pain-hour score.

The idea is that the creature should be governed by this plan. It won't, for example, care about it's own survival. Suppose the options sketched above represent the creature's entire future. It chooses between a future life of moderate pain that lasts about four hours and then ends in painless obliteration, and one in which it feels mild pain for about two and a half days and then is obliterated. Presumably the creature should still choose the moderate pain.

I take it the creature could be designed (by random variation and natural selection, or by a team of engineers) to operate in the proposed way. There is, however, a possible drawback to the plan. The creature may come to see that the best way to minimize its pain-hour score is to destroy itself as soon, and as painlessly, as possible. A carefully managed suicide can yield a score close to zero. Continued existence will almost certainly yield many pains, some of them very unpleasant.

Alternatively, the creature might discover some way of removing, shutting off, or destroying, its pain-system. That's another way to get a future pain-hour score of zero. Any of these self-destructive procedures is likely to frustrate the purpose the pain-system is designed to serve. The system is there, we imagine, to help the creature survive and do the job for which it (the creature) was designed. In all likelihood, neither Mother Nature, nor a team of engineers, would want the creature to maim or destroy itself at the first good chance it gets.

Here is another plan. The creature is designed to maximize 'non-pain.' The degree of 'non-pain' at a given time, t, is the greatest possible degree of pain (viz. 10) *minus* the intensity of pain at t. So, for example, when the creature feels a pain that scores 2.5 on the intensity scale, its 'non-pain' scores 7.5.

Our revised creature pictures the moderate pain experience in some such way as this:

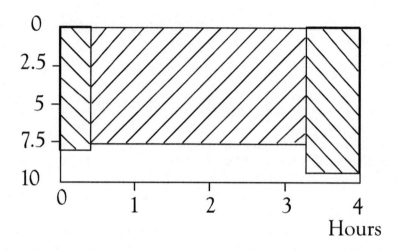

First, there are about 20 minutes of degree 8 non-pain. Then there are 170 minutes of degree 7.5 non-pain. And, finally, there are 50 minutes at 9.95 degrees.

$$(20 \times 8) + (170 \times 7.5) + (50 \times 9.95) = 1932.5 \text{ non-pain-minutes}$$
$$= \text{about } 32.2 \text{ non-pain-hours}$$

On the other hand, the *mild* pain yields:
60 X 9.85 = 591 non-pain-hours
(An alternative way of arriving at this score would be to subtract the pain-hour score (9) from the maximal amount of pain 60 hours can contain (60 X 10).)

Under the new proposal, the creature tries to maximize the non-pain-hours in its future. So, apparently, it ought to prefer the mild pain. (591 is greater than 32.2.)

This result makes sense on the assumption that both options end in the creature's destruction. Clearly, in these circumstances, a maximizer of non-pain-hours should choose the mild pain, while a minimizer of pain-hours should choose the moderate pain.

On the other hand, suppose once the pains are over, the creature will live just as long, with about the same amount of pain either way. In that case, we have miscalculated the number of non-pain-hours offered by the moderate pain. Just to make things simple, pretend the creature will be obliterated in two and a half days (60 hours) no matter which choice it makes. If the creature chooses the moderate pain, it will have a bit more than two days of pain-free life after the pain stops. Hence, it should add, say, 56 hours of degree 10 non-pain to the moderate pain score.

$$(56 \times 10) + 32.2 = 592.2$$

Now the policy of minimizing pain-hours yields the same result as the policy of maximizing non-pain-hours. The moderate pain-experience is preferable.

The first policy may urge the creature to act in ways that strike us as mad. It recommends indifference between 15 minutes of future life, and 15 days, or 15 years, provided all three offer the same 'amount of pain'—i.e. total score in pain-hours. On the other hand, under the second policy the creature would much prefer the 15 years to the 15 days, and the 15 days to the 15 minutes, given that the total score in pain-hours remains the same. The three options yield very different scores in non-pain-hours. As I have already suggested, engineers may have good reasons for 'hard-wiring' the second policy rather than the first. They may want the creatures to remain alive and do their job.

Benevolent engineers might find the second policy unacceptable. Creatures who maximize non-pain-hours will prefer any torture that includes a few moments of something less than ultimate agony to immediate, painless, obliteration. Such creatures would, for instance, prefer six weeks of torture (ending in death), with only a few tolerable minutes now and then, to present, painless, death.

One way to avoid this limitless 'tough-it-out' behavior would be to have the creature aim at maximizing non-pain-hour scores *minus pain-hour scores*.[5] On this plan, the creature would prefer immediate, painless, death to any stretch of time of more than 5 degrees pain ending in death. For instance, suppose the benevolently designed creature is offered instant death or four hours of 7.5 degree pain followed by death.

$$(2.5 \times 4) - (7.5 \times 4) = -20$$

Since zero is more than negative twenty, the creature will prefer immediate death.

What should we say is ultimately 'bad' from the point of view of the rational, pleasureless, pain-feeling, creature? The answer is obvious: its own pain is 'bad'. And what is 'good'? I have suggested that it may well make engineering sense to have the creature make some effort to maximize non-pain. For such a creature, 'non-pain' would be 'good'. This, in effect, would give the creature some inclination to preserve its own life. (Would that make *survival* another 'good' relative to the creature?)

I also said that if the engineers want to minimize the creature's potential agony without impairing its pain-system, they might have it try to maximize *non-pain-hours minus pain-hours*. (Things tend to get complicated.)

Creatures With Both Pleasures and Pains

Let's try to imagine a creature in regard to which something like the primitive Cyreniac theory of pleasure and pain is absolutely right.

It has a 'pleasure-pain' region in its thinking apparatus. This region has ten distinct sub-regions. At any given moment, each sub-region is in just one of three possible states: (1) 'rough' motion; (2) 'smooth' motion; (3) at rest. The creature is in maximal bliss when all ten sub-regions are in smooth motion. Call that 'degree 10' pleasure. Similarly, 'degree 10' pain is all ten sub-regions in 'rough' motion. 'Degree 5 pleasure' is 5 sub-regions in smooth motion, and so on.[6]

We want this creature to 'maximize pleasure'. Given what has been said about pain, we already have some idea as to how the creature should proceed. Degree and duration are both relevant. Presumably, the creature ought to maximize *pleasure-hours*.

Given a choice between twenty minutes of degree 5 pleasure and forty-five minutes of degree 3 pleasure, it should prefer the less intense, but longer lasting, experience.

How should the creature deal with options that include both pleasure and pain? At this point we need a single intensity scale for both kinds of experience. Let's assume we have one. The creature is indifferent between one minute in the 'zero' state (no pleasure, no pain) and one minute of degree 1 pleasure and degree 1 pain, or one minute of degree 2 pleasure and degree 2 pain, and so on up to the maximally intense equal mix of the two (e.g. 5 degrees of each).

It may also be useful to have some way of comparing (weighting) pleasure-hours against non-pain-hours. Should a creature that cares about non-pain-hours value one non-pain-hour as much as one pleasure-hour? Should it be indifferent, given a choice between the two? Just for the fun of it, let's have creatures that care about non-pain-hours value a pleasure-hour twice as much.

Given this set-up, how should the creature order its preferences? Here are three general strategies:

- Pure Hedonism: Maximize pleasure-hours minus pain-hours.
- Tough Hedonism: Maximize pleasure-hours plus (non-pain-hours/2).
- Halfway Hedonism: Maximize pleasure-hours plus (non-pain-hours/2) minus pain-hours.

Pure Hedonism generates the problem we found in the policy of minimizing pain-hours. A creature operating on Pure Hedonism prefers immediate painless death to any experiential sequence in which the total pain-hour score is larger than the total pleasure-hour score. (I assume the creature is always, or at least often, able to destroy itself.) The creature's designers might well prefer a different approach.

Tough Hedonism goes to the opposite extreme. A creature governed by this policy is indifferent between immediate painless death and *any* finite amount of maximal torture. Offered a choice of death now or five years of maximal torture (ending in death), the creature has no preference—perhaps it flips a coin to decided the matter.

Suppose, our creature is given a choice between immediate, painless, obliteration, and four days in which there is a lot more pain than pleasure. To be a bit more precise, suppose there will be two and half days of degree 8 pain, one day of degree 9 pleasure, half a day of degree 1 pleasure, and a bit more than half a day of degree 1 pain ending in obliteration. Here is a graph of the experience:

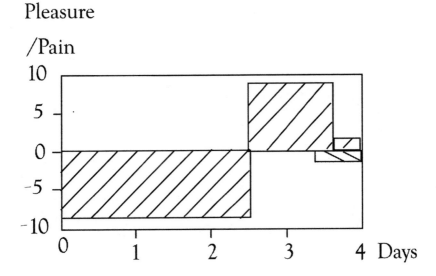

Pleasure-days = (1 X 9) + (.5 X 1) = 9.5
Pain-days = (2.5 X 8) + (.6 X 1) = 20.6
Non-pain-days = (4 X 10) – 20.6 = 19.4
Pleasure-days minus pain-days = 9.5 –20.6 = –11.1
Pleasure-days plus (non-pain-days/2) = 9.5 + (19.4/2) = 19.2
Pleasure-days plus (non-pain-days/2) minus pain-days = 19.2 – 20.6 = –1.4

If the creature follows the Pure Hedonism plan, it will prefer immediate painless death to this experience. A score of zero is better than –11.1. On the other hand, the policy of Tough Hedonism would have the creature accept these pleasures and pains. A score of 19.2 is better than zero.

Halfway Hedonism produces a fairly close call. If the creature follows this policy, it will, again, prefer immediate death. Zero is better than –1.4. But suppose the degree 1 pain had not been in the offing, and suppose the pleasure of the last half day would have been twice as intense (.5 X 2). In that case, the Halfway policy would have had the creature be indifferent between the two options. Add a tiny bit more pleasure to the picture, and the creature will choose to endure those four days.

It is a mistake to confuse a creature's *utility* with its own pleasure or absence of pain. They are not the same thing. For medicinal purposes against this potential confusion, imagine a pair of creatures that normally try to maximize their own pleasure and minimize their own pain following the Tough Hedonism plan, but, now and then, for a month or so, they *switch policies*, so to speak. During this stretch each one only tries to maximize the *other's* pleasure and minimize the *other's* pain according to the TH [Tough Hedonism] plan for that other person. (They tend to go into this state when they are engaged in the joint project of constructing a new creature much like themselves.)

Consider such a pair: Ping and Pong. When Ping is busy trying to maximize Pong's TH score, he is *not* trying to maximize her utility. Nor, I presume, is he trying to maximize his own. But, if he is successful, he maximizes his own utility. He does it, e.g. by maximizing her TH score. And similarly for Pong. In maximizing Ping's TH score, she maximizes her own utility. In effect, they swap utility functions. When they are in this state, Ping's utility function is a rough approximation of what used to be Pong's utility function, and visa versa. (If there are worries about how they could have learned enough about each other's pleasures and pains to do this job well, it might be helpful to imagine that these creatures involuntarily change color—like chameleons—in ways that reveal their hedonic state.)

The picture of pleasure and pain presented in this chapter is absurdly simplistic and mechanical. Real pleasures and pains (miseries, sorrows, joys, and so forth) are often much more complex and difficult to evaluate. I have sacrificed verisimilitude for the sake of simplicity and adherence to something like traditional hedonism.

NOTES

1. Fredrick Lange called this tradition 'Ethical Materialism.' He explores its development and its association with science, empiricism, and materialism in *The History of Materialism*, first published in 1866. See, for example, the third edition, translated from the German by E. C. Thomas, Harcourt, Brace & Company, Inc. London, 1925, First Book, section four, chapters 2 and 3.

2. See Diogenes Laertius, *Lives of Eminent Philosophers*, translated by R. D. Hicks, the Loeb Classical Library, London & New York, 1925, Vol I, p. 473.

3. The best sketch of the *human* pain system I know of is the somewhat fanciful version offered by Daniel Dennett in his book *Brainstorms*, Bradford Books, 1978, sec. 11, "Why You Can't Make a Computer that Feels Pain," pp. 1902–29.

4. A friend of mine tells me that he finds it annoying that the number of pain hours can be greater than the number of hours one suffers. I agree that this is annoying; but I don't see any easy way of avoiding it. Increasing the 'height' of the pain-scale, to say 50, or 100, would, I think, give 'non-pain' too much weight.

5. The creature's 'tough-it-out' behavior could be fine-tuned by *weighting* the pain-hour score to be subtracted. Thus, for example, multiplying the pain-hour score by 0.25 and then subtracting would 'toughen' the creature up a bit—make it prefer four hours of 7.5 pain to immediate painless death.

6. Of course this is nothing like actual pleasure systems or pain systems. For one thing out of many, in regard to mammals we would have to take into account the role, or roles, of the insula cortex.

CHAPTER FIVE

Brutes and Hobbots

obbots (Hobbesian Robots) are rational creatures, who, when they are acting rationally, are governed by what Joseph Butler sometimes calls 'cool self-love.'[1] The following rough draft of their psychological constitution is derived mostly from Butler. To a large extent, Hobbots are just Butler's 'men' minus a conscience.

It may seem odd to use Butler's moral psychology in trying to model rational creatures in a way appropriate to the disenchanter tradition. After all, Butler was a Platonist and one of the disenchanters most troublesome critics.[2] I employ Butler in this project because I think he can make a useful contribution to the tradition he attacks. A moral psychology for disenchanters is enriched, and made more plausible, by acceptance of something like Butler's picture. In particular, Butler helps us see that disenchanters need not, and, I think, should not, accept psychological hedonism, at least not in any straightforward form, and probably should not hold that our motives are always selfish.[3]

Platonists might well think of Hobbots as creatures halfway between sentient, non-rational, entities and full-fledged, morally accountable, people. In this chapter, we will take a quick look at some absurdly simplified wiring diagrams for Hobbots and sentient non-rational creatures.

Since Hobbots have roughly the psychological constitution Butler ascribes to human beings, except that their conscience is missing, we might approach our topic by outlining Butler's view of human nature, and proceed by amputation. However, I prefer to begin with brutes and work upward by various additions.

Brutes

We can imagine sentient creatures that are 'designed' to be governed by their inclinations. Such creatures might be the products of engineering, or the results of random variation and natural selection. Let's call them 'brutes.'

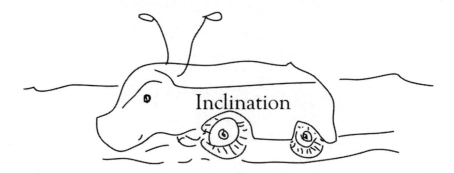

These creature's 'Inclinations' should be thought of as first-order desires, needs, wants, passions, and so forth. Second-order desires are desires in regard to desires. Thus, for example, someone might wish that she didn't have a craving for cigarettes. A craving for cigarettes is a first-order desire, and the wish that one lacked that craving is a second-order desire. Harry Frankfurt has written several important papers on this topic.[4] He calls a creature that has first order desires, but lacks all higher order desires, a 'wanton'. Brutes and wantons appear to be much the same thing.

How should brutes act? I take it there is an objective, scientifically acceptable, answer to this. They should do what the dominant inclination of the moment urges them to do. A cat stalking a mouse is behaving as it should. That is to say, it is acting as it was 'designed' to act. It is operating properly. A very crude block diagram for the 'wiring' of such a creature might go like this:

Notice that I have said nothing about pleasure and pain. As in chapter two, the supposition is that there are, or could be, sentient creatures that have no pleasures or pains. Perhaps they are driven this way and that by measurable features of their environment (e.g. degrees of light or heat) and of their own bodies (e.g. the need for food).

Our creatures can be made more complex by adding a pain system. Such a system can be useful in a variety of ways. Thus, for instance, severe pain could immobilize an injured creature while repairs were underway.

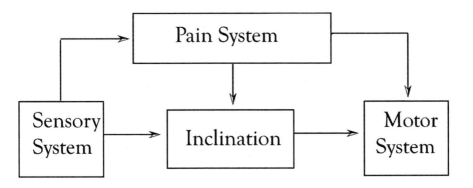

More interesting from our present point of view is the fact that pain might well serve to modify a creature's repertoire of inclinations. Thus the creature might come to avoid places and situations that have caused it pain in the past, and thereby avoid present dangers. On observing its behavior, we might think the creature foresees future pain and tries to avoid it; but, if we understood the mechanism, we might be more inclined to hold that present perceptions of certain places and situation have themselves become painful, and it is just this that induces avoidance.

(How does this work? Perhaps a strong inclination to avoid severe pain, and situations which have been linked with severe pain in the past, is, so to speak, part of the pain system.)

A pleasure system would, presumably, be useful in roughly the opposite way. Places and situations that yield pleasure will create, or strengthen appetites and affections. Both systems are likely to have powerful, and complex, effects on a creature's repertoire of inclinations. Inclinations will, so to speak, become loaded with information about the creature's environment.

Particular Appetites, Passions, & Affections

Butler does not mention an inclination module. He speaks of *particular* affections, and so on, and contrasts these with Self-Love, Conscience, and sometimes Benevolence. For the moment, we will neglect the more authoritative modules. The object of a particular affection is always *some particular external object* towards which the affection tends, and of which the creature has some particular idea or perception. Particular affections, and so on, pursue external objects as ends in themselves.

Butler denies that particular affections, and so on, have pleasure (or the avoidance of pain) as their objective. Hence, he would presumably say, a creature equipped with pleasure and pain systems, but propelled through life by its particular affections, would not be pursuing pleasure and trying to avoid pain.

Some of our particular affections, and so on, aim at harm to another (for instance *resentment*), others aim at promoting another person's good (*benevolence*); some, of course, are difficult to classify (*love of the arts*).[5]

Butler's discussion of particular affections, etc., is, I think, based in part upon what I suppose was in his day a well-known account of animal movement, desire, love, appetite, and so on. This account was derived mostly from Aristotle,[6] and had been brought to fruition by Aquinas.[7] In its final form, it is complex and sophisticated; but the underlying model is simple enough. Consider two bodies, A and B. Either B attracts A or repels A.[8] Suppose B attracts A.

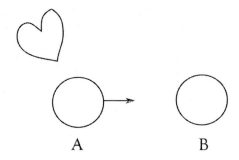

Under this supposition, there are three distinct states of response.

- A has a tendency, or inclination, to move towards B. But there is, as yet, no actual movement.
- A moves towards B.
- A comes to rest next to B.

The model was used in the following way: Suppose some object attracts a creature's appetite (*appetitus*)—i.e. the object is 'good' with respect to the appetite.

- The inclination of the appetite towards the object—the sense that they are naturally fitted for each other, the sense of affinity between them— is *love*.
- If the object is not yet possessed, and nothing prevents its possession, the appetite will be moved towards that which it loves. This movement is *desire*, or *lust*.

- Finally, if the object is obtained, the appetite rests—finds repose—in its possession, and this is *pleasure*, or *joy*.[9]

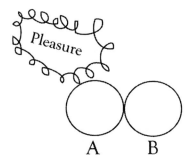

The model of repulsion mirrors the model of attraction and goes something like this:

- When the appetite is in possession of an object it hates, we have *sadness*, or *grief*.
- Movement away from such an object is *aversion* or *disgust*.
- Finally, the appetites' disinclination towards an object—its sense of non-affinity for it—is *hatred*.

For Aquinas (and Aristotle), a person's appetite (*appetitus*) is, as it were, an entity that is attracted towards certain objects (e.g. cheese) and repelled by others (e.g. worms). Desire and aversion, love and hatred, pleasure and grief are explained in terms of the appetite's situation with respect to such objects.

Butler seems to have this model in mind when, for example, he argues that since the pleasure arising from the gratification of a particular appetite is due to a 'prior suitableness' between the appetite and its object, the *object* of the appetite must be something other than pleasure. We enjoy eating food more than we enjoy eating stones because there is this sort of 'prior suitableness' in the one case and not in the other.[10]

Is this a persuasive argument? Of course the whole topic is very murky, but it seems to me that Butler's conclusion is at least partially right. There could be creatures that have various appetites, or whatever, and yet lack a pleasure system. Those appetites are not aimed at pleasure. A creature can perceive its need for fuel, and feel a strong urge to go and get some, without pleasure (or pain) entering the picture. Hence, some possible appetites are 'toward external things themselves,' and not toward pleasure arising from the attainment of those things.

On the other hand, consider affections that spring from, or have been nourished by, associated pleasure. For instance, Alice is enjoying Wanda's company because Wanda is an old and cherished friend. Butler tells us that Alice's fondness for Wanda has found, achieved, and 'come to rest in', its object (viz. Wanda, or Wanda's company). But why shouldn't we say Alice has an 'appetite' *for the pleasure* of Wanda's company, and it is in that pleasure that she has come to rest? Or, to put it another way, why should we insist that there is no appetite of that sort here? (Analytic Psychologist: "When you haven't seen each other for a while, do you have (a) a craving to be with Wanda, or (b) a craving for the pleasure of being with Wanda?" It seems wrong to insist on either answer to the exclusion of the other.)

Perhaps pain yields a clearer case. Don't we have an immediate, non-reflective, avoidance reaction to pain itself? Don't we want to get rid of *the pain?*

Quick review: Butler thinks (1) that all particular appetites, passions, and affections have external things—things distinct from one's own pleasure or pain—as their objects, and (2) that no particular appetite, passion, or whatever, has one's own pleasure or pain as its object. I don't see why we should accept either claim.[11]

Butlerian Self-love

Roughly speaking, the job of the self-love module of a given creature, C, is to urge behavior favorable to C's long-term well being, or happiness. It's as if the module were a little person who loves only C, and works full time trying to figure out how to make things go well for C. Self-Love doesn't care at all about *morality.* It has no interest in whether C is virtuous or not. Nor does it worry about how C's behavior might affect other creatures, except in so far as this would have an effect on C's well being.

Once again Aquinas may be helpful. In the present context, Aquinas' division of the powers of the soul seems relevant. He divides these powers into three layers, the vegetative, the sensory, and the intellectual. The powers of the sensory and intellectual layers are, in turn, divided vertically into appetites (in a loose sense) and cognitive powers.[12] If we omit the vegetative layer, the resulting diagram looks like this:

	Appetites	Cognitive Powers
Intellectual	Rational appetite (Will)	Powers of intellectual cognition (Reason)
Sensory	Sensory appetite (the particular passions)	Powers of sensory cognition

This diagram still lurked at the back of the minds of at least some educated people in Butler's day. Hutcheson complains of confused harangues to the effect that there is a war within us between reason and the passions—reason presumably being good and the passions bad. Those who discuss such topics should remind themselves of "the common divisions of the faculties of the soul."[13] There are, he says, (1) Reason which presents the natures and relations of things; (2) the will, or *appetitus rationalis*, which is the disposition of the soul to pursue what is presented by the cognitive powers as good, and to shun what is presented as evil; (3) the *sensus*, and (4) the *appetitus sensitivus*, in which are grouped the particular passions. And, in another place, while discussing the relation between the 'particular passions' and 'general desires', Hutcheson says that the schoolmen express this distinction by talking of the *appetitus rationalis* and the *appetitus sensitivus.*[14] Presumably 'general desires' are rational appetites—i.e. states of Will.

Butler often appears to be taking these 'common divisions of the faculties of the soul' as his point of departure. Butlerian Self-Love is plainly a 'rational appetite.' Every man, Butler says, has a *general* desire for his own happiness.[15] This general desire is radically different from any particular affection, etc. It has as its object something *internal,*—namely our own happiness, enjoyment, or satisfaction—and does not require us to have any distinct particular perception of what it is that would make us happy. Self-Love can only exist in rational creatures; i.e. creatures that have some sort of internal representation of themselves, and can form the abstract notion of their own long-term interest or happiness. When Self-Love pursues some external thing, its end is not that thing itself. The external object is, for Self-Love, only a means to happiness.

A Butlerian Self-Love module could be designed to operate on any of the hedonic policies described in the preceding chapter. It could, for example, be governed by Pure Hedonism. In that case, roughly speaking, it would endorse choices that maximize pleasure-hours minus pain-hours across the foreseeable future.[16]

A '*standard*' Hobbot is often torn between the urgings of Self-Love and the urgings of its particular affections, appetites, and so on (i.e. Inclination). Such Hobbots have a module called the 'Chooser' that decides whether they will be governed by Self-Love or by inclination when there is conflict between the two.[17]

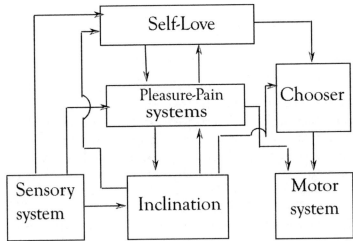

Supernaturalists (like Butler) can suppose that there is something paranormal at work in the Chooser—a spirit perhaps. Naturalists will insist upon something more mundane. The Chooser might, for example, randomize on the basis of the present strengths of the urgings of the conflicting modules.[18] If, on a given occasion, Self-Love scores 6 and an inclination 8 (both on a single scale from 1 to 10) then, as it were, the Chooser puts 6 black marbles and 8 red ones in an urn, stirs them up, and draws one at random. If the marble is black, Self-Love wins. If the marble is red, the creature acts on its inclination. That is to say, the Chooser sets up a situation in which there is roughly a 0.43 chance of Self-Love winning and a 0.57 chance for Inclination to win.

There could be Hobbots that *cannot* act in ways contrary to the dictates of self-love (unless they breakdown in some way, or loose self-control due to intense pleasure or pain). Let's call them 'Determined Hobbots.' When the self-love module of a Determined Hobbot decides it would be foolish to obey the urgings of a particular inclination, the creature cannot succumb to that inclination. These Hobbots are designed in such a way that Self-Love governs their behavior when they are in control of themselves. Here is a block-diagram for Hobbots of this kind:

The Determined Hobbot

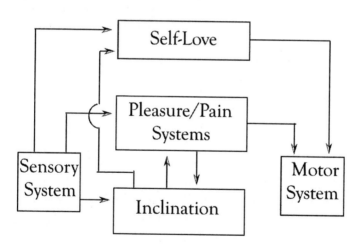

Notice that the two wires to the Motor System carry signals from the Pleasure-pain systems, and from the self-love module. The only way Inclination can determine behavior is via Self-Love (or, perhaps, via pleasure or pain).

One of the interesting features of Determined Hobbots is that good engineers can say a lot about how Determined Hobbots ought to act. They are sometimes useful to disenchanting theorizers because their behavior is so predictable.

We have made a start towards understanding Hobbot psychology. Now let's take a quick look at two inter-related questions: (1) is *all* Standard Hobbot behavior just pursuit of pleasure and avoidance of pain? (2) Can a Standard Hobbot feel, and act upon, genuine, non-selfish, concern for someone else's well being?

In some circumstances, a Standard Hobbot's behavior is controlled by Self-Love, and not by any particular passion, or whatever.[19] Suppose the Self-Love module is operating on the Pure Hedonism policy. In such cases, clearly, the Hobbot is trying to maximize pleasure and minimize pain. More precisely, it is trying to maximize pleasure-hours minus pain-hours. On the other hand, if the Self-Love module is operating on the Tough Hedonism policy, then, we might say, the creature is trying to maximize pleasure, minimize pain, and stay alive. Let's assume that Self-Love operates on Pure Hedonism.

Sometimes Standard Hobbot behavior is in compliance with a particular passion, in spite of Self-Love's vigorous protest. (Similarly, a human may devour half a cheese-cake, knowing full well that such behavior will tend to make him a bit fatter and may well increase the contempt his sweet-heart already feels for him.) Butler holds that in cases like this, the creature is not pursuing pleasure or trying to avoid pain. The creature's ultimate objective is allegedly just the non-hedonic, external, object of the particular passion (*cheesecake*, or whatever).

The line of thought seems to be something like this: The creature is under the control of the particular passion, and not Self-Love. The particular passion has a non-hedonic, external, target. Hence, that non-hedonic, external, target must be what the creature is going for.

It is not obvious that Butler is right about this. Remember Alice and Wanda.

Nevertheless, perhaps we can derive Butler's conclusion via a different route. Suppose the Hobbot has a particular passion such that the gratification of this passion yields no pleasure (and no pain). And suppose it is this passion that triumphs over Self-Love. The result would be a clear case in which the Hobbot is not pursuing pleasure or trying to avoid pain.

In many cases, Self-Love endorses the urgings of a pleasure-yielding particular passion. Thus for instance, a Hobbot might have an urge to re-charge its batteries by basking in the sun, and Self-Love might agree that this is a good idea. Why does the Hobbot bask in the sun? Is it simply pursuing pleasure and/or trying to avoid pain? Of course that may be the whole story so far as Self-Love is concerned. But what does the particular passion want? (Think of it as a little person.) Well, at least in part, it wants some basking in the sun, and recharged batteries—not just the pleasure. Egoistic hedonism is, at best, a simplistic account of Hobbot behavior.

Let's try the second question. Can Hobbots be genuinely concerned about the well being of other Hobbots? Are such Hobbots possible? Could a fantastically clever engineer design and build such a creature?

Pretend an engineer has designed and built some Standard Hobbots that have powerful benevolent passions. For instance, they have an urge to help other Hobbots in distress. They also have an urge to have a good friend, and be a good friend in return, and so on. These benevolent passions yield 'mental' (as opposed to physical) pleasures and pains. For instance, a Hobbot of this sort would be deeply unhappy if its friend were destroyed, or removed. Such a Hobbot feels pleasure in the company of its friend, and joy when the friend is particularly lucky, or does something particularly well.

We watch one Hobbot help another to the repair shop—a time-consuming job. Why did the Hobbot do it? Well, of course, a benevolent passion urged it to do so. After that either one of two things happened: Possibility One: Self-Love thought that yielding to the benevolent passion would generate a better score in pleasure-hours minus pain-hours than any feasible alternative, so it concurred with the passion, and thus the Chooser had no choice. Possibility Two: Self-Love decided it would be a bad idea to help the other Hobbot; but the Chooser yielded to the benevolent passion.

Some people think that seeking one's own pleasure makes sense, while helping others—being benevolent, acting altruistically—does not. Butler is very clear and persuasive in attacking this idea.[20] His main point is that while Self-Love and benevolence are different principles, there is no more conflict between them than between self-love and any particular appetite, passion, or affection. Crucial to this argument is the assumption that benevolence is a particular passion, or a set of particular passions. If it were general, like self-love, there would, perhaps, be no pleasure in its gratification and it would certainly appear to rival self-love (i.e. it would urge a different policy in decision making). Does Butler regard benevolence as a general passion? Perhaps he uses the term ambiguously. Sometimes, at least, there is no doubt he takes benevolence to be a rational principle, and he pictures it as ruling a cluster of particular passions, such as love of family, friends, country, etc.[21] At other times, by 'benevolence' he seems to mean just that cluster of passions.

Butler does, I think, show that there is no special rivalry between self-love and particular benevolent affections. That is to say, self-love can urge a creature to gratify a benevolent affection (and thus gain pleasure) just as it sometimes urges the gratification of 'selfish' appetites (like love of hot baths). The idea that self-love would have good Hobbots gratify only their selfish appetites is absurd.

In fact, on Butler's view, we were designed, in part, to serve our fellow creatures and in turn to be dependent upon them. We were not designed for solitary self-sufficiency. The theory that we are 'single and independent' is the same absurdity as thinking that hands or feet do not naturally work in coordination with the rest of the body.[22]

I take it that this social-dependence view of our nature (or of Hobbot nature) is entirely compatible with a disenchanting approach to moral psychology and ethics. Disenchanters need not deny the existence of particular, altruistic, benevolent, passions in Hobbots or in human beings.

Desirous Hobbots

Roughly speaking, Self-Love urges the pursuit of maximal pleasure and minimal pain over the long haul. An interesting and as of now more popular alternative urges maximal satisfaction of one's desires, wants, needs, and so on (of whatever order). Let's call a device of this sort a 'Desire-Resolver'.

How does the Desire-Resolver work? Here is one possibility. Each present desire assigns a desirability score to each of the presently perceived possible pay-offs. (For example, a desire for food might rank the options according to how much food the agent would get.) The contending desires differ in strength. The Desire-Resolver finds the weighted score for each option as judged by a given desire by multiplying the raw desirability scores by the strength of the desire. The options are then ranked by summing the weighted scores for each option.[23]

Most people have very strong and persistent desires to have various kinds of pleasures both now and in the future. And most people want very much to avoid pain, misery, boredom, and so on, both now and in the future. If these desires have no serious competitors, a Desire-Resolver will act much like a Self-love module.

On the other hand, some people seem to have at least some desires that are not closely linked to their own pleasures and pains. A Desire-Resolver takes these desires into consideration too. In this regard, desire driven Hobbots may be more like us than standard Hobbots.

In addition, let's give these Hobbots various other high order desires. (I mean other than the desire to do a good job of gratifying one's own desires). For instance, they may have an altruistic desire to alleviate the suffering of other Hobbots. Here's a block diagram of (some of the modules of) this new kind of Hobbot.

The Desirous Hobbot

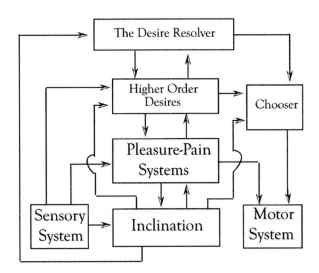

In subsequent chapters I will generally take the term 'happiness' to mean *either* satisfaction of desires *or* lots of pleasure and little pain.

Are we to suppose that *all* of a Desirous Hobbot's overt choices are, ultimately driven by desires? Is this true of us?

Let me spell this problem out a bit. Aristotle has taught us that some, but not all, desires are *deliberate*.

> The object of choice being one of the things in our own power which is desired after deliberation, choice will be deliberate desire of things in our own power; for when we have decided as a result of deliberation, we desire in accordance with our deliberation.[24]

If Alice decides to go to Chicago, she has a deliberate desire to go to Chicago. She 'wants' to go there in the sense that she has so decided. This deliberate desire is, presumably, grounded in a *non*-deliberate desire—a 'basic' desire— for instance, a desire to see some of the paintings at the Art Institute. Given that she chooses to go to Chicago, it would be a mistake to conclude that she must have a non-deliberate desire to go to Chicago.

Deliberate desires provide us with a spurious argument for the theory that all choices are grounded in desire. If Alice chooses to go to Chicago, she must have a desire to go there. She is driven by her desire. This line of thought springs from confusion.

The real question as to whether all our choices are grounded in our desires is not a question about deliberate desires. It's a question about non-deliberate, basic, desires. For instance, given Alice's decision to go to Chicago (and her deliberate desire to get there) can we conclude that she must have some non-deliberate desire that can best be fulfilled by going there? The traditional view has been that this conclusion would be legitimate. Every choice, rational or not, (and thus every deliberate desire) is ultimately grounded in some present non-deliberate desire or cluster of desires.

One might worry about the Chooser's choices. Suppose some Hobbot's Chooser decides to go along with some inclination even though the Desire Resolver and all the Hobbot's other higher-order desires are opposed. Presumably the Hobbot's choice is grounded in the inclination; but what about the Chooser's choice? Was that based upon some non-deliberate desire the Chooser has? This seems the wrong way to go. Perhaps the Chooser has some sort of policy it follows. Or perhaps it acts more or less mechanically. (If it is, so to speak, a very small rational person, then, perhaps, it's a Hobbot, and it too has a Chooser. And so on ad infinitum.) In any case, our question was a question about the choices made by whole people and whole Hobbots, not about the choices made by their real or imaginary modules.

Thomas Nagel reminds us that rational creatures often have reason to act now in such a way as to bring about the eventual gratification of desires they believe they will have, but do not presently have. For instance, someone setting out on a long hike might well bring along water, even though she isn't now thirsty. She knows she will be thirsty.

Following Nagel's reminder, we might install a more or less permanent, general, second order, desire to the effect that our creature's future desires be fulfilled. The Desire Resolver sometimes endorses this second order desire and urges the Hobbot to make provision for the gratification of it's future desires. In this way, the second order desire gives the Hobbot reason to do these things.

Or, alternatively, we could re-design the Desire Resolver, or perhaps the Chooser, so that it can, on its own so to speak, take future desires into consideration.

I will assume that we have adopted the first option (i.e. we have installed a second order desire). This seems more in line with the standard disenchanting view.

Nagel argues that we are sometimes motivated by reasons that are not grounded in present desires of any kind. (So far as I know, he doesn't discuss Hobbots.) I do not find his argument altogether persuasive (see Appendix A); but, of course, his conclusion may true.

NOTES

1. See, for example, Joseph Butler's *Fifteen Sermons Preached at the Rolls Chapel*, sermon 11, "Upon the Love of Our Neighbor", pars. 4-20. By 'Self-Love' Butler generally means '*Cool Self Love*'—rational, reasonable, self-love—rather than a potentially excessive affection for oneself.

2. More specifically, Butler seems to have been an Intuitionist. My guess is that he thought our conscience perceives rightness and wrongness more or less as Clark had said. His work and Clark's supplement each other. See his Preface to the sermons, paragraph 12.

3. By 'Psychological Hedonism' I mean the theory that our actual choices are in fact always governed by our desire to maximize our pleasure and minimize our pain.

4. See for example, Frankfurt's "Freedom of the Will and the Concept of a Person", *The Journal of Philosophy*, 68 (1971) pp. 5-20, and "Necessity and Desire", *Philosophy and Phenomenological Research* 45, 1984, pp. 1-13. Daniel C. Dennett discusses creatures that have desires and beliefs of various orders in his *The Intentional Stance*, Bradford Book, MIT Press Cambridge, Mass., 1987, Chapter 7.

5. These examples of 'particular affections' are provided by Butler himself: Sermon 11, par. 13.

6. See Aristotle's *De Anima*, Bk. III: Ch. 10.

7. See, for example, Aquinas, *Summa Theologiae*, Ia2ae, Q. 23, Art. 4. The physics, as well as the psychology, is basically Aristotelian.

8. One might add, as a option, that the appetite might just feel indifferent—neither love nor hate.

9. " Pleasure is repose of the appetite in some good..", Aquinas, op. cit. Q. 34, Art. 2.

10. Sermon 11, par. 6.

11. One might think that (1) entails (2); but I am entertaining the possibility that some particular appetites can equally well be described as having something 'external' as their object or as having the pleasure of attaining that thing as their object. If this is so, then (1) might be true and (2) false.

12. See Eric D'Arcy's discussion of these divisions in Aquinas' *Summa Theologiae*, Blackfriers, New York, vol. 19, pp. xxiv-xxv.

13. Hutcheson, in *British Moralists*, op. cit. vol. I, p. 405.

14. Ibid. p. 400, footnote.

15. Butler, ibid. ser. xi, par. 3.

16. I say 'roughly speaking,' because this description does not accurately describe how the Pure Hedonism policy works when *chance* (probability) enters the picture.

17. So far as I can tell, this is a departure from the versions of moral psychology sketched by Hobbes, Locke, and Helvetius. And, it must be admitted, Butler himself makes no mention of such a module. The fact is that something somewhat like the *Kantian will* seems to have crept in here.

18. What determines the strength of Self-Love's urging on a given occasion? One solution would be to have the strength depend upon the amount of difference between the *best* and the *worst* pleasure minus pain score presently available. If the difference is small, Self-Love doesn't care much. If the difference is huge, Self-Love cares a lot.

19. Butler provides a nice example. "Suppose [a] man to go through some laborious work upon promise of a great reward, without any distinct knowledge what the reward will be; this course of action cannot be ascribed to any particular passion." [Sermon 1, footnote (5) to par. 7.]

20. See, for example, ibid. Sermon XI, par. 20.

21· See, Sermon v, par. 10, and sermon I, par. 6.

22. Butler, Sermon 1, par. 10.

23. I assume that a 'negative' desire for x, (i.e. a positive desire for *non-*x) will assign a negative number to x.

24. Aristotle, *Nicomachean Ethics*, 1113a 9–13; translated by W. D. Ross.

Rational Decision Making

Pretend we have designed and constructed some sophisticated brutes— brutes that feel pleasures and pains, which tend to modify their inclinations. Now we turn these creatures into Hobbots by adding a self-love module and a chooser. How will they, or should they, behave? The standard Butlerian self-love module operates on the Pure Hedonism policy. It tries to maximize the creature's pleasure-hours minus pain-hours (PMP) over the foreseeable future. To keep things simple, our creatures follow this policy.

Some Easy Decisions

Imagine a Standard Hobbot—Minnie—who is only called upon to make two decisions in her whole life. Imagine, moreover, that there are only six possible pleasant or unpleasant experiences in Minnie's possible futures. Finally, pretend that chance doesn't enter the picture. The future depends entirely on Minnie's decisions.

She begins by estimating the pleasure-hours and/or pain-hours of her possible experiences. (Given her limited background, I have no idea how she manages to do this.) As she sees it, she faces the following network of possible futures:

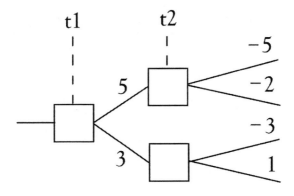

At t1 Minnie must choose between one hour of degree 5 pleasure and one hour of degree 3 pleasure. If she chooses the more intense pleasure, then at t2 she must choose between an hour of degree 5 pain and one hour of degree 2 pain. If, on the other hand, at t1 she chooses the less pleasurable experience, then at t2 she will have the opportunity to choose between one hour of degree 3 pain and one hour of degree 1 pleasure. Let's assume that some particular passion strongly urges her to go for the degree 5 pleasure.

Obviously, Self-Love must tell her to choose the lesser of the two possible pleasure experiences in the immediate future in order for her to avoid misery in the future. How does Self-Love arrive at this recommendation? The answer is obvious. It just adds up the PMP scores of the pleasures and miseries along each of her possible routes and thus obtains a number indicating each route's over all score.

Route:	5 + –5	5 + –2	3 + –3	3 + 1
Total score:	0	3	0	4

Since 4 is the best total, Self-Love prefers this outcome to the other three. The next best is 3, and the two 0's are least desirable. Given that Minnie is operating properly, and that her Chooser 'decides' to be governed by reason (i.e. Self-Love) rather than by inclination, she will choose the route that yields one hour of degree 3 pleasure and then the hour scoring 1.

Should she be governed by Self-Love? Note that pure engineering does not yield any such 'should'. Engineering only says that Minnie should be governed by whichever component her Chooser selects.[1] If we did not intend that she should sometimes be overcome by a particular passion, why did we install a wire from Inclination to the Chooser?[2]

Platonism, or some other objectivist theory, can creep in here. We may feel that Minnie *ought* to make the choices she (i.e. her Self-Love) sees to be in her interest. It would be dumb for her to choose the 5 PMP experience. She ought to play it smart.

The Standard Theory of Choice

In Chapter Three, in the section on Ramsey, we began our examination of something like present-day decision theory. Here is a bit more on the topic. According to a common view of the matter, rational decision making has two basic components. First there is a theory about the requirements that must be met by a rational set of preferences. Second there is a theory about how rational creatures should behave given a set of preferences that meets those standards. Let's take quick look at both components.

Remember the situation just described in which Minnie must choose between four futures. Label them *a*, *b*, *c*, and *d*. Does reason itself put certain constraints upon her ordering of these outcomes? One common supposition is that reason imposes the following three prescriptive constraints:

Completeness:

First a rational creature's set of preferences in a particular situation should have the property of 'completeness'. That is to say, in regard to every pair, x and y, among the outcomes under consideration, either x is preferred to y, or y is preferred to x, or the agent is indifferent between x and y. (The 'or' here is taken to be exclusive. That is to say, 'P or Q or R' is taken to require and permit the truth of *just one* of the three.)

What constraints does this impose on Minnie? Well, for one thing, she can't just *ignore* some of the outcomes. ("What about *b* ? Do you prefer that to *a* ?" "I don't want to think about *b*. Forget that one.") In addition, she is not allowed 'contradictory' preferences. If she prefers *a* to *b* she cannot also (at the same time) prefer *b* to *a*, or be indifferent between them.

Transitivity:

The 'transitivity' conditions might be written as follows:

T1] If x is preferred to y and y is preferred to z, then x is preferred to z.

T2] If x is preferred to y and the agent is indifferent between x and z, then z is preferred to y.

T3] If x is preferred to y and the agent is indifferent between y and z, then x is preferred to z.

T4] If the agent is indifferent between x and y and between y and z, then the agent is also indifferent between x and z.

The standard argument in defense of these transitivity conditions uses a set up called a 'money pump'. Suppose some simple creature had been confronted with three different flavors of ice cream. She prefers *vanilla* to *chocolate*, *chocolate* to *strawberry* and *strawberry* to *vanilla*. (Her preferences go in a circle.) Is this rational? Pretend a bowl of *chocolate* ice cream is now in her possession. She would prefer *vanilla*. So, presumably, she would be prepared to sacrifice something to make the change. Perhaps she would pay us a nickel. Suppose she does so. Now she has a bowl of *vanilla*. But, of course, she would prefer *strawberry*. For another nickel, we will let her make the trade. Poor creature! Once she has the *strawberry*, she will be willing to pay five cents to acquire her original bowl of *chocolate* ice cream. How can she stop? Apparently her preferences require her to go round and round giving us money at every step. But, the argument says, rationality should prevent her from being caught in this sort of loop. The source of the trouble is her violation of T1. Hence, presumably, rationality requires compliance with that constraint.[3]

(There is a difficulty in regard to T4. We can imagine three medical procedures, f, g, and h, such that patients cannot discern any difference in degree of painfulness between f and g, or between g and h, but such that many patients *do* discern that f is (slightly) more painful than h. Given a choice among these procedures (other things being equal), it does not appear to be wildly irrational to be indifferent between f and g, and between g and h, and yet prefer h to f.)

Independencee

Obviously, a set of preferences, S_1, (for example Minnie's *a*, *b*, *c*, and *d*) has subsets (for example *b*, *c*, and *d*). Independence conditions concern relations between a set of preferences and its subsets.

I1] Given that S_2 is a subset of S_1, if x is a member of S_2, and is the highest rated member of S_1, then x is also the highest rated member of S_2.

Here is a closely related condition:

I2] Given that S_2 is a subset of S_1 and that x and y tie for first place in S_2, then one of them (e.g. x) cannot be a highest rated member of S_1 unless the other (e.g. y) is too.[4]

According to I1, if the best basketball player at the university is a sophomore, then he must also be the best *sophomore* basketball player at the university. According to I2, if Peter and Paul tie as the two best sophomore basketball players at the university, than if Peter is one of the highest rated basketball players at the university, Paul must also be one of the highest rated basketball players at the university.

Notice that a 'rational' set of preferences can be weird. Fred's preference for eating pebbles as opposed to potatoes may be perfectly 'rational' in the sense under consideration.

We turn now to the second major component of the Standard Theory. How are such preferences relevant to rational decision making?

Up to this point, we have been assuming that our creatures have perfect knowledge of the future. Of course this is wildly unrealistic. Things are chancy—the future is often, to a large extent, unknown. How can Hobbots (or anyone else for that matter) choose wisely in such a world? Decision theorists, and most if not all thin rationalists, recommend the policy of *maximizing expected utility.*[5]

Suppose that George is invited to play a game with two pennies. The pennies will be flipped. If, on landing, both show heads, George must pay forty cents. If they show one head and one tail, he must pay twenty cents. Finally, if they show two tails, George wins three dollars and 20 cents. George must decide whether to enter the game. His situation may be pictured like this:

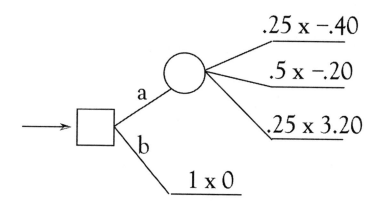

Remember, expected value is determined by multiplying probabilities by values and then summing the results. When we sum the products of probabilities times values in the game George has been asked to enter, we see that entering the game (route *a)* has an expected monetary value of sixty cents.

$$((.25 \times .40) + (.5 \times -.20) + (.25 \times 3.20)) = .60$$

Since 60 cents is considerably more than 0 cents (the expected monetary value of route *b)*, it would seem that George should play the game.

Perhaps, then, Butlerian self-love should urge a creature to do x if, and only if, the expected PMP [Pleasure Minus Pain] value of x's consequences is greater than the expected PMP value of the consequences of each of the feasible alternatives. Perhaps it should urge the creature *not* to do x if, and only if, there is some alternative act whose score in expected PMP value is greater than that offered by x.

Even in this simple form, the theory would have a considerable degree of plausibility. It would explain, for example, why some Hobbots who are probably in for more misery than pleasure nevertheless should not kill themselves. Imagine such a creature—call him "Alfred". Suppose Alfred knows that the chances are three out of four that he will have a short and unhappy future—a future whose total PMP score is, say, -100. If he commits suicide (painlessly) his score will be zero. And yet, if he lives on, there is one chance in four his future will be happy and of normal length—say 1,000 PMPs (1,000 units of pleasure minus pain). What does self-love urge him to do?

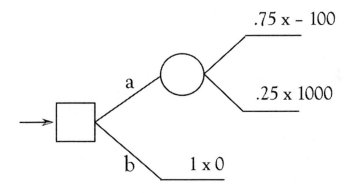

The expected PMP value of route *a* is 175. The expected PMP value of the suicide is zero. Hence standard self-love should urge Alfred not to commit sui-

cide, even though he is probably in for more misery than pleasure by not doing so.

Risk-Aversion

Butlerian self-love, as I have described it, takes utility to be directly proportional to PMP value. Suppose the greatest possible PMP score Alfred can
achieve is 1,000. Now consider a series of acts that give Alfred an increasing
good chance to win that maximal score and an increasingly small chance of a
zero score. One act, for example, gives him a fifty-fifty chance of scoring 1,000
or scoring 0. Another gives him a .75 chance of scoring 1,000 and a .25
chance of scoring 0, while a third gives him a .90 chance for the maximal score
and a .10 chance for 0. If we plot the PMP value to Alfred of these acts, the
result will presumably be a straight line. Furthermore, we assume that a .5
chance to win a score of 1000 (together with a .5 chance to come up with a
score of 0) is just as desirable as a *guaranteed* score of 500. The basis for this
assumption lies in the fact that the expected PMP values of these two paths are
exactly equal.

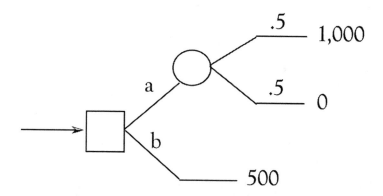

Alfred is *indifferent* in regard to choosing between route *a* and route *b*.

To take another example in the same series, a .75 chance to win a score of
1,000 (together with a .25 chance to win 0) will be just as desirable as a guaranteed score of 750. In fact, if we mark the points of equal desirability, we can
calibrate the desirability of this series of bets in units of guaranteed PMPs.

Chance

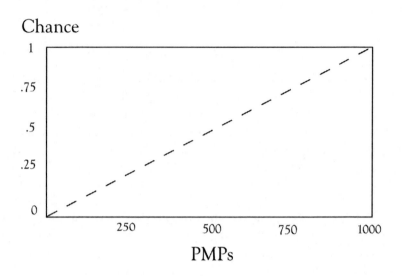

PMPs

If someone were to ask how much Alfred would value a ticket to a lottery giving him a .25 chance to win 1,000 PMPs and a .75 chance of winning 0 PMPs, we could say he values this at 250 PMPs—using PMPs to measure the value of the lottery. Conversely, if we were asked how much he values 250 PMPs, we could say, he values this at .25 in the 0-1000 lottery—using this probability as a way of measuring the utility score of 250 PMPs.

Now I want to claim that there is no good reason why a self-love module should go for pleasure and try to dodge pain in this simple minded, straightforward, way. It would be at least equally feasible to have the module be a bit *risk-adverse* where pay-offs are PMP scores.

Consider a fancier kind of self-love module. Suppose some such modules take PMP scores to exhibit diminishing marginal utility. That is to say, imagine Hobbots who do *not* value PMPs in direct proportion to their amount. Perhaps one such Hobbot values a PMP of 20,000 a bit *less* than twice as much as a PMP of 10,000. For this Hobbot, PMPs exhibit diminishing marginal utility.

A 'risk-adverse' Hobbot of this sort might prefer a guaranteed score of 500 to a .5 chance at a score of 1000 and a complementary chance of being killed painlessly on the spot. This creature might be indifferent between the .5 chance and a guaranteed score of 250. Such a Hobbot's 'curve of indifference' is, at least partially, convex. It may look like this.

Chance

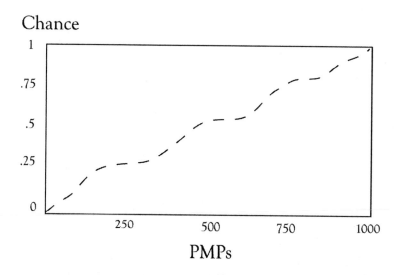

Pmps

In some situations, some possible Hobbots would avoid the route into the future with the best score in expected PMP value because that route is just *too risky*.

Problem: can something which is good in itself relative to a creature, have diminishing marginal utility for that creature? One might be tempted to hold that this is impossible. I think the temptation should be rejected. Pleasure is good in itself at least relative to the creature that feels it, and yet it is, I believe, rational permissible, if not mandatory, to be a bit risk-adverse in regard to possible future pleasures.

Imagine that some strange looking person you meet on the street tells you that he is the long awaited Holy One, and offers you infinite pleasure infinitely prolonged on the condition that you show your faith by cutting off the little finger of your left hand. Suppose you are not *absolutely* certain that he is not who he says he is. Perhaps you think there is one chance in 10^{10} that he is right. Under these conditions, does rationality require you to start cutting? I don't think so. The value to you now of infinite pleasure infinitely prolonged may be finite, and small enough to be made negligible when it is multiplied by 1 divided by 10^{10}.[6]

Risk aversion in regard to pleasure (and the absence of pain) is an interesting topic. Nevertheless, I will, for the most part, disregard it.

Hobbots and Prudence

The basic elements of Hobbot moral-psychology are now before us. So how should a Hobbot live? What, if anything, should be it's aim in life?

Here is one obvious suggestion. Hobbots should be governed by self-love. Certainly *Determined* Hobbots should conduct themselves in this way—that is to say, they *do* live this way when they are operating properly and are in control of themselves. But *Standard* Hobbots have to choose between self-love and inclination. The suggestion is that, all things considered, Standard Hobbots ought to be prudent—ought to make self-love dominant over inclination. They are likely to do better if they operate in this way—be happier, live longer, have more viable 'offspring', or whatever.

By definition, thin rationalists hold this view. Roughly speaking, they think it 'makes sense' to choose to be governed by self-love, and doesn't make sense to choose to be governed by inclination. A clear-thinking standard Hobbot should be able to see that, all things considered, it ought to be governed by reason (in this case Self-Love).

The *total* disenchanters disagree. Why shouldn't a Standard Hobbot favor its inclinations? For that matter, why shouldn't it operate on any weighting of self-love and inclination that strikes its fancy? Why *should* it pick a decision-making policy likely to be beneficial to itself?

Naturalistic total disenchanters are likely to add that this 'should' set's off alarms. Is it a leftover bit of theism? Who issued this commandment? Where does the obligation, or whatever, come from?

Disenchanters and Platonists can perhaps agree that prudence is likely to be a good thing relative to a Standard Hobbot (i.e. that it is likely to be good for the Hobbot). But this does not imply that the Hobbot ought to be prudent.

Platonists about morality can say that, other things being equal, it is objectively better if Hobbots are happy than if they are not. Prudence tends to be conducive to happiness. Hence, such realists can say, it would be a good thing if Standard Hobbots were prudent. In this sense, Hobbots 'ought' to be prudent.

As a warm-up for the next chapter, let's take a quick look at a well known, and somewhat puzzling, story.

The Prisoner's Dilemma

The 'Prisoner's Dilemma' was invented in 1950 (or thereabouts) by Merrill M. Flood and Melvin Dresher. The story might be told as follows:

A pair of Hobbots, H1 and H2, have been accused of a robbery. They are now in solitary confinement, unable to communicate with each other. The prosecuting attorney offers each them the following deal: "I have enough evidence to send you to the slammer whether anybody confesses or not. If you and your buddy remain silent, I'll put the two of you away for a year. If you confess and he doesn't, I'll let you go free, and throw the book at him –10 years. Of course I'm offering him the same deal. If it turns out you *both* squeal, you'll get nine years each. Think it over. I'll be back in an hour for your answer "

From H1's point of view, the situation looks like this:

	H2 Doesn't Squeal	H2 Squeals
Don't Squeal	One Year	Ten Years
Squeal	Go Free	Nine Years

In a way, the solution is obvious. Either H2 is going to squeal or he isn't. Suppose he keeps his mouth shut. In that case, it's a lot better to go free now than to spend a year in jail. So, if H2 is going to keep quiet, H1 should squeal. But suppose H2 Squeals. Clearly it would be better (from H1's point of view) to spend nine years in jail than to be locked up for ten. So no matter what H2 decides to do, it is to H1's advantage to squeal. Squealing 'dominates' not squealing.

Now the dilemma emerges. H2 is just as good as H1 at figuring the angles. He too sees he should squeal. Consequently (as both foresee) both will squeal, and both will be put away for nine long years. Is there some way they can avoid this? We will work on this problem in the next chapter.

Meanwhile, it is important to see that the root of the dilemma *isn't* the natural 'selfishness' of our Hobbots. Another case brings this out.

The Imprisoned Lover's Dilemma

Imagine a similar situation applied to two people (Bonnie and Clyde) who are 'Other-Lovers'. Each one is only concerned about the fate of the other. Now both lovers are (separately) offered this deal by the prosecutor:

"If you both squeal, you'll each get one year in jail. If you squeal and your partner doesn't, I'll set you free (and throw the book at him/her). On the other hand, if you keep quite, and he/she squeals, I'll throw the book at *you*— ten years in jail. If neither one of you squeals, you'll both get nine years."

Here is the situation from Bonnie's point of view:

	Clyde Squeals	Clyde doesn't Squeal
Squeal	One Year	Go Free
Don't Squeal	Ten Years	Nine Years

But, of course, Bonnie is only concerned about what will happen to Clyde (and visa versa). So bonnie thinks of the pay-offs like this:

	Clyde Squeals	Clyde doesn't Squeal
Squeal	Clyde gets One Year	Clyde gets Ten Years
Don't Squeal	Clyde goes Free	Clyde gets Nine Years

Hence, her ordinal utility assignments for these outcomes are as follows:

	Clyde Squeals	Clyde doesn't Squeal
Squeal	Second	Fourth
Don't Squeal	First	Third

Notice that her preferences have exactly the same configuration that H1's had in the original Prisoner's Dilemma. Now, however, *not* squealing dominates *squealing*. That is, it appears that things will go better for Clyde, if Bonnie refuses to squeal (no matter what Clyde decides to so). Unfortunately, Clyde is thinking of Bonnie in just the way Bonnie is thinking of Clyde. He too is compelled to keep silent by his concern for her well being. Neither will squeal. The result is that Bonnie and Clyde spend nine years in jail. Once again we have a genuine 'prisoner's dilemma'; but it certainly isn't generated by any kind of selfishness.

Relevant Books

Michael D. Resnik, *Choices*, University of Minnesota Press, Minneapolis, 1987. This is an excellent introduction to decision theory intended primarily for people interested in its philosophical aspects and its relevance to philosophical matters.

Howard Raiffa, *Decision Analysis*, Addison-Wesley Publishing Co., Reading, Mass., 1970. Intended primarily for people interested in business, engineering, administration, and so on. Not for those who don't like arithmetic.

NOTES

1.   Of course this is not an ethical 'should.' All we mean when we say this sort of thing is that this is the way she was designed to act—this is how these creatures were meant to operate.

2.   That wire represents the fact that occasionally we are governed by an inclination in spite of the protests of self-love (and conscience). But this leaves us with the question: does this feature of our design serve any useful purpose? And, if so, what?

3.   For a critical discussion of this and the other alleged constraints, see "Are the preference axioms really rational?" by Paul Anand, *Theory and Decision*, Vo. 23, No. 2, Sept. 1987, pp. 189-212. Patrick Maher offers a strong objection to the Money Pump argument (pp. 36-38) but later makes it part of his account of rational choice (p. 60). See his *Betting on Theories*, Cambridge University Press, 1993.

4.   Both I1 and I2 are taken (with trivial modifications) from Amartya Sen's *Collective Choice and Social Welfare*, Holden-Day, Inc. San Francisco, 1970, p. 17.

5.   For an introduction to the use of this strategy, see Resnik's, *Choices*, op. cit., or Howard Raiffa's *Decision Analysis*, Addison-Wesley Publishing Company, Reading, Mass., 1970. Richard C. Jeffrey's *The Logic of Decision* (University of Chicago Press, 1965) is a classic in the area.

6.   The decision problem discussed in this paragraph is, of course, related to Pascal's Wager. Pascal (mistakenly, I think) assumes that infinite happiness infinitely prolonged is, or should be, infinitely valuable to us now. See Blaise Pascal's, *Pensées*, Part two, section two.

CHAPTER SEVEN

'One Shot' PD

O ne of the projects of those who are interested in using computer simulations to study problems in political theory, sociology, and ethics, is to simulate the emergence and breakdown of cooperation in social interaction—in effect, the Hobbes Project. Imagine a million freshly manufactured standard Hobbots wandering around loose on the surface of Ganymede. They are totally unorganized—no administrative set-up, no rules, or laws, no economic system, no folk ethics, in operation among them. And, unfortunately, some of the things they need are in very short supply. According to the Hobbesian version of the story, this initial phase of Hobbot history is chaotic. The Hobbots just grab whatever they want from each other by trickery or violence. Many are 'killed'—trapped and stripped down for valuable parts. (The manufacturers replace defunct Hobbots with new ones so as to keep the population at roughly one million.) In short, the Hobbots find themselves in a state of war, each Hobbot against all the others. Their lives, as Hobbes says of humans in a 'state of nature', are "solitary, poor, nasty, brutish, and short".[xcii]

This scenario seems to pre-suppose that wide-ranging, benevolent passions in these Hobbots are very weak, or non-existent. Suppose each of the Hobbots very much wants all Hobbots to be healthy and happy. Suppose the misfortune of any Hobbot causes great ('mental') pain in all of those who become aware of it. Wouldn't strong, general, passions of this sort greatly reduce the horrors of a Hobbot 'state of nature'?

On the other hand, *narrow*, sharply focused, benevolent passions might do no good or even make things worse. The Hobbots might form small, tightly knit, gangs that do terrible damage to each other.

Let's assume that the Hobbots lack, or have only very weak, hard-wired, general, benevolent passions. After all, we want them to represent us, and human history seems to indicate that general benevolence—benevolence towards all of mankind or all sentient creatures—is not one of our most obvious characteristics.

Can the Hobbots find a way out of the state of nature? Some philosophers (Locke and Helvetius, for instance) seem to have thought that the transition from a state of nature to an organized society is relatively easy. Can't humans, or Hobbots, simply agree to set up some form of government, some equitable system for the distribution of scarce goods, and so on?

But why should rational creatures do what they have agreed to do, when, in a particular instance, it is to their advantage to stab someone else in the back (so to speak)? Why should Hobbots obey the Hobbot analog of Hobbes' Third Law of Nature, namely *that men perform their covenants made?* (By 'convenants' Hobbes means contracts, agreements, promises, and so on.)

Hobbes imagines a 'fool' who thinks, and sometimes even says out-loud, that there is no good reason why we should not do whatever we think is conducive to our own survival and contentment; and thus no reason why we shouldn't keep, or not keep, our covenants simply on the basis of whether or not it will benefit us to do so.[2]

Surely the fool's claim has a considerable degree of plausibility? But, that being so, how can any human, or Hobbot, trust another to keep an agreement? At least two means of escape have been suggested. First, if the creatures could somehow bring it about that all, or at least most, agreement-breakers were severely punished, that would *change the pay-offs* for breaking agreements—make such behavior very expensive. This would reduce the occurrence of agreement breaking. (Let's call this the *Political* Solution.) Second, perhaps the creatures will get the idea that it is in their interest to *reform their character* (or change their strategy) in a way that makes them cooperative under certain circumstances [the *Reformation* Solution].

Some advocates of the Reformation Solution view the state of nature as a one-shot Prisoner's Dilemma. David Gauthier thinks of it that way.[3] Others think of it as involving many interactions between particular players of the game ('iterated' interaction). In this chapter we will focus on one-shot PD.

The idea is, in effect, that the Hobbots on Ganymede can be represented by a single pair of Hobbots who discover that they can resolve the one-shot prisoner's dilemma by undergoing a transformation of character— 'constraining' their Self-Love, and thus becoming (somewhat, sort of) *moral* before the game begins. Presumably, Hobbot Self-Love itself urges all, or at least most of the Hobbots on Ganymede to undergo the same reformation, and this leads to an escape from the state of nature.

How is this supposed to work? The story is a bit tricky. Let's go back to basics.

A pair of determined Hobbots, H1 and H2, are about to play one round of PD. They will then collect their payoffs and that will be the end of them— they will be obliterated. The game is *terminal.* (Both of them know this.) Here are their pay-offs in PMPs (Pleasure hours Minus Pain hours, in case you have forgotten).

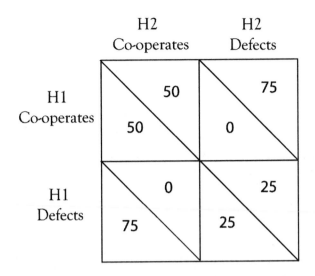

The upper left-hand box shows that if H1 and H2 both choose to cooperate they will each receive 50 PMPs. On the other hand, if H1 cooperates and H2 defects, then (upper right-hand box) H1 will get nothing, and H2 will get the big prize—75 PMPs. Moving down-stairs, if H1 defects and H2 cooperates, H1 gets the big prize and H2 gets nothing (lower left-hand box). Finally, if both Hobbots defect, they each get 25 PMPs.

Given the problem as stated, it seems clear that they should both defect. Look at the situation from H1's point of view. H2 is either going to cooperate or defect. Suppose he is going to cooperate. In that case, H1 will win the big prize, if she (H1) defects. Suppose H2 is going to defect. Then, again, it would be better for H1 to defect—that way she gets 25 PMPs. If she were to cooperate, she would get nothing. So either way, it looks as though H1 should defect. There's no surprise here. It's a simple PD. Defecting dominates cooperating. If they are thinking clearly, both H1 and H2 will defect, collect their 25 PMPs, and be obliterated.

(The fact that these are determined, rather than standard, Hobbots makes this prediction plausible. In trying to figure out what H2 is going to do, we don't have to worry about the possibility that his Chooser will endorse some inclination contrary to Self-Love. We are dealing with determined Hobbots rather than standard ones in order to avoid this worry.)

Let's change the story. Suppose now that H1 and H2 can each acquire a character (i.e. adopt a strategy) that will determine how he or she will act in a one-shot PD situation. Each character (or strategy) is associated with a color. Everybody knows what the basic colors mean. There are many such characters. But, for the moment, let's give our Hobbots just four options:

> (1) *Nasty* creatures always defect. The perceived character of their opponent makes no difference. Nasties are bright red.
>
> (2) *Patsies* always cooperate. Like the Nasties, they pay no attention to the character of their opponent. Patsies are pale blue.
>
> (3) *Selfers* cooperate with all creatures they take to be like themselves (i.e. other selfers), and defect in all other cases. Selfers are green.
>
> (4) *Self-Haters* cooperate with all creatures they take to be *unlike* themselves, and defect when they encounter creatures they take to be Self-Haters. Self-Haters are yellow.[4]

(Note that in these one-shot games an 'unmodified' determined Hobbot will defect no matter what. Hence, for present purposes, these Hobbots can be lumped with the Nasties and painted red.)

H1 and H2 are trying to decide which character to adopt. What should they do?

I take it we can forget the Self-Haters. They are losers. For instance, when a Self-Hater meets a Nasty, the Self-Hater cooperates, even though she can see that the other player is red. Thus she scores zero. H1 and H2 are not going to become Self-Haters.

Here is a table showing the pay-offs that each of the remaining three characters score against their own kind and against the others.

	Nasty	Patsy	Selfer
Nasty	25	75	25
Patsy	0	50	0
Selfer	25	75	50

The first row (25, 75, 25) shows the PMPs a Nasty scores against another Nasty (25), and against the other two characters (75 and 25). The second row (0, 50, 0) shows a Patsy's pay-offs, and so on.

Given a choice among just these three characters in this set-up, what should H1 and H2 do? Think of the problem from H1's point of view. Suppose that, initially, H1 thinks it equally likely that H2 will choose any one of the three characters. In that case the expected PMP values of H1's three options are roughly:

Nasty = 125/3 = 41.7
Patsy = 50/3 = 16.7
Selfer = 150/3 = 50

Clearly, becoming a Patsy is not a serious option. So the real choice is between becoming a Nasty or a Selfer. Both H1 and H2 must be aware of this. On the supposition that H2 might equally well choose either of the two remaining characters, H1's choice reduces to:

Nasty = 50/2 = 25
Selfer = 75/2 = 37.5

It seems obvious that H1 should become a green Selfer. And, since both Hobbots are almost certainly reasoning in the same way, in all probability they will both become Selfers and thus will cooperate. As rational decision-makers, this is what they ought to do in the present situation.

I have made it sound as though H1 and H2 can only guess what the other is likely to do. But, in fact, there is no particular reason why the problem should not be worked out in candid conversation. They have nothing to loose by helping each other see where their interests lie.

Why do Determined Selfers cooperate when they find themselves in a one-shot PD with someone they take to be another Selfer? Two general kinds of reasons, or grounds, come to mind.

First, the Selfer may have made a move towards something like loyalty to a group (namely, all Selfers). Selfers who have made this move genuinely want to be helpful—cooperative—when they are dealing with other Selfers. (Of course each Selfer knows that it will not be harmed by cooperating with another Selfer.) When a Hobbot becomes a Selfer of this sort, it may well be that her utility function is modified. Given a choice between a situation in which both she and her fellow Selfer get 50 PMPs and one in which she receives 50, while he receives only 25, she positively prefers that her fellow Selfer should gain the

50 PMPs. Or, perhaps, what she prefers is that she should be cooperative in dealing with other Selfers rather than not being cooperative, other things being equal.

The other general possibility is that the Selfer has simply chosen to set up in herself a compulsion, which will induce other Selfers to be cooperative. Selfers of this sort do not particularly *want* to be cooperative. They are, so to speak, operating mechanically.

In either case, it must be possible for other Selfers to be quite sure that their partner will cooperate. The psychological set-up might look something like this:

Output from the Self-Love module is filtered through the Selfer Strategy. If the creature sees itself as being in a PD of the sort we are considering, then it is governed by the Selfer Strategy. When the situation is not perceived as a PD of this kind, the Selfer Strategy module simply passes the output of Self-Love along to the Motor System.

The Selfer

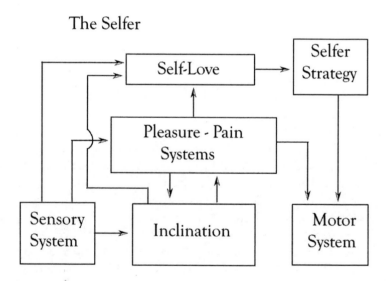

Here is an interesting variant of the one shot PD game. Instead of the Hobbots making their moves simultaneously, the moves are made one after the other sequentially. One of the Hobbots is chosen at random to make the first move. She cooperates or defects. The other Hobbot sees what the first Hobbot has done, and then makes his move.[5]

H1 and H2 have become Selfers. They are going to play terminal PD sequentially. H1 makes the first move. Since she has every reason to think that H2 is a Selfer (after all, he's green), H1 chooses to cooperate. Now it's H2's turn. What should he do?

Presumably, Self-Love would now urge H2 to defect. That way he gets 75 PMPs. He gets only 50 if he chooses to cooperate. On the other hand, if he now wants to be cooperative more than he wants those extra 25 PMPs (if he is *that* kind of Selfer), then he will cooperate. (His utility function departs from the function dictated by Self-Love at this point.)

The same result can be obtained by a sort of compulsion, without any general affection for Selfers.

Given a particular finite set of alternative characters, we can test them in the following way. Each character is assigned to two Determined Hobbots. Each character type gets one round of standard (i.e. non-sequential) PD with itself and with a representative of each of the other character types. Then the total score for each character type is added up. (This is sometimes called a 'tour' of characters.[6])

Let's try it with Nasties, Patsies, and Selfers. First two Nasties play a round of one-shot PD. Then a Nasty plays a patsy. Then a Nasty plays a Selfer. Next, a Patsy plays a Nasty. And so on. Using the same old pay-offs, here's how it looks:

	Nasty	Patsy	Selfer
Nasty	25 / 25	0 / 75	25 / 25
Patsy	75 / 0	50 / 50	75 / 0
Selfer	25 / 25	0 / 75	50 / 50

The payoffs for a player representing each character (or strategy) are as follows:

Nasty = (25 + 75 + 25) = 125
Patsy = (0 + 50 + 0) = 50
Selfer = (25 + 75 + 50) = 150
(We have seen these numbers before.)

Given just these three characters, and any number of tours, Selfers do better than Nasties. And Nasties do better than Patsies. (No surprises here.)

Let's try something similar on Ganymede. We assume, for now, that our creatures are determined Hobbots. They are divided into three equal groups. Each group is assigned one of the three characters and painted the appropriate color. Then they are turned loose to play standard, one-shot, PD, with the pay-offs as specified above, in randomly selected pairs. The process is repeated over and over again. That is to say the Hobbots wander around, form new random pairs, and play again. They keep repeating this process.

In the long run, the pay-offs of the Nasties, Patsies and Selfers should tend to approximate the ratio given above: 125:50:150 (i.e. 5:2:6). The Selfers should tend to do best, the Nasties next best, and the Patsies worst. Under these circumstances, cooperation with one's own kind and defection when one meets alien kinds tends to pay off. Given a chance to be one of the players in this set-up, it would make sense to want to be a Selfer.

There are possible characters who are 'nicer' than Selfers. For instance:

(5) *Cautious Cooperators* cooperate with any creature they take to be like themselves (i.e. a Cautious Cooperator), and with any creature they think will cooperate with them. Otherwise, they defect. Cautious Cooperators are violet.[7]

Cautious Cooperators do not exploit Patsies, since, after all, they expect them to cooperate. Consequently, they do less well than Selfers in a tour of all four characters.

	Nasty	Patsy	Selfer	Cautious Cooperator
Nasty	25 / 25	0 / 75	25 / 25	25 / 25
Patsy	75 / 0	50 / 50	75 / 0	50 / 50
Selfer	25 / 25	0 / 75	50 / 50	25 / 25
Cautious Cooperator	25 / 25	50 / 50	25 / 25	50 / 50

(Note that Cautious Cooperators do not cooperate with Selfers. This is because they are aware that Selfers will regard them as non-selfers, and won't cooperate.)

Here are the scores:

Nasty = (25 + 75 + 25 + 25) = 150
Patsy = (0 + 50 + 0 + 50) = 100
Selfer = (25 + 75 + 50 + 25) = 175
Cautious Cooperator = (25 + 50 + 25 + 50) = 150

A slight modification of the Cautious Cooperator strategy yields another interesting character.

Anti Patsies cooperate with any creature they take to be an Anti-Patsy, and with anyone else they think will cooperate, *except* someone they take to be a Patsy.[8] Anti Patsies are orange.

None of my Hobbots are mind readers.[9] They have information about how the various basic characters behave—they know how these characters act in PD situations—and they can see the colors of the creatures they confront. On the basis of these perceived colors, and their information, they decide whether to cooperate or defect.

In a tour of all five characters the pay-offs look like this:

	Nasty	Patsy	Selfer	Cautious Cooperator	Anti Patsy
Nasty	25 \ 25	0 \ 75	25 \ 25	25 \ 25	25 \ 25
Patsy	75 \ 0	50 \ 50	75 \ 0	50 \ 50	75 \ 0
Selfer	25 \ 25	0 \ 75	50 \ 50	25 \ 25	25 \ 25
Cautious Cooperator	25 \ 25	50 \ 50	25 \ 25	50 \ 50	50 \ 50
Anti Patsy	25 \ 25	0 \ 75	25 \ 25	50 \ 50	50 \ 50

The scores are:

Nasty = (25 + 75 + 25 + 25 + 25) = 175
Patsy = (0 + 50 + 0 + 50 + 0) = 100
Selfer = (25 + 75 + 50 + 25 + 25) = 200
Cautious Cooperator = (25 + 50 + 25 + 50 + 50) = 200
Anti Patsy = (25 + 75 + 25 + 50 + 50) = 225

Selfers have dropped back a bit. They now do no better than Cautious Cooperators. This is because Cautious Cooperators cooperate with Anti Patsies, but Selfers don't.

We have looked at three tours. Each one can be taken as representative of a possible situation on Ganymede. Selfers do best in the first two situations. Anti Patsies do best in the third. Both Selfers and Anti Patsies are sometimes cooperative. Does this show that some kinds of moral self-constraint tend to pay off? Not quite. It is far from obvious that genuine *morality* is required here at all. Selfers and Anti Patsies are not nice. They take advantage of Patsies. Furthermore, from the point of view of people who believe in genuine morality, there may well be nothing at all moral in their cooperation. Why do they cooperate? Is it, for example, because they want to be helpful to creatures of their own kind? Perhaps. On the other hand, they may cooperate simply because a compulsion to do so has been installed. The compulsion would work just as well as a desire to be helpful. Clearly their reason for cooperating is *not* that it is morally right to cooperate in these circumstances. We have found no evidence that instrumental rationality requires a bit of morality.

I am about to introduce the topic of Hobbot mimics—Hobbots who present themselves as being what they are not. But before we get into that, I want to outline an argument to show that there is no generally dominant character (strategy) among non-mimicking, 'transparent,'[10] Hobbots in the kind of PD set-up we have been exploring. The argument was devised by Leslie Burkholder.[11]

First, consider non-mimicking characters that cooperate in some situations. This group includes Patsies, Selfers, Self-Haters, Cautious Cooperators, and Anti Patsies. (Every possible character is either a sometimes cooperator or a Nasty.) It is easy to show that none of these characters can be generally dominant (i.e. always do at least as well as any other character, and sometimes do better). The argument is the following:

For any sometime cooperator, imagine a tour of three characters, namely (1) the sometime cooperator, (2) a Nasty, (3) a *gray* character who cooperates with anyone it takes to be a Nasty, and defects with everyone else (this includes its own kind, of course)— a *Nasty Lover. In all such tours, the Nasties do best.*

For instance, here are the scores (same old pay-offs) for a tour made up of Nasties, Anti Patsies, and Nasty Lovers:

Nasty (25 + 25 + 75) = 125
Anti Patsy (25 + 50 + 25) = 100
Nasty Lover (0 + 25 + 25) = 50

Clearly, then, none of the sometimes cooperators, including the Nasty Lovers, can be dominant. But, as we have seen elsewhere, Nasties are not dominant either. For instance, we have seen a tour in which Anti Patsies do better than Nasties. Hence, no non-mimicking (non-deceptive) character (strategy) is generally dominant.

Impostors

As in the natural world, mimicry can be very rewarding among Hobbots. Nasties and Patsies have a lot to gain from successful mimicry. In particular, it would pay to resemble an Anti Patsy or a Cautious Cooperator.

(Obviously, there is a lot of fakery in ordinary human life. For instance, some bad people are very successful at pretending to be good.)

Consider a Hobbot who cooperates no matter what, but is yellowish-orange rather than pale blue. Of course this is just a Patsy with something close to Anti Patsy coloration. Let's call it a *'Patsy Fake.'* Suppose the mimicry is good enough to fool everyone. A creature like this would do better than an ordinary Patsy when playing against Anti Patsies.

A *Nasty Fake* is a much more serious matter. These Hobbots always defect, and are a reddish violet or reddish orange in color (i.e. they look a lot like Cautious Cooperators or Anti Patsies).

Suppose, again, that the mimicry is good enough to fool everyone.

Nasty = (25 + 75 + 25 + 25 + 25 + 25) = 200
Patsy = (0 + 50 + 0 + 50 + 0 + 0) = 100
Selfer = (25 + 75 + 50 + 25 + 25 + 25) = 225
Cautious Cooperator = (25 + 50 + 25 + 50 + 50 + 0) = 200
Anti Patsy = (25 + 75 + 25 + 50 + 50 + 0) = 225
Nasty Fake = (25 + 75 + 25 + 75 + 75 + 25) = 300

There are at least two important points to notice about Nasty Fakes. First, if the mimicry is a complete success, or even anything near it, Nasty Fakes do very well indeed. In fact, in the six-character tour just listed they get the best score. I take this to show that there are circumstances in which rational Hobbots should become (or try to become) Nasty Fakes. (This sense of 'should' is obviously the same as that in which, in other circumstances, a Hobbot 'should' become a Selfer, or an Anti Patsy. Instrumental rationality urges the transformation.)

The other point is that Nasty Fakes do serious damage to other players of the game. In this last tour, the Anti Patsies do no better than Selfers. More importantly perhaps, the characters that depend upon reliable information about the character of their opponent now have reason to be worried.

Think again of the situation on Ganymede. Suppose the six characters listed above are equally represented in the population. Now, when a Selfer is matched against another Selfer, neither one can be perfectly confident that the other really *is* a Selfer. They have to learn to estimate the chances, or just guess.

Is some sort of mimic generally dominant in the sort of set-up we have been considering? I don't think so. In any case, it is easy to show that the Nasty Fake isn't dominant.

Consider a tour in which the characters are (1) Nasties, (2) Nasty Fakes, and (3) Nasty Lovers. Here are their scores:

Nasty = (25 + 25 + 75) = 125
Nasty Fake = (25 + 25 + 25) = 75
Nasty Lover = (0 + 25 + 25) = 50

In this tour, Nasties do better than Nasty Fakes because the Nasty Lovers recognize the Nasties but take the Nasty Fakes to be Cautious Cooperators or Anti Patsies.

My guess is that there is no dominant character of any kind in this one shot sort of set up. If I am right, then, one assumes, there is also no generally dominant character in the Ganymede situation we have been imagining. As we have seen, there can be particular situations at a given time, or in a given locale, such that, there and then, it would be wise for a Hobbot to choose such and such a character. But there is, I think, no character it would always, everywhere, make sense to adopt and maintain.

Summary of Results

- It has been shown that there are situations in which Self-Love urges a Hobbot to become a creature who is cooperative to some extent in PD encounters. (It has *not* been shown that the resultant cooperative creature is, or is on the way to becoming, genuinely moral.)
- It has been shown that Self-Love urges Hobbots to take advantage of Patsies.
- It has been shown that no non-deceptive ('transparent') character is dominant in all one-shot PD tours.
- It has been shown that Self-Love sometimes urges a Hobbot to become a Nasty Fake.

If we were to take this experiment (or whatever it is) to show how we should act in various social contexts, the up-shot would appear to be that there is no one sort of character—no one strategy—that reason recommends. We should be nice when that is what is required to get the people around us to act the way we want them to act, and we should be nasty when we can get away with it to our own advantage. In addition the experiment would seem to show that it is often a good idea to deceive others into believing that we are nicer (more willing to cooperate) than we really are.

We have been looking at one shot PD—single games between pairs of players. Or, if there have been re-matches, our Hobbots have paid no attention to the past records of their opponents.

In *iterated* PD, the situation is quite different. Here, Hobbots regularly form pairs that play each other repeatedly. Typically, they respond to the way their opponent has behaved in previous matches. This is our topic in the next chapter.

NOTES

1. Thomas Hobbes, *Leviathan*, Basil Blackwell, Oxford, 1955, Part 1, chap. 13, p. 82.

2. Ibid. Part 1, chap. 15, p. 94.

3. See his *Morals by Agreement*, Clarendon Press, Oxford, 1986, Ch. VI.

4. One might think of these four characters as the start of an infinite series of characters defined by how they respond to other characters in the series. The first pair doesn't pay any attention to character. They just do their own thing. The second pair recognize their own kind and 'others.' The third group of characters will recognize themselves and the four characters already defined. All remaining characters are just 'others.' The fourth group will recognize themselves and all the characters previously defined. And so on.

5. This is what Peter Danielson calls "extended PD." See his *Artificial Morality, Virtuous Robots for Virtual Games*, Routledge, 1992.

6. Again, this is a term from Danielson. See ibid.

7. My Cautious Cooperators are basically the same as Peter Danielson's Conditional Cooperators and David Gauthier's Constrained Maximizers. See Danielson's "Closing the compliance dilemma: How it's rational to be moral in a Lamarckian world," in *Contractarianism and Rational Choice*, Edited by Peter Vallentyne, Cambridge University Press, New York, 1991, pp. 291-322. Note especially p. 298, and footnote 8.

8. Anti Patsies are cheap and easy substitutes for Danielson's more interesting, but also more problematic, Reciprocal Cooperators. See his "Closing the Compliance Dilemma", ibid. p. 299, and pp. 309-314.

9. Some of Danielson's creatures (and perhaps Gauthier's too) are flawless, or at least tolerable, mind readers. They 'see' the actual program that determines their opponent's behavior in PD. See Holly Smith's "Deriving morality from rationality", in *Contractarianism and Rational Choice*, (ibid.) for a nice attack on this feature of the Gauthier/Danielson project.

10. This is a reference to the mind-reading property discussed by Gauthier and Danielson. The idea is that some characters are 'transparent,' or at least 'translucent,' to others. One can, so to speak, see into their hearts. Other characters are more or less 'opaque.' One cannot see how they will act.

11. The Burkholder argument was produced in the course of controversy in an e-mail PD discussion group. I have modified the argument slightly to suit the characters under consideration in this chapter.

Iterated PD

In iterated PD, at the end of each round there is some likelihood that the same players will immediately confront each other again. For instance, in a given tournament there might always be a 0.7 chance of this happening. Given that two players have met before, we assume that they remember what happened in the previous game. Typically, they will cooperate or defect on the basis of those memories. In this sense, iterated PD is 'behavioristic' decisions are made on the basis of previous behavior—no revealing (or concealing) coloration, no reading of minds.

The two simplest strategies in iterated PD are deviant in this regard. They are not responsive to what happened in previous games. *Nasties* and *Patsies* don't need any memory. They just keep on defecting or cooperating, unless they make a mistake. (In realistic computer models of social interaction it is common to allow a few mistakes—random errors in the execution of a players strategy.)

A slightly more complicated group of 'no memory' strategies is based on randomization. For instance, the player might flip a coin and defect when the coin lands heads, cooperate when it lands tails. That is to say, the strategy might be to cooperate or defect with a random 50/50 chance of doing either one. Another such strategy would be to cooperate 75 percent of the time and defect the other 25 percent, on a random basis. And so on.

Then there are strategies that only depend upon remembering what the *opponent* did in the previous round. Here, for example, is the well known *Tit-for-Tat* strategy:

$$0 \longrightarrow C$$
$$C \longrightarrow C$$
$$D \longrightarrow D$$

The Tit-for-Tater begins by cooperating. Thereafter she simply does whatever her opponent did in the previous round.

Suspicious Tit-for-Tat begins by *defecting* and then proceeds as a Tit-for-Tater:

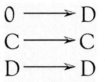

The opposite strategies are, for obvious reasons, called 'Anti-Tit-for-Tat':[1]

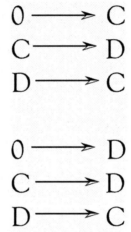

A creature following one of these strategies defects in response to the opponent's previous cooperation and cooperates in response to defection.

One can, so to speak, mix strategies. Thus, for instance, one could cooperate on the first move, and continue to cooperate unless, and until, the opponent defects. At that point one might turn nasty and defect for as long as the series of games continues (The *Sorehead* strategy).

There are no end of possible probabilistic ("impure,' 'stochastic') responses to the opponents move in the previous game. Thus, for instance, there is the strategy of (a) responding to the opponent's cooperation by randomizing with a 0.4 chance of cooperating (and, of course, a 0.6 chance of defecting); and (b) responding to the opponent's defection by randomizing with a 0.1 chance of cooperating (and a 0.9 chance of defecting).

$$C \longrightarrow 0.4$$
$$D \longrightarrow 0.1$$

The strategy space composed by these probabilistic strategies has been explored in considerable detail, and some interesting results have emerged. Thus, for instance, it turns out that given a very low error level, and a very high probability that the game will be repeated, *Generous Tit For Tat*, is the optimal strategy.[2]

Generous Tit For Tat

$$C \longrightarrow 1$$
$$D \longrightarrow 0.33$$

The Generous Tit for Tater always responds to cooperation by cooperating. In response to defection, she randomizes in such a way as to cooperate about 33% of the time (and defect about 67% of the time).[3]

I take an 'optimal' strategy to be one which gets the highest over-all score, or tends to get such a score, in a given population of alternative strategies. An 'optimal' strategy, in this sense, need not be dominant—it need not do better than, or even as well as, every other strategy in every one of it's matches.

We turn now to strategies that require memory of *both* player's moves in the previous game. There are four possible both-player outcomes in a single PD game.

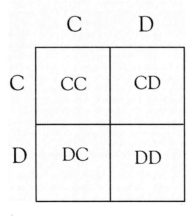

	C	D
C	CC	CD
D	DC	DD

Suppose that Player One and Player Two have just played a match. Player one cooperated and player two defected. From Player One's perspective, the outcome was **CD.**

Here is a nice strategy for players of iterated PD.

Pavlov:

$$CC \longrightarrow C$$
$$CD \longrightarrow D$$
$$DC \longrightarrow D$$
$$DD \longrightarrow C$$

Pavlovians repeat their previous move if it paid off in the previous round (i.e. if they got positive reinforcement for it). Hence, if there was mutual cooperation, she cooperates again. If defection paid off (the other player cooperated), she defects. On the other hand, if she was punished by getting one of the two lower scores, then she switches to the **alternative** response. "Win-stay, lose-shift."

There are 16 deterministic (non-probabilistic) ways of responding to the four possible previous outcomes–16 deterministic strategies.

D	D	D	D	D	D
D	D	D	D	C	C
D	D	C	C	D	D
D	C	D	C	D	C ...and so on.

What about the moves in the first game of the series? Don't the players have anything worked out for this situation? Well, of course, they can either cooperate or defect. So there are two variants for each of the 16 strategies.

(Note that these 16 [or 32] strategies include most of the deterministic strategies we have already defined. For instance DDDD is the Nasty strategy, and CCCC is the Patsy. Tit for Tat has two variants: CCDCD and DCDCD.)

Genetic Algorithms

Clearly, players of iterated PD that can 'remember' what happened in the previous round of the game—what they themselves did and whether their opponent cooperated or defected—sometimes have an advantage over those that don't. Their strategies can be more complex. Things get even more interesting if the players are allowed to 'remember', say, the previous two or three rounds. Now the 'search space' of strategies to be considered becomes very large.

Consider the possible deterministic strategies available to a player that can respond on the basis of two previous rounds of the game (once the two initial two rounds have been played out):

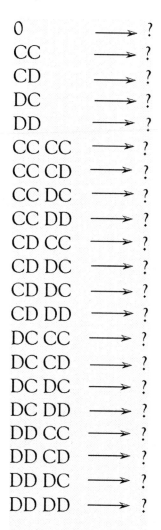

$$
\begin{array}{lcl}
0 & \longrightarrow & ? \\
CC & \longrightarrow & ? \\
CD & \longrightarrow & ? \\
DC & \longrightarrow & ? \\
DD & \longrightarrow & ? \\
CC\ CC & \longrightarrow & ? \\
CC\ CD & \longrightarrow & ? \\
CC\ DC & \longrightarrow & ? \\
CC\ DD & \longrightarrow & ? \\
CD\ CC & \longrightarrow & ? \\
CD\ DC & \longrightarrow & ? \\
CD\ DC & \longrightarrow & ? \\
CD\ DD & \longrightarrow & ? \\
DC\ CC & \longrightarrow & ? \\
DC\ CD & \longrightarrow & ? \\
DC\ DC & \longrightarrow & ? \\
DC\ DD & \longrightarrow & ? \\
DD\ CC & \longrightarrow & ? \\
DD\ CD & \longrightarrow & ? \\
DD\ DC & \longrightarrow & ? \\
DD\ DD & \longrightarrow & ? \\
\end{array}
$$

Each different way of filling in the column of question marks with twenty-one Cs and/or Ds represents a possible deterministic strategy. There are, then 2^{21} (i.e. 2,097,152) such strategies.. And we want to know how well they do when played off against each other in various possible combinations. Clearly the 'search space' here is large.

In this sort of case, 'genetic algorithms' tend to do well. A genetic algorithm is a computer simulation of Darwinian evolution. In the present situation, we might begin with a population of twenty different random sequences of twenty one Cs and Ds.

Robert Axelrod often uses eight particular strategies as a sort of fixed standard environment by which to measure the success or failure of new non-designed strategies produced by a genetic algorithm.[4] Each genetic strategy is paired off against a standard strategy, and they all play, say, 155 rounds of PD. The scores are recorded. Then each genetic strategy is paired off with a different standard strategy, and again the pairs play 155 rounds of PD, and so on, until each genetic strategy has been tested against each of the eight standard strategies, and its average score in the eight matches has been noted.

Now comes the interesting part. Strategies that have done conspicuously badly are scraped.[5] Very successful individuals are allowed four offspring.[6] Average individuals are allowed just two. (of course, very successful individuals only mate with other very successful individuals.) The mating involves both mutation and 'crossover.' A *mutation*, in this case, is a change of a C to a D, or a D to a C at a few randomly selected location in a strategy-string ('chromosome'). A *crossover* is brought about by cutting two strategy-strings at the same location, and switching the parts above (or below) the cut. Thus a string of 21 letters might be mated to another such string by cutting both strings just below the 10th letter down, and switching the two 10 letter pieces. The result, generally speaking, is two new strategies.

The new generation of strategies is then played off against the standard eight strategies, just like the first generation. And again the successful strategies are mated. This process is continued for, say, 50 generations.

Axelrod has used this sort of procedure to explore strategies that 'remember' the *three* previous rounds of PD. (This generates chromosome strings of 70 Cs and Ds. Hence, the number of possible distinct strategies is 2 to the 70th power. The results surprised him. The genetic algorithm often produced strategies that were more successful than Tit for Tat against the standard strategies. Axelrod writes:

> Although most of the runs evolve populations whose rules are very similar to TIT FOR TAT, in eleven of the forty runs, the median rule actually does substantially better than TIT FOR TAT. In these eleven runs, the populations evolved strategies that manage to exploit one of the eight representatives at the cost of achieving somewhat less cooperation with two others. But the net effect is a gain in effectiveness.

These very effective rules evolved by breaking the most important advice developed in the computer tournament, namely, to be 'nice,' that is never to be the first to defect. These highly effective rules always defect on the very first move, and sometimes on the second move as well, and use the choices of the other player to discriminate what should be done next. The highly effective rules then had responses that allowed them to 'apologize' and get to mutual cooperation with most of the unexploitable representatives, and different responses that allowed them to exploit a representative that was exploitable.[7]

The evolution just described took place in a fixed environment. The problem to be solved, so to speak, was to arrive at an optimal strategy for iterated PD played against the standard eight opponents. Axelrod, and others,[8] have run simulations in which strategies evolve in games played against other evolving strategies, rather than against the standard eight. This, of course, makes the situation much more complex. Typically, at first, the tendency is for there to be less and less cooperation. Very few of the early, more or less random, strategies regularly cooperate in response to cooperation. Hence, cooperation doesn't pay, and the evolving strategies tend to become even less cooperative. Eventually, however, some players begin to 'figure out,' so to speak, how to cooperate with those willing to cooperate while still being quick to retaliate to those who defect in response to cooperation. Reciprocators become common, and, in the long run, there tends to be lots of cooperation.[9] (Presumably, many, if not most, of these reciprocating strategies are also able to locate exploitable cooperators, and take advantage of them.)

These experiments are relevant to the project on Ganymede. If the Hobbots there are able to identify each other and remember past interactive behavior, then it makes sense for them to adopt strategies that tend to bring about long periods of cooperative interaction, unfortunately punctuated sometimes by periods of social disintegration and lack of cooperation. The computer experiments lead us to expect this result.

One of the most common objections I have heard to disenchantment theory is that, given the disenchanter's assumptions about ethics and human nature, a prosperous society would be impossible. Each person would be out for himself or herself and a Hobbesian state of nature would be inescapable. The computer experiments described in this chapter seem to show that this claim is overly pessimistic.

NOTES

1. See Kristian Lindgren's "Evolutionary Phenomena in Simple Dynamics,," in *Artificial Life II*, Ed. by Christopher Lagton, Charles Taylor, J. Doyne Farmer, and Steen Rasmussen, Addison-Wesley Publishing Company, Redwood City, Cal. 1992, pp. 295–312, esp. p. 299.

2. See Karl Sigmund, *Games of Life*, Oxford University Press, 1993, pp. 193-4.

3. See Karl Sigmund, ibid.

4. See Robert Axelrod, *The Complexity of Cooperation*, 1997, Princeton University Press, Princeton, New Jersey, pp. 16-22. Success against these eight strategies emerged as a good predictor of success in Axelrod's PD tournaments.

5. A 'conspicuously bad' score is one that is one standard deviation below the average score among the competing genetic strategies.

6. A 'very successful' individual is one whose score is one standard deviation above the average.

7. Ibid. p. 21.

8. See, for instance, Karl Sigmund's *Games of Life*, Oxford University Press, 1993, Ch. 8.

9. Axelrod, op. cit. pp. 22-23.

Hobbot Rationality

C an Hobbots be fully rational? The principal problem in regard to Hobbot rationality is that Hobbots of all kinds lack a conscience. They have no sense of moral rightness and wrongness. They are totally unaware of that aspect of things. Some philosophers take, or seem to take, this to entail that Hobbots cannot be rational at all, let alone be fully rational.

For instance, Richard Price writes:

> A rational agent void of all moral judgment, incapable of perceiving a difference, in respect of fitness and unfitness to be performed, between actions, and acting from blind propensions without any sentiments concerning what he does, is not possible to be imagined.[1]

Apparently he holds that moral judgment is a necessary condition for being a 'rational' creature. Of course Hobbots may well have sentiments concerning what they do. Suppose that a Hobbot succumbs to an inclination in spite of strong protests from Self-Love. Such a Hobbot might well feel shame or anger at itself—might think, correctly, that the deed was foolish. Perhaps Price would regard this as enough for the Hobbot to pass the test. On the other hand, Price seems to lump a capacity for this sort of approval or disapproval of actions together with an ability to perceive moral rightness and wrongness in actions. If this is part of the requirement, Hobbots are not rational.

Imagine a race of alien creatures who design space-ships, compose music, dance, write poetry, are good at mathematics and physics, and so on, but have no sense of humor. Of course they are lacking something. Perhaps we wouldn't want to invite them to our parties. But, surely, they may be fully rational? Not all spiritual-intellectual impairments impair one's rationality.

It seems clear that Hobbots are more rational than brutes. This is not to say that their choices are more likely to show that the creature's preferences are 'rational.' I take it that the choices of well-designed brutes could be more or less 'rational' in *that* sense. Hobbots are 'rational' in the minimal sense that they are able to act in conformity to Self-Love (or a Desire Resolver). This requires reasoning in regard to what ought to be done, and an appraisal of one's possible deeds. A Hobbot must have a conception of itself as it is at present and a conception of itself as it will be in the future. It must be able to imagine how it *would* feel *if* such and such happened to it. In this sense, a Hobbot is certainly more rational than a brute. Furthermore, we have been supposing that Hobbots are free to choose various possible strategies for attaining their hedonic goal. Moreover, we have allowed them to select their own general policy in regard to acting from inclination or from Self-Love. All of this seems to support the view that they are rational and have some form of 'practical reason.'[2]

Can a Hobbot *have good reason* to do what it does?[3] Surely, in any ordinary sense, it can. Imagine a Hobbot who wants very much to spend the day basking in the sun, and, after reflection, decides to so because that is what it wants to do and because this desire is endorsed by the long-term calculations of Self Love. That's a good reason (or two good reasons) to make the choice, one would think.

Let's say a creature, C, 'has reason' *or* 'has good reason,' to do D if, and only if, C has *a* reason for doing D, and that reason *justifies* the doing of it. (It follows that one can have *a* reason for doing D, *without* 'having reason' to do D.) Let's also say that C 'has no reason' to do D if, and only if, C has no *good* reason to do D—no reason that *justifies* the doing of D.[4] (Again, it follows that one can have *a* reason for doing D, even though one 'has no reason' to do D.) And, of course, C has prima facie reason to do D if, and only if C has prima facie justification for the doing of D.

By hypothesis, Hobbots do not take their own 'reasons' for acting as '*agent-neutral*' reasons.[5] The Hobbot we have been considering does *not* believe that it's reason for basking in the sun, by its very nature, gives other Hobbots a prima facie reason to aid and abet its basking.

J's reason for doing D is *agent-neutral* if, and only if, for every rational agent, R, knowledge of J's reason for doing D gives R prima facie reason to aid and abet J in doing D. J's reason is *agent-relative* if, and only if, it gives J reason for doing D. Note that someone's reason for doing something can be both agent-relative and agent-neutral. The relevant properties are not mutually exclusive. If we find ourselves needing a term for reasons that are agent-relative and *not* agent-neutral, we can say that the reason is *strictly* agent-relative (or subjective).

Let's try another kind of case. It seems to me that any person's pain gives that person prima facie reason to try to make it stop.[6] That is to say, this reason is at least agent-relative. Does J's pain give all of those who know about it prima facie reason to try to make it (J's pain) stop? Perhaps it depends on the kind of pain. Consider the pains of remorse and guilt. In some cases we may well have reason to approve of, and encourage, pain. ("Well you *ought* to feel guilty. You did the child harm from which she may never recover!")

Philosophically inclined Hobbots presumably hold, or tend to hold, that agent-neutral practical reasons don't make sense. If a Hobbot has good reason to reduce someone else's pain, that must be because the Hobbot likes that person, or wants to impress someone, or hopes to be repaid some day, or perhaps he just *likes* helping people.

Obviously, this is a long way short of being a full account of these technical terms. I have only described their application to two kinds of reasons; but I think this will suffice for present purposes.

Egoistic Hedonists (Egoists, for short) should deny that reasons, by nature, are agent-neutral. In particular they should deny that something's being conducive to J's long-term happiness gives everyone who knows this fact prima facie reason to help J get, or achieve, that thing.

Moore's Attack on Egoism

In *Principia Ethica*, G. E. Moore argued that 'Egoism as a form of Hedonism' is self-contradictory. What does he mean by 'Egoism'?

In section 58 he says:

> Egoism, as a form of Hedonism, is the doctrine which holds that we ought each of us to pursue our own greatest happiness as our ultimate end.

But, a little way into section 59 he describes Egoism as holding that rationality urges each of us to believe that:

> My own greatest happiness is the only good thing there is: my actions can only be good as means, in so far as they help to win me this.

I think sophisticated Egoists (and philosophically inclined Hobbots) should emend this formulation. They should say something like the following: "My own greatest happiness is, ultimately, the only good thing *relative to me.*" They might add: " And similarly, for any rational creature, C, C's greatest happiness is, ultimately, the only good thing relative to C." The obvious corollary is that, for standard Hobbots "it was endorsed by my Self-Love" is the ultimate 'good reason' for action.

Moore's 'refutation' of Egoism depends upon a *non*-relative 'only good thing' formulation:

> ... when ... I talk of a thing as 'my own good' all that I can mean is that something which will be exclusively mine, as my own pleasure is mine...is also *good absolutely;* or

rather that my possession of it is *good absolutely*...The only reason I can have for aiming at 'my own good,' is that it is *good absolutely* that what I so call should belong to me—*good absolutely* that I should *have* something, which, if I have it, others cannot have. But if it is *good absolutely* that I should have it, then everyone else has as much reason for aiming at *my* having it, as I have myself. If, therefore, it is true of *any* single man's 'interest' or 'happiness' that it ought to be his sole ultimate end, this can only mean that *that* man's 'interest' or 'happiness' is *the* sole good, *the* Universal Good, and the only thing that anybody ought to aim at. What Egoism holds, therefore, is that *each* man's happiness is the sole good—that a number of different things are *each* of them the only good thing there is—an absolute contradiction! No more complete and thorough refutation of any theory could be desired.[7]

The implicit theory of practical reason being affirmed here is that a good reason for doing something must, ultimately, be a justification in terms of *absolute, universal*, good, not in terms of *relative, individual*, good. This Platonistic, or, at least, Realist, theory of practical reason is not absurd; but it is not self-evident. Moore begs the question at issue.

It's as if he is convinced that the 'logical form' of 'goodness' attributions can only be *monadic*. Thus for instance, he might think that the underlying form of 'Strawberries are good' could only be:

$$(x) [S_x \text{-}\blacksquare \quad G_x]$$

(For every x, if x is a strawberry, then x is good.)

Whereas, those who see this kind of 'goodness' as relative think that the judgment thus expressed may well contain a concealed (or presupposed) entity or class of entities *relative to whom* strawberries are good. The concealed form might be something like the following:

$$(x) (y) [(S_x \& P_y) \quad \blacksquare \quad Grel_{xy}]$$

('For every x and every y, if x is a strawberry, and y is a primate, then x is good relative to y.')

Egoists should reject Moore's notion of a 'Universal Good' if by that Moore means a general state of affairs, S, or a best of all possible worlds, W, such that, ultimately, the only good reason anybody has for doing anything is that it tends to push the actual world towards S or W. To put it plainly, Egoists should hold that all good is *Relative* good.

It seems obviously true that something can be good relative to A, and not good relative to B. Scoring a touchdown is good for (relative to) the team that scores, but bad for (relative to) their opponents. Generally speaking, in itself, a touchdown by team A is neither good nor bad in the relevant sense.

Suppose the coach of team A decides to tell the quarterback of his team to throw a long pass to Johnson. He does this because he thinks that such a pass will set up the team's only chance for a badly needed touchdown. This reason in itself is not agent-neutral. The good to be achieved is only good relative to team A. The coach of team B has no reason to aid and abet the pass, or to help team A achieve the touchdown. Does the reason I have ascribed to the coach of team A justify his telling the quarterback of his team to throw the pass? According to Moore's theory, it does not.

However, Moore could insist that the coach's reason may have been wrongly described. Perhaps, when spelled out in full, his reason can be linked to the Universal Good. He wants football to be a source of widespread innocent pleasure, and, consequently, he wants this particular game to be a good one. Hence, he hopes that both teams play well. In the case of his team, this means doing what they can to score a touchdown now. If this is the case, then he has good reason to call for the pass.[8] If he had no such reason in mind, if, say, he hopes that the opposing team will fall apart and the game in that respect will be a bad one, then, on Moore's view, he *doesn't* have reason to call for the pass. But this seems to me counter-intuitive.

I think Moore's view forces him into departures from ordinary usage in regard to 'having reason', and 'having good reason.' Of course that's a long way from being a decisive objection. And the theory does give us a start towards an account of what it is that justifies intentional action.

It is important to note that Platonists in regard to morality need not accept Moore's theory in regard to 'having reason.' There are alternatives. Here is one. Many Platonists have thought that *both* one's own happiness *and* 'Universal Good' provide justifiable ultimate reasons for action.[9] On this view, one can have good reason to do D (for instance, that doing D is, or appears to be, conducive to one's own long-term happiness) even if that reason is not conducive to the general happiness. Suppose that doing D will be conducive to Jones' long-term happiness, but at the cost of serious pain for many others— pain that greatly outweighs Jones' happiness. In a case like this, a Platonist can hold, Jones has good reason to do something that is *not* conducive to Universal Good.

In the quotation above Moore says:

> The only reason I can have for aiming at 'my own good,' is that it is *good absolutely* that what I so call should belong to me—*good absolutely* that I should *have* something, which, if I have it, others cannot have.

But, as I have just in effect suggested, it is far from obvious that this is true. No doubt, like the rest of us, Moore had a strong, natural, innocent, desire to be happy. Self-love urged him towards happiness, and, perhaps, gave him reason to seek it, *whether or not* his attaining it was *absolutely* good, and part of 'Universal Good.' If, in fact, his happiness was only good *relative to himself*, that might still be sufficient reason to seek it. Platonists need not hold that the only good is absolutely and objectively so.

Roughly thirty years before Moore wrote these words, Henry Sidgwick had claimed that the Egoist can, perhaps, be shown the error of his ways *if* he accepts

> implicitly or explicitly, the proposition that his happiness or pleasure is Good, not only for him but from the point of view of the Universe,— as (e.g.) by saying that 'nature designed him to seek his own happiness." [In *that* case,]"... it becomes relevant to point out to him that his happiness cannot be a more important part of Good, taken universally, than the equal happiness of any other person. And thus, starting with his own principle, he may be brought to accept Universal happiness or pleasure as that which is absolutely and without qualification Good or Desirable: as an end, therefore, to which the action of a reasonable agent as such ought to be directed. [10]

On the other hand, Sidgwick says,

> If the Egoist strictly confines himself to stating his conviction that he ought to take his own happiness or pleasure as his ultimate end, there seems no opening for any line of reasoning to lead him to Universalistic Hedonism as a first principle; [Footnote: It is to be observed that he may be led to it in other ways than that of argument: i.e. by appeals to his sympathies, or to his moral or quasi-moral sentiments.] it cannot be proved that the difference between his own happiness and another's happiness is not for him all-important." [11]

In the Concluding Chapter of *The Methods of Ethics* Sidgwick wrote:

> ...[W]e have discussed the rational process (called by a stretch of language 'proof') by which one who holds it reasonable to aim at his own greatest happiness may be determined to take Universal Happiness instead, as his ultimate standard of right conduct. We have seen, however, that the application of this process requires that the Egoist should affirm, implicitly or explicitly, that his own greatest happiness is not merely the rational ultimate end for himself, but a part of Universal Good: and he may avoid the proof of Utilitarianism by declining to affirm this. It would be contrary to Common Sense to deny that the distinction between any one individual and any other is real and fundamental, and that consequently "I" am concerned with the quality of my existence as an individual in a sense, fundamentally important, in which I am not concerned with the quality of the existence of other individuals: and this being so, I do not see how it can be proved that this distinction is not to be taken as fundamental in determining the ultimate end of rational action for an individual. [Ibid. sec. 1 of Concluding Chapter]

In section 60 of *Principia Ethica*, Moore attacks Sidgwick's claims.

> What does Prof. Sidgwick mean by these phrases 'the ultimate rational end for himself,' and for him all-important'? He does not attempt to define them; and it is largely the use of such undefined phrases which causes absurdities to be committed in philosophy. ...
>
> Is there any sense in which a thing can be an ultimate rational end for one person and not for another? By 'ultimate' must be meant at least that the end is good-in-itself—good in our undefinable sense; and by 'rational,' at least, that it is truly good. That a thing should be an ultimate rational end means, then, that it is truly good in itself; and that it is truly good in itself means that it is a part of Universal Good. Can we assign any meaning to that qualification 'for himself,' which will make it cease to be a part of Universal Good? The thing is impossible: for the Egoist's happiness must either be good in itself, and so a part of Universal Good or else it cannot be good in itself at all: there is no escaping this dilemma. And if it is not good at all, what reason can he have for aiming at it? How can it be a rational end for him? That qualification 'for himself' has no meaning unless it implies 'not' for others'; and if it implies 'not for others,' then it cannot be a rational end for him, since it cannot be truly good in itself: the phrase 'an ultimate rational end for himself' is a contradiction in terms.

This barrage should not silence those of us who think that Sidgwick's stance in the dispute is basically correct. Perhaps our reply should be that the Egoist's end may be 'ultimate' simply in that we need no further explanation of why she chooses to do something.[12] The idea is that an 'ultimate' end, in this sense, can be strictly agent-relative.

Is the Egoist's end 'rational'? Presumably, the Egoist's end is 'rational' in that it is universalizable. For each agent, A, it is rational for A to pursue A's happiness. It doesn't follow from this that anyone's happiness is good in itself or that it is part of Universal Good.

Must Hobbots Hold That They Have 'Intrinsic Value'?

According to Christine Korsgaard,

> Kant saw that we take things to be important because they are important to us—and he concluded that we must therefore take ourselves to be important. In this way, the value of humanity itself is implicit in every human choice. If complete normative skepticism is to be avoided—if there is such a thing as a reason for action—then humanity, as the source of all reasons and values, must be valued for its own sake.[13]

I cannot find this argument where Korsgaard apparently finds it.[14] In any case, I hope it wasn't Kant's line of thought. Surely a philosophically sophisticated Hobbot could realize that he desperately needs something (say a quart of oil) and yet insist (quite reasonably) that oil is only good, relative to entities like himself—that his need for oil only makes oil good *relative to himself*. This view does *not* require sophisticated Hobbots who need oil to hold that they themselves are important or valuable (in some absolute and intrinsic sense). Something can be valuable relative to an entity E, even though E itself has no intrinsic value.

Philosophically sophisticated Hobbots will not regard themselves as intrinsically valuable. Of course this does not mean that they, in fact, lack this property. I assume that Platonists who ascribe intrinsic value to wolves and elephants would ascribe at least the same kind and amount of value to Hobbots.

A Kantian Attack on Hobbots

In his *Groundwork of the Metaphysics of morals* (published in 1785) Kant offered a line of thought that could be taken to show that Hobbots cannot be rational creatures. To put it crudely, the sequence seems to go like this:

(1) A rational creature must think of itself as *free*—as having *free will*.
(2) The idea of free will entails the idea of *autonomy*.
(3) Thinking of oneself as autonomous entails thinking of oneself as bound by the *universal principle of morality*.

By hypothesis, Hobbots cannot think of themselves as bound by that principle. Hence, (3) tells us, they cannot think of themselves as autonomous. But then, according to (2), they cannot think of themselves as having free will. And thus, according to (1), they cannot be rational creatures.

Kant says:

> As a rational being, and thus as a being belonging to the intelligible world, the human being can never think of the causality of his own will otherwise than under the idea of freedom; for, independence from the determining causes of the world of sense (which reason must always ascribe to itself) is freedom. With the idea of freedom the concept of *autonomy* is now inseparably combined, and with the concept of autonomy the universal principle of morality, which in idea is the ground of all actions of *rational beings*, just as the law of nature is the ground of all appearances. [4:452–453]][15]

The line of thought seems to suggest that we could work our way to the idea that we are bound by the universal principle of morality by working out the implications of our own rationality. If we are rational we must be bound by that principle. Hobbots seem to show that this is false.

Subsequently, Kant seems to reverse an important part of this line. He came to hold that we only discover that we have free will by working out the consequences of the fact that we are bound by the moral law.

Kant writes:

...freedom is real, for this idea reveals itself through the moral law.

But among all the ideas of speculative reason freedom is also the only one the possibility of which we *know* a priori, though without having insight into it, because it is the condition of the moral law, which we do know[16]

A footnote to this last sentence reads as follows:

Lest anyone suppose that he finds an *inconsistency* when I now call freedom the condition of the moral law and afterwards, in the treatise, maintain that the moral law is the condition under which we can first *become aware* of freedom, I want only to remark that whereas freedom is indeed the *ratio essendi* of the moral law, the moral law is the *ratio cognoscendi* of freedom. For, had not the moral law *already* been distinctly thought in our reason, we should never consider ourselves justified in *assuming* such a thing as freedom (even though it is not self-contradictory). But were there no freedom, the moral law would *not be encountered* at all in ourselves. [5:4-5:5]

I take Kant to be saying that where there is no Kantian freedom—no noumenal free will—there cannot be any moral obligation. On the other hand, a creature's knowledge, or assumption, that it has Kantian freedom can only be based upon, and justified by, that creature's consciousness of having moral obligations.

Let's return to the more threatening sequence of thought. Two questions come to mind: (1) Must rational creatures (for instance, Hobbots) think of themselves as 'free' in Kant's sense of that term? (2) Could a Hobbot think of itself as 'autonomous' without thinking of itself as bound by the moral law?

At the very least, rational creatures seem compelled by their rationality to think of themselves as at sometimes confronting various options—various alternative, mutually exclusive, things they can do. They regard themselves as having at least this much freedom.

Remember the absurdly simple story of Minnie in Chapter Four. She faced a choice between doing something, A, which would result in a PMP score of 5, and something else, B, which would result in a PMP score of 3. (There were also subsequent choices to be made.) Hence, presumably, she thought these were her two initial options. The choice was up to her. But this line of thought, I take it, is compatible with the belief that she is a decision making 'machine' of some kind, and that she lives in a deterministic world. That is to say, she need not think of herself as having Kantian freedom.[17]

I shift now to a brief discussion of a different, but closely related, topic. Thin rationalists are committed to the idea that some of our decisions are defective in that they are less than fully rational (in the thin sense). After all, they have a positive theory about how rational creatures 'should' proceed. Furthermore, their theory is meant to apply to us, and we do in fact sometimes make stupid, senseless, decisions. Hence, I take it, they want, and need, a theory of rationality that permits defective decisions of this sort.

The block diagrams of Hobbot psychology show some ways in which this is possible. By hypothesis, Self-Love and the Desire Resolver urge decisions that yield a nice utility function. Thus, these modules are 'rational' in two senses: (a) their operation requires rational thought e.g. thought that conforms to logic and probability theory, and (b) their urgings (actual and counterfactual) at a given time form a rational preference set. If a Hobbot regularly makes decisions that comply with such a module then, presumably, they will be making decisions that are 'rational' in the decision theoretic sense. On the other hand, there is no guarantee that choices made at the urging of some inclination in opposition to Self-Love, or the Desire Resolver, will yield such a function. On the contrary, we should expect their output to be disorderly. For instance, the choices made in this way may well constitute a non-transitive set of preferences.

Thin rationalists presumably hold that thinly rational creatures generally make their choices on the basis of policies or procedures that yield nice utility functions. For instance, thinly rational Desire Driven Hobbots generally make their choices in compliance with the Desire Resolver. Their occasional nonrational choices typically occur when the Chooser lets an inclination, or some higher-order desire, override the urgings of the Desire Resolver.

A Hobbot could be rational in the sense that at any given time the choices it would then make form a rational preference set, and yet be a wildly erratic Hobbot. Suppose that there is a complete, random, replacement of its basic desires every three minutes. The Desire Resolver makes rapid readjustments and urges a radically different set of choices. The Hobbot, being 'rational,' almost always complies with the current urgings of the Desire Resolver.

Of course the resultant behavior may well be mad. The Hobbot may find it almost impossible to complete any project that takes more than three minutes to accomplish.

Perhaps thin rationalists should hold that rational creatures must maintain some of their non-deliberate desires over fairly long stretches of time (days? weeks?). They might add that basic desires may die out and be replaced by others; but there must be substantial over-lapping continuity across such changes.

NOTES

1. Richard Price, *A Review of the Principal Questions in Morals*, Edited by D.D. Raphael, Clarendon Press, Oxford, 1974, Chapter I, Sect III, pp. 48–49. The first edition of Price's book appeared in 1758.

2. Kantian 'pure practical reason' deals with full-fledged morality and the 'categorical imperative.' Hobbots presumably have 'empirical practical reason,' but lack 'pure practical reason.' John Rawls uses the terms 'rational' and 'reasonable' to mark this distinction (See *Lectures on the History of Moral Philosophy*, p. 167.) Hence, in Rawls' terminology, Hobbits are 'rational' but not 'reasonable.' Nevertheless, I do not see why Hobbots cannot be reasonable and unreasonable (in Hobbot, non-human, ways, so to speak). For more on Rawls' use of these terms, see Samuel Freeman's Introduction to *The Cambridge Companion to Rawls*, Edited by Samuel Freeman, Cambridge University Press, 2003, pp. 31–32.

3. The O.E.D. offers the following definition of 'reason' (in the relevant sense): "A statement of some fact (real or alleged) employed as an argument to justify or condemn some act, prove or disprove some assertion, idea, or belief."

4. Oddly enough, "*I* have no reason to do D" seems to mean just what it says. The speaker does not have a reason to do D. On the other hand "You had no reason to do D" typically seems to mean something like: "You had no *call* to do D." "Your doing D was totally unjustified."

5. In *The Possibility of Altruism*, Chapter Seven, Thomas Nagel introduced the important distinction between 'objective' and 'subjective' reasons. In *Reasons and Persons*, Derek Parfit made use of Nagel's distinction, but used the terms 'agent-neutral' and 'agent-relative.' In *The view from Nowhere*, (see pp. 152–153) Nagel adopted Parfit's terms in place of his own. I am (more or less) following Nagel and Parfit. Christine Korsgaard in *The sources of Normativity* speaks of 'public' and 'private' reasons. 'Public' reasons, she says, are, 'roughly' agent-neutral reasons, and 'private' reasons are roughly agent-relative. See *The Sources of Normativity*, p. 133.

6. Korsgaard holds the somewhat surprising theory that pain just *is* the perception of a reason to revolt against a threat to the preservation of one's identity. (See ibid. pp. 147–50.)

7. G. E. Moore, *Principia Ethica*, Cambridge University Press, Cambridge, 1991, p. 98.

8. David Rowland forced me to see this.

9. Henry Sidgwick is an obvious example. I discuss this sort of 'dualism of practical reason' in Chapter Fourteen.

10. Henry Sidgwick, *The Methods of Ethics*, 1874, book IV, Ch. II.

11. Ibid.

12. See Elizabeth Anscombe on this point. "Because it seemed conducive to my long-term happiness" is, in Anscombe's phrase, a 'desirability-characterization.' It gives a final answer to 'What for?' questions in regard to an action. The notion of a 'desirability-

characterization' is discussed in her book, *Intention*, Harvard University Press, Cambridge, Mass., 2000, sections 37–39. This important work was first published in 1957.

13. Christine M. Korsgaard, *The Sources of Normativity*, Cambridge University Press, Cambridge, 1996, p.122.

14. Kant's *Foundations of the Metaphysics of Morals*, 4:427–28.

15. For those who don't recognize it, the '4' indcates the *Groundwork of the Metaphysics of Morals*, and the number that follows specifies the relevant page in the standard German edition of Kant's works. The '5' in subsequent references indicates that we have shifted to Kant's *Critique of Practical Reason*.

16. Kant, *Critique of Practical Reason*, 5:4.

17 . Daniel Dennett's *Elbow Room*, [The MIT Press, Cambridge, Massachusetts, 1985] is relevant here.

General Comments on Disenchanting Theories

Disenchanting theories of ethics have two components, one negative and the other (sometimes, sort-of) positive. The negative component is a flat-out rejection of genuine, objective, morality. Disenchanters claim that there are no objective, absolute, moral principles. The positive component tells us how, according to this view, we should conduct our lives—or, perhaps, it says there are no general principles of this sort at all.

Our discussion of disenchanting theory has been focused almost entirely on thin rationalism. Thin rationalists offer us a normative theory of instrumental reasoning. They hold that such reasoning should govern our choice making.

Total disenchanters, on the other hand, reject even this 'should.' Their positive theory of ethics simply isn't normative in this sense. A total disenchanter who accepted naturalism might, for instance, sketch Hobbot 'moral psychology,' and draw conclusions about how such creatures 'should' act; but the 'should' here would be strictly mechanical or biological. The creature 'should' act this way if it is working properly. ("If you throw this switch, the light should go on.")

Hobbots and Morality

It would appear that morality is simply not applicable to Hobbots. For instance, it is absurd to think they could have a moral obligation to sacrifice their happiness. That is to say, *fullstrength* morality plainly does not apply to them. They are, so to speak, mechanically incapable of compliance with it. It's incompatible with their wiring.

But many of us are willing to go further. We have the idea that Hobbots cannot have any genuine moral obligations at all. In this regard, we think, they are like brutes, plants, and machines.

Imagine a society of Hobbots that has developed a 'folk-ethics.' Surely this is possible? It would make good sense for them, just as it makes good sense for us, to have such a system. But, I suppose, there will be crucial differences. Presumably the Hobbots know they are Hobbots. I mean they know that they are driven by Self-Love, or by Desire Resolvers, by pleasure and pain, and by their inclinations. They do not expect any other sort of behavior from each other.

Suppose one Hobbot makes an appointment with another and then doesn't keep it—and doesn't later make any sort of apology or excuse. Has the Hobbot done something *morally wrong?*

There may well be some sort of 'punishment' (in a broad sense of the term) for violations of the ethical rules. Perhaps, for instance, the Hobbots tend to shun Hobbots that regularly fail to fulfill promises. Presumably they do this, in part, in order to modify the calculations, the pleasures and pains, or the inclinations, of the violator.[1] If they are clear headed about these things, the 'punishment' is purely 'remedial', not retributive. The idea of wickedness doesn't enter the picture.

Neither we, nor the Hobbots themselves, would expect a properly functioning Hobbot to do something which is (a) known by the Hobbot to be required by the ethical rules, (b) will be unpleasant, and contrary to inclination, and (c) is such that the Hobbot can (almost certainly) get away with not doing it. This, I take it, is in contrast to our idea of genuine morality. We think, or tend to think, that an ordinary human being (not a Hobbot) *ought* to do what morality requires even under these conditions.[2]

Hobbots are not 'reasonable' in Rawls' sense,[3] nor, I think, in the sense that is basic to Scanlon's 'contractualist' account of right and wrong. They do not, perhaps, give weight to 'the suitability of certain principles to serve as the basis of mutual recognition and accommodation.'[4] Nevertheless, it seems to me that their decisions are often 'reasonable' in a fairly ordinary sense of the term.[5]

Disenchantment theory seems correct in regard to Hobbot ethics. That's one of the principal reasons for thinking about such creatures. They help us see what it would be like for the disenchantment theory to be clearly true.

Given that a community of Hobbots might well find it useful to construct and maintain a system of ethics, why shouldn't *disenchanters* be interested in, and enthusiastic about, some such social construction for human communities? By definition, disenchanters reject genuine morality as bogus; but this does not mean that they must deny the potential usefulness of a folk ethics designed for humans (as viewed by disenchanters).

The fact that disenchanters of this kind are possible makes it difficult to place some ethicists on our chart of theories. For instance, it seems fairly clear that Helvetius was a disenchanter who was intensely interested in constructing a reasonable ethical system. Jeremy Bentham got his Utilitarianism from Helvetius; but is Bentham a disenchanter?

Divine Command Theories and Disenchantment

Are Divine Command theorists like Paley disenchanters?[6] Roughly speaking, Paley thinks that we are Hobbots. Genuine morality is simply not applicable to Hobbots. So, If I am right, Paley should reject genuine morality. On the other hand, of course, he asserts the existence of moral laws not made by us—laws that are 'objective' in that sense—and claims that we are obliged to comply with those laws.

I am inclined to stipulate that disenchanters reject any kind of objective, absolute, non-man-made, morality, and thus that Paley does not qualify for the title, even though (whether he admits it or not) he should deny that we have *genuine* moral obligations.

Platonism in Regard to Thin Rationalistic Disenchantment

There are at least two places where Platonism might lurk within Thin Rationalism, and thus within a disenchanting theory of ethics. These places were briefly mentioned in Chapter Four. First, one might hold that it is simply an irreducible Platonistic fact that Self-Love, (or a Desire Resolver) should dominate a creature's inclinations. Self-Love has greater 'authority' (in some Platonistic sense) than does any inclination or combination of inclinations. Second, one might hold that it is an irreducible Platonistic fact that one's preference set should be 'rational.' That is to say, it should be 'complete.' The preferences should be 'transitive', and so on.

Suppose that many Hobbots are like us in that they often sacrifice their own happiness to "...fancy, inquisitiveness, love or hatred, any vagrant inclination."[7] Both the Hobbots themselves and observers of their behavior might well say that they 'should not' act in this way, that they 'ought' to comply with the dictates of self-love (or their Desire Resolver). Their behavior seems 'unreasonable.'

Platonistic thin rationalists presumably take this obligation (or quasi-obligation) to be irreducible.[8]

Platonists in regard to *morality* may, or may not, hold that prudential (Hobbot-like) rationality is 'irreducible' to naturalistically acceptable properties—that is to say they may or may not be Platonists in regard to prudential reason.

Total disenchanters might hold that 'irrational' choices don't 'make sense' simply because we employ something like the theory Ramsey used (but said was false) in trying to understand behavior. On this view, there is no real normativity here, just a departure from our standard way of understanding each other.

NOTES

1. See Axelrod's interesting discussion of norms in *The Complexity of Cooperation*, Chapter 3.
2. Arthur Melnick pointed this out to me as a difference between Hobbot ethics and genuine morality. In his book, *What does it all Mean?* Oxford University Press, 1987, Thomas Nagel suggests that we would *resent* it if someone stole our umbrella, especially if this happened on a rainy day. (A similar case is discussed in Nagel's *The Possibility of Altruism*, pp. 84-85.) This resentment seems to show that we think the thief had good reason not to do it. Presumably, then, we think that we ourselves have good reason not to steal anyone's umbrella [pp. 64-67]. This seems right. But *Hobbots* do *not* feel the resentment that leads down this road. They understand the [Hobbot] reasonableness of the theft, given that it is raining and all. (This does *not* mean that they are not often furious at being inconvenienced in this way.) P. F. Strawson, in his important and influential paper "Freedom and Resentment," contrasts the 'purely objective view' to the 'participant reactive attitudes' we humans typically adopt. Resentment, he claims, is one such attitude. [See his, *Freedom and Resentment*, Methuen & CO, LTD, 1974.]
3. I described this briefly in Chapter Nine, footnote 2.
4. T. M. Scanlon, *What We Owe to Each Other*, Harvard University Press, Cambridge, Mass., 1998, p. 198. Scanlon's use of 'reasonable' seems nearer to ordinary usage than Rawls'. An additional point of interest for us is that, as Scanlon himself in effect says, his contractualism can be read as grounded in a Platonistic notion of 'being a reason for.' [See p. 11.]
5. Sidgwick says: "...it is hardly going too far to say that common sense assumes that 'interested' actions, tending to promote the agent's happiness, are prima facie reasonable: and that the *onus probandi* lies with those who maintain that disinterested conduct, as such, is reasonable." [*The Methods of Ethics*, p. 120.]
6. William Paley (1743-1805) was the English moral philosopher and theologian who invented (or at least made famous) the still popular 'watch' argument for the existence of God.
7. Butler, *Sermons on Human Nature*, Preface, 40. This phrase from Butler is also quoted, in regard to the same topic, by Arthur Prior in *Logic and the Basis of Ethics*, p. 38.
8. Sidgwick (who, of course, is *not* a Disenchanter) takes this line in regard to this 'ought.' See his *Methods of Ethics*, I, iii. 4. Again, I am just repeating a point made by Prior. See Prior, op. cit. pp. 38-39.

• Part Two •

Platonistic and Reductive Realists

CHAPTER ELEVEN

Introduction to Part Two

Some moral realists are *reductive* realists. To put it crudely, they hold that moral facts, properties, and so on, are, basically facts, properties, or whatever, of some other kind. They deny the 'autonomy' of morality. Platonists, on the other hand, assert that autonomy, and reject all kinds of reduction.

Here, for instance, is Henry Sidgwick (a Platonist) attacking Herbert Spencer:

> In discussing Spencer we shall be dealing with an attempt to 'establish Ethics on a scientific basis.' Now this, I hold, cannot be done to the extent and in the manner in which Mr. Spencer tries to do it. 'Science' relates to what is, has been and will be, Ethics to what ought to be: therefore the fundamental principles of the latter must be independent of the former, however important and even indispensable Science—especially Biology and Sociology—may be in the working out of the system of rules. And Science—in particular Psychology and Sociology—may trace the origin of moral sentiments and ideas, but it cannot itself supply a criterion of the validity of moral principles, or authority of moral sentiments.[1]

I take the 'autonomy' of morality to imply both (1) *realism* in regard to at least some moral facts and properties, and (2) the irreducibility of at least some of those real facts and properties.

One traditional form of reductionism is *supernaturalistic*. Morality is reduced to alleged facts about God's commands. In principal there could be other forms of supernaturalistic reduction. One could hold, for instance, that moral properties reduce to features of Karma, or to 'health' of soul.

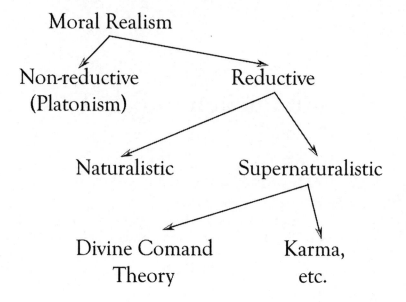

The metaethical battlefield is complex. Realists confront anti-realists. Both groups are themselves divided and sub-divided by internal factions. Reductive realists reject Platonism. Naturalistic reductive realists reject supernaturalistic reductive realism. Some Platonists are intuitionists; others are not, and so on.

As I mentioned in the general Introduction, Platonism is nowadays often dismissed as untenable. But suppose reductive realism turns out to be implausible or incoherent. In that case, the fate of realism will depend upon Platonism. For those of us committed to realism, that possibility in itself provides a reason to keep Platonism in contention.

There is another reason. Platonism may be the only view that can support 'full scale' morality. If that is the case, then people who favor full-scale morality, or at least do not want to see it dropped from the list of options, should reconsider Platonism.

Why does Platonism in regard to morality tend to be neglected and abused? Of course it has its difficulties and embarrassments. For instance, like Platonism in regard to mathematics, it seems to have epistemic problems. How can we have knowledge of non-natural facts and properties? But, to a large extent, Platonism is dismissed simply because it is incompatible with *Naturalism*.

Naturalism underlies a large share of the best work done in philosophy during the last century or so. It has strong roots in the 17th and 18th centuries. No less a figure than Isaac Newton (1642–1727) urged *methodological* naturalism. Both Hartley and Helvetius advocated 'scientific procedure' (i.e. some form of naturalism) in ethics.

In spite of this early start, the major intellectual adjustment to Naturalism occurred during the last two hundred years. Many people have found the effect devastating. The naturalistic 'news' seems almost entirely negative:

(1) There is no God.

(2) There are no angels, no gods, or goddesses.

(3) There are no wizards, witches, or real magicians. No genuine *magic* in the world.

(4) We lack souls, and supernatural 'minds.' We are, in fact, *physical objects*—animals.

(5) There is no life after death, no reincarnation, no resurrection, no Heaven.[2]

(6) There is no salvation, no Nirvana, no satori.

... and so on.

It is important not to exaggerate the gloom. Many of those who found the evidence against the general world-view in which they had been nurtured more or less conclusive felt like prisoners suddenly set free. Ludwig Feuerbach (1804-1872) is an outstanding example. Naturalistic realism in regard to ourselves and the world around us cures 'self-alienation', and thus makes a rich, rewarding, and thoroughly good, form of human life possible, he said. This up-beat message made Feuerbach's writings very popular in the mid-19th century.

Nevertheless, the difficulties were genuine. Many are still unresolved. For instance, consider Platonic Forms, and the 'Eternal Verities'. These were generally taken to be ideas in the mind of God. Suppose there is no God. What happens to the truths of logic, mathematics, and morality? For many people the 'news' that God is non-existent, yielded, among other things, the conclusion that there is no such thing as genuine, objective, morality. "If God is dead, everything is permitted."

When it was generally believed that God had created us, or at least supervised our construction, it was reassuring to think he had implanted in our minds a propensity to work out mathematics and morals correctly. Random variation and natural selection are less reliable. Given the nineteenth century's 'bad news,' is there any guarantee that our mathematics mirrors mathematical reality or that our 'moral truths' reflect non-natural moral facts?

Naturalistic moral realism seems too good to be true. The idea is that one can accept naturalism and yet be a robust realist about morality. It's almost as if someone said that we can have the consolations of religion and yet be naturalists. (That's fairly close to what Feuerbach did in fact say.)

Moral properties seem 'queer' to many naturalists.[3] They don't fit in. They don't seem natural. Many Platonists, in a sense, agree. On their view, the world contains things that have both natural and non-natural properties, and some of those non-natural properties do seem a bit 'queer.' All naturalistic *reductive* realists disagree. Moral properties do not seem 'queer' to them; they seem natural.

If naturalism were obviously correct, Platonism would indeed be out of the running. But naturalism (or at least *hardcore* naturalism—i.e. physicalism) has its own problems.[4] Science needs mathematics. But mathematics seems to deal with abstract (non-physical) entities. Is an adequate, naturalistic, reductive account of mathematics possible?

Science develops theories that we hope are substantially true. That's the aim of the enterprise. Presumably then, naturalists need a naturalistically acceptable account of language and truth—one that doesn't employ irreducible semantic terms (like 'reference' and 'meaning' perhaps). Can there be such a theory?

So much for intellectual history. We turn now to a direct study of the contrast between moral realism and disenchantment in ethics. As I hinted in the general Introduction, it seems to me that full-scale Platonism is intellectually permissible; nevertheless, some of the objections to it are formidable, and disenchanting alternatives are more plausible than many realists are willing to admit.

NOTES

1. Henry Sidgwick, *Lectures on the Ethics of T..H. Green, Mr. Herbert Spencer, and J. Martineau,* MacMillan and Co, London, 1902, p. 1. This passage is cited in Arthur N. Prior's *Logic and the Basis of Ethics,* Clarendon Press, Oxford, 1949, p. 107.

2. Those who relish the idea that wicked people will be punished even when there is no chance that those wicked people will be improved by it, can add the 'news' that there is no Hell.

3. See, for instance, J. L Mackie, *Ethics Inventing Right and Wrong,* Penguin Books, 1977, pp. 38-42. For a Platonist's *total* rejection of the accusation see Philip Stratton-Lake's Introduction to Ross' *The Right and the Good,* 2002, pp. xxiii–xxiv.

4. Some of the difficulties Naturalism faces are discussed in *Naturalism: A Critical Appraisal,* Edited by Steven J. Wagner and Richard Warner, University of Notre Dame Press, Notre Dame, Indiana, 1993.

CHAPTER TWELVE

Trees and Brutes

I n this chapter we take a quick look at some questions about things that are good and bad with respect to plants and other non-rational entities. In particular we are interested in what Platonists and naturalistic disenchanters can say about these matters.

Admittedly, no sane, well-educated, contemporary person thinks that plants have duties. And, I suppose, very few people hold that plants (e.g. trees) have 'rights.' Nevertheless, it is not obviously absurd to think, for example, that the existence of plants and non-rational animals is objectively and absolutely (i.e. not relatively) a 'good thing.' or that their wanton destruction is objectively and absolutely a 'bad thing,' apart from the effect on *us*, or on any other rational creatures. Nor, for that matter, is it obviously absurd to deny that it is our attitudes, beliefs, preferences, evaluations, or whatever, that makes these things true.[1]

(It is tiresome to keep repeating the phrase 'objectively and absolutely.' For the most part hereafter I will use the term 'objective' for things that are objective but perhaps not absolute, and the term 'absolute' for things that are both objective and absolute. That is to say, something is 'absolutely' good, as I use the term, if it is objectively good, and its goodness is not just goodness relative to some individual, group, species, or whatever.)

Trees

There is a fairly clear sense in which something can be bad for a tree. For example, pealing a large section of bark from the trunk of a living tree is likely to cause disease in the tree, or kill it outright. But is the 'untimely' death of a tree an unfortunate event in some absolute sense?[2] I am not asking whether it is bad for the ecological system of which the tree is (or was) a part, or bad for the planet as a whole, or bad for people who love trees. Having a good portion of its bark stripped off is plainly bad with respect to the tree. But is this endangering of a tree's life a bad thing (period)? No doubt there are people who will say it is. If they follow the dictates of common sense, they are likely to add that this evil is sometimes outweighed by a greater good requiring the risk to the tree. A prima facie evil can be good all things considered—i.e. a necessary component of some greater good.

We can imagine a mildly eccentric tree-lover arguing as follows:

(a) It is prima facie an absolutely bad thing for a tree to be destroyed.
(b) In most circumstances, peeling the bark from a living tree makes it much more likely that the tree will suffer an untimely death.
(c) Hence, in most circumstances, peeling the bark from a living tree is *prima facie* an absolutely bad thing to do.

It seems to me that all disenchanters should reject this argument. Premise (a) is unacceptable from the disenchanter's perspective. Platonists can either accept or reject it.

Why do I think disenchanters should reject (a)? Perhaps it is because I associate the view in question with an 'extreme case' invented by G. E. Moore (a Platonist if ever there was one). Moore invites us to consider two planets, one exceedingly beautiful, and the other simply a 'heap of filth.' And then he adds the stipulation that no one will ever see either planet. No sentient being will ever enjoy the beauty of the one, or be disgusted by the nastiness of the other. Given these suppositions, Moore asks whether it would be irrational to think it would be 'better' if the beautiful planet existed than that the heap of filth should exist. He himself thinks it would *not* be irrational.[3]

Following Moore's lead, we might imagine a somewhat simpler pair of planets: the surface of one is bare rock and ocean—no life at all. The surface of the other is exactly the same, except for one big, mature, healthy, tree and enough soil for its roots. Leaving aside the possibility of anyone ever actually seeing either planet, would it be absolutely better that the one-tree planet should exist? It seems to me that only eccentric Platonists can say that it would be. Others can express their own *preference* for the one situation over the other and leave it at that.

Questions for those eccentric Platonists: If the existence of one tree is absolutely a good thing, would the existence of *two* trees be even better? If so, *how much* better? Would it, for example, be twice as good? Does this goodness increase in direct proportion to the number of trees, without limit? Perhaps there are some people who hold that given *any* finite number of trees, it would be better, other things being equal, that one more tree should exist.

Let's try to clarify for ourselves the strictly disenchanting view of these matters. Can disenchanters hold that it is an absolute fact that stripping the bark from a living tree is bad *with respect to the tree?* (Analogous question: can it be an absolute (non-relative) fact that two particular events, e₁ and e₂, are simultaneous *relative to coordinate system S?*)

Imagine a tribe that regards the stripping of the bark from a tree as a pure and unmixed blessing conferred upon it—a liberation. Are they *wrong?* Some philosophers will be relativists here. They will say that different people, or different tribes, are at liberty to view the situation in different ways. From some perspectives, the stripping of bark is bad relative to the tree. From others, it is good. From still others, it is neutral. According to these philosophers, it all depends upon one's point of view. There is no absolute right, or wrong here.

When we say that pealing large strips of bark from a living tree is bad for it, or that putting nitrogen in the soil near its roots is likely to be beneficial, our claims can be justified in scientific terms (provided we are fairly tolerant in regard to what is, and what isn't, genuine science.) We can explain the ways in which the first sort of event endangers the life of the tree, while the second is conducive to the tree flourishing (for example, developing new, healthy, branches). Realism in regard to what is good and bad for trees looks very plausible. If some subjectivists, or whatever, say this is *not* an objective matter, then, to that extent their view looks implausible.

As I have said, stripping bark from a living tree tends to be bad for the tree in that it may well lead to disease or death. But it does not follow that the untimely death of a tree, or it's being diseased, is a bad thing (absolutely, in itself). Nor do I see how such absolute (objective, non-relativistic) claims could be justified in scientifically acceptable ways.

The up-shot would appear to be that both disenchanters and Platonists in this domain can, and probably should, agree, at least to some extent, about what is good and bad for trees. Both kinds of theorists can hold, for example, that it is an absolute fact that stripping the bark from a tree is likely to be bad for it.

Platonists, subjectivists, and others, can, if they like, go on to say that the untimely and unnecessary death of a tree is, at least prima facie, a bad thing. Imagine someone, say Randolph, making this claim. According to subjectivists, he is just expressing his own, slightly peculiar, 'values'. And perhaps this is how he himself views what he is doing. (He himself may be a subjectivist.) But then he should be prepared to acknowledge a crucial distinction between the claim that having its bark stripped is bad for the tree, and the claim that the ensuing death of the tree is (in itself) prima facie a bad thing. The first claim is (putatively) absolute, and naturalistically acceptable. The second is (on his view) an expression of his own values.

On the other hand, Randolph may say he means to be stating another absolute fact. He may even go on to say that this fact (if that's what it is) is in no way dependent upon his, or anyone else's, beliefs, evaluations, practices, or whatever. In short, he may turn out to be a realist, and perhaps a Platonist, in regard to the evil he claims to discern here.

I hope I have not given the impression that Platonists, as such, hold, or ought to hold, that the existence of trees is in itself an absolutely good thing, and that the untimely death of a tree is absolutely something prima facie bad. Many, if not most, card-carrying Platonists would regard both claims as silly.

Before we shift our attention to brutes, let's think for a moment about *groups* of trees. If some procedure is beneficial with respect to each tree in a collection of trees, then, presumably, it is beneficial relative to the whole collection. (Suppose the trees form a grove. When I say the 'collection' benefits, I do not mean that the *grove* must benefit—the procedure in question may require moving the individual trees to different forests and thus destroying the grove.)

To generalize a bit: consider a set of things that might happen to some trees. Suppose that one outcome, O_1, is better than another, O_2, with respect to *each* of these trees in a naturalistically acceptable sense of 'better'. In such a case, it seems naturalistically legitimate to say that O_1 is better than O_2 relative to the whole *aggregate* of trees. (This does *not* mean that O_1 is *absolutely* better than O_2.).

Imagine an outcome that is bad relative to one tree, but good relative to the vast majority of the aggregate. Is this procedure good relative to the aggregate? We do not, as yet, have enough information to answer this question. If the procedure kills one tree outright, and only benefits five others in a very small way, perhaps we should say that the procedure isn't beneficial with respect to the aggregate as a whole. But look what is happening. We are using some sort of *inter-arboreal* scale of benefit and harm. Is a disenchanter allowed to use this devise? I don't know; but let's be permissive if possible. Suppose the outcome of a certain procedure is that one tree looses five healthy leaves (out of several thousand) while nine other trees gain a healthy root system. This outcome seems plainly beneficial with respect to the ten trees.

Brutes

Consider a hungry cat and a fat mouse. We need not suppose that it would be good in some absolute sense for the cat to catch the mouse. From the mouse's point of view, it would be a disaster. Presumably, we should say it is absolutely good relative to the cat, and absolutely bad relative to the mouse. What is 'absolute' here are *relational* facts. These things are said to be 'absolute' in that they are not themselves relative matters and not matters of opinion. A demon looking at our universe from 'outside' who hopes to understand what is going on should perceive these ethical, or quasi-ethical, facts. Here again (as with trees), we seem to be dealing with some form realism in regard what is good and bad. But again we must be careful. It seems unlikely that disenchanters can defend the claim that the well being of some brute is absolutely good simplicitor. As I see it, they can claim that it is an absolute fact that doing such and such is good *relative to* some particular brute, or group of brutes. (Obviously, disenchanters and other non-realists in regard to morality can have personal, or socially shared preferences in regard to the outcome.) On the other hand, Platonists, and perhaps some other realists, can if they like hold that some possible outcomes of cat and mouse encounters are absolutely better than others. Platonism *permits* this view. I am *not* saying that there is something intrinsic to Platonism that would encourage it.

The suggestion is that all of these people (disenchanters, realists, subjectivists, and so on) can, in principle, explain what is good with respect to the cat and bad with respect to the mouse in scientifically acceptable terms. The cat is a carnivore, it needs meat; it's mouse-catching ability has survival value; and so on. But, so far as I can see, anyone who holds, for example, that it would be best (absolutely) that the mouse should escape (or, at least, not be tormented) *cannot* explain in naturalistically acceptable terms why this is (absolutely, in itself) the best outcome. (Both disenchanters and subjectivists are likely to think that such a person is simply expressing a preference for non-violent outcomes or something like that.)

If we hold that undeserved pain, misery, terror, and so forth are intrinsically and absolutely evil—that the world will be a better place if the cat does not 'play' with the mouse since there will then be less undeserved pain—we seem once again to commit ourselves to something like Platonism. (Again, I am not saying that Platonists should take this line. Platonism is perfectly compatible with the view that brutish pain is not, absolutely, a bad thing, and that brutish pleasure has no absolute, intrinsic, value whatsoever.)

In very general terms, what kinds of things are good, or bad, for a brute? More specifically, how can a brute *benefit* or *harm* itself? There may be cases in which it is intrinsically indeterminate whether or not some outcome was good or bad (or in between) for a brute. I don't mean there is an answer; but we don't know it. I mean there is simply *no answer*. Consider, for example, a sentient bomb, i.e. a bomb that is an artificial brute. Suppose there is nothing in the world the bomb wants more than to hit its target dead center. But hitting its target means annihilation. So would this be good relative to the sentient bomb or not? (Notice, 'Good relative to the bomb' doesn't mean 'perceived as good by the bomb'.) So far as I can see, there is no good, straightforward, answer to this question. The proper response to the question would go something like this: "Hitting its target would fulfill the bomb's primary desire, and in that sense be good (relative to the bomb); on the other hand, it would obliterate the bomb, and in that sense be bad (relative to the bomb). There is no fact of the matter in regard to whether the good outweighs the evil, or *visa versa*, (relative to the bomb)."

Should naturalists, or for that matter Platonists, hold that all behavior that harms a brute is bad relative to the brute? Think of a male coyote driving a rival away from his mate. Suppose he gets a few scratches in the process. Would this make the behavior bad relative to himself? Of course not. We mustn't be misled by misplaced tenderheartedness.

Here is a rough start towards a theory of what is good or bad with respect to brutes. An event is *good* relative to B if, and only if, it benefits B (e.g. is good for B's health, sustains B's life, and so on) or B wants it to occur, and it does B no harm, or the harm done is outweighed by the importance in B's life of the inclination towards the event. An event is *bad* relative to B if, and only if, B does not want it to occur, and any good it does B is outweighed by this want, or it does B harm which outweighs the importance in B's life of the inclination towards the event.

There are at least two problems here. One is finding an objective criterion for judging the degree of importance of brutish inclinations. The other is finding the appropriate scale by which to measure and compare degrees of harm and degrees of importance. In regard to the first problem, and perhaps the second as well, the 'purpose' which guided the 'design' of the brute seems highly relevant. Roughly speaking, natural brutes, like coyotes and cats, are 'designed' in such a way as to maximize the likelihood of their having offspring that will survive to produce offspring of their own. Hence, for example, a disposition to drive away rival males is an important trait in male coyotes. To some extent, the goodness or badness of acting from a given inclination and the benefit or harm likely to ensue could be measured by their effect on 'reproductive utility' (i.e. probability times number of viable offspring). Nevertheless, it seems clear that *some* behavior with high reproductive utility tends to harm the creature exhibiting the behavior.

I think the strictly naturalistic view must be that what is good relative to a particular brute has no absolute value whatsoever. But what should a Platonist hold in this regard? There is no 'should' here. Nevertheless, there are no doubt some Platonists who believe that if x is good with respect to a given brute, then x is a prima facie absolute good. If Peter Rabbit would benefit from vitamin C, then it would be a good thing (at least prima facie) that Peter Rabbit gets some vitamin C. Other things being equal, a world in which this happens is a better world than one in which it doesn't, whether or not any rational being believes this to be so.

This is certainly not Kant's view. As Kant sees it, a world that contains no life, or contains living things, but only plants, brutes, and (roughly speaking) Hobbots, *has no worth at all*. This is because there wouldn't be anyone who has the *concept* of 'worth.'[4]

The claim is ambiguous. Kant might be taken to mean that brutish and Hobbot well-being has no absolute worth unless, or until, it is given worth by being seen as valuable by some rational, accountable, being. This view would be compatible with the claim that such beings *should* assign value to brutish and Hobbot well being.

I do not think this is Kant's theory. As I understand him, he holds that there is no absolute good in a brute's or a Hobbot's attainment of what is good relative to itself. If we see this as absolutely good, we are making a serious mistake.

Our line of thought suggests a somewhat surprising conclusion. A well-designed brute is doing what it 'should' do (what it will do if it is operating properly) when it acts as it was designed to act. But we can imagine badly (or malevolently) designed brutes that are regularly and predictably destroyed or at least maimed by obedience to relatively trivial inclinations. It seems perverse to hold that such behavior is good relative to the dead, or injured, brute. Apparently, then, there are cases in which a brute does what it 'should' do, even though what it does is not good relative to itself. For brutes, at least, doing what one 'should' do is not the same thing as doing what is, or tends to be, best relative to oneself.

We turn now to cases involving two or more non-rational entities of radically different natural kinds. Think of a porcupine and a young spruce tree. During the coming day, the porcupine might spend its waking hours eating the some of the tree's branch-tips, or it might devour most of its bark. Suppose these alternative diets would be equally beneficial to the porcupine. Isn't it fairly clear that it is best with respect to *tree and porcupine* (considered together) that the porcupine should eat the branch-tips? This solution of the problem is *'strongly Pareto optimal.'* That is to say, the proposed outcome is at least as good for the porcupine as the outcome of any other alternative under consideration (there is only one), and is no worse for the tree than any other alternative (again just one).[5]

In a situation like this, I think it is permissible for naturalists (and everyone else) to say that the first outcome is better than the second relative to the tree-porcupine pair.

Is it absolutely better? Once again, it looks as though naturalists must deny that one of these outcomes is just plain better. Naturalists cannot provide naturalistically acceptable justification for this sort of absolute (unrelativised) claim. Platonists have the option of accepting or rejecting an absolute view of the matter.

Suppose there is one young tree and one porcupine on an island. The porcupine is desperately hungry. The tree is a healthy spruce. If the porcupine eats a good portion of the tree, he will have enough strength to swim to the mainland and so live out his life; but the spruce tree will die. On the other hand, if he does not eat a good part of the tree, it will live; but he will starve to death. Which outcome is better, at least prima facie, for the tree and porcupine pair? Presumably, we all agree that it is better *for the tree* not to be eaten, and better *for the porcupine* to eat the tree. But which outcome is better for the tree and porcupine combined?

There is no naturalistically acceptable answer to this question. No doubt there are a fair number of Platonists who will say that porcupines 'outrank' young spruce trees (in normal circumstances). Porcupines 'count' more. This is meant in a sense which entails that the untimely death of a porcupine is, somehow, more *serious*—worse—than the untimely death of a young tree. Consequently, (on this view) it would be better (absolutely, or, at least with respect to the tree and porcupine pair) that the porcupine should live and the tree die. On what grounds could one hold this? I suppose the claim would be that porcupines are *sentient* beings. They can perceive the world around them. They have their own peculiar joys and sorrows.

Many people hold that sentient beings are of greater intrinsic value than non-sentient things. Clearly this is not a *scientific* fact. But what is it? There are various options. Here are two of them: (1) It is an expression of a personal, or social, preference (Subjectivism or Groupism), (2) It is a *non*-scientific fact and yet, nevertheless, a fact that is not dependent upon, beliefs, preferences, or whatever (Platonism).

Footnote on Aquinas

Aquinas (and other medieval philosophers) would have said the worth of spruce trees and porcupines is shown by the relevant 'Porphyrian Tree'. Such a tree 'grows' upwards from the most general category (e.g. 'substance', that is to say individual things) *via* a series of two-way 'branchings.' Each branching, sub-divides the previous category by means of a positive and a negative differentia. Thus, for example, individual things are divided into *physical* (corporeal) individuals (e.g. planets), and *non*-physical individuals (e.g. angels). Physical individuals are, in turn divided into *living* things (e.g. mushrooms) and non-living (planets again), and so on.

How might the Porphyrian Tree help us with our problem? Eleanor Stump and Norman Kretzmann explain:

> Since each dichotomy in the tree is generated by the application of complementary characteristics, and since (setting aside the complicated case of the first dichotomy) all the characteristics applied involve capacities, one of the species (or genera) encountered in any pair after the first is characterized by a capacity its counterpart lacks. But, given Aquinas's views on being and actuality, an increment in capacity (or potentiality) constitutes an increment in being; and because of the supervenience of goodness on being, a species (or genus) with more capacities of the sort that show up in the differentiae will have potentially more goodness than one with fewer.[6]

The idea would be, for example, that a porcupine 'counts' for more than a spruce, other things being equal, because the porcupine has a positive capacity, power, or ability—a positive potentiality—which the tree lacks. The porcupine is a sentient, living, corporeal, individual while the spruce tree is a living, but *non*-sentient, corporeal individual. Similarly (as Kretzmann and Stump say) the destruction of a human being is a greater evil than the destruction of a dog (other things being equal) because the human is a rational, sentient, living, corporeal, creature, while the dog is just a non-rational, sentient, living, corporeal creature.

These traditional assumptions may be correct; but the Porphyian Tree as interpreted by Aquinas does not establish their correctness. One can imagine a similar Tree designed by a fanatic plant-lover. Living, corporeal, individuals are divided into those inherently capable of performing photosynthesis and those incapable of this trick. The upshot would appear to be that the life of a spruce tree 'counts' for more than the life of either a human being or a porcupine. Or again, a fanatic bird-lover might design a Porphyrian Tree that divides living, corporeal, creatures into those inherently capable of flight and those who lack this ability. Then creatures capable of fight might be divided into those who are able to lay eggs and those who aren't. According to this fanatic, female rob-ins 'count' for more than cats or bats.

Porphyrian Trees do not justify absolute rankings. The resultant rankings appear to reflect prior 'perceptions' of value. The Trees do not justify those 'perceptions', or make them more credible.

NOTES

1. My topic here is a form of what Korsgaard calls 'Objective Realism,' although I do not take it to entail that 'subjective values are derived from objective ones.' (See Christine M. Korsgaard, *Creating the Kingdom of Ends*, Cambridge University Press, Cambridge, 1996.) Korsgaard rejects Objective Realism—see footnote 17, p. 305.

2. What would make the death of a tree 'untimely' ? Is the death of a young tree that is crowded and killed by the fierce competition of forest growth 'untimely'?

3. G.E. Moore, *Principia Ethica*, Cambridge, at the University Press, 1959, pp. 84–85, see also pp. 188–189.

4. Immanuel Kant, *Critique of Judgment*, Hafner Press, 1951, p. 300.

5. For discussion of Pareto optimality, see, for example, Michael D. Resnik's *Choices*, University of Minnesota Press, Minneapolis, 1987 (e.g. pp. 151–152).

6. Eleonore Stump and Norman Kretzman "Being and Goodness", in *Divine & Human Action*, Edited by Thomas V. Morris, Cornell University Press, Ithaca, 1988, pp. 281–312. The quotation is from p. 294.

Accountability and Goodness

In Book One, Observation I, of his dark and deep *Religion Within the Limits of Reason Alone*, Kant divides 'the original predisposition to good in human nature' into three elements:

1. The predisposition to *animality* in man, taken as a *living* being;
2. The predisposition to *humanity* in man, taken as a living and at the same time a *rational* being;
3. The predisposition to *personality* in man, taken as a rational and at the same time an *accountable* being.

In an important footnote to element (3), Kant says:

> We cannot regard this as included in the concept of the preceding [i.e. being 'human'–being alive and rational (HO)], but necessarily must treat it as a special predisposition.... The most rational mortal being in the world might still stand in need of certain incentives, originating in objects of desire, to determine his choice. He might, indeed, bestow the most rational reflection on all that concerns not only the greatest sum of these incentives in him but also the means of attaining the end thereby determined, without ever suspecting the possibility of such a thing as the absolutely imperative moral law which proclaims that it is itself an incentive, and, indeed, the highest.[1]

We are, Kant thinks, animals, 'humans', and 'persons'. But these classes (and the related concepts) are quite distinct. In effect, he invites us to imagine creatures of three different kinds.

Think of them lined up in a zoo. The first cage contains a non-rational brute—a living animal with first-order wants and needs, but no higher order desires, and lacking reason. The second cage contains a 'human' who is not a brute and not a 'person'. This strange creature is clearly rational—indeed, as Kant says, he might be the most rational mortal in the world (i.e. the universe); but he is governed by his inclinations and something like self-love. The idea of 'genuine morality' (as opposed to the idea of rules and values imposed upon him by the creatures around him and his early training) strikes him as nonsensical. It seems harsh to label such creatures 'non-people'. In fact, the creature appears to be a Hobbot of some kind.

The third cage contains a 'person,' that is to say, a living, rational, creature who is able to perceive, or construct, absolute moral imperatives he is morally obliged to obey. I suppose naturalists and disenchanters will interpret this creature as some peculiar kind of unaccountable person.[2] The concept of 'accountability', (and thus 'personhood') in Kant's sense, seems to presuppose non-naturalism and some serious enchantment.[3]

Apparently, at least sometimes, Kant held that rationality per se is compatible with non-accountability.[4] There could be whole planets populated by rational creatures who have no reason to be 'genuinely moral'. But if this is true, then we need not ask whether reason per se requires rational creatures to be moral, or, alternatively, to be self-interested, or perhaps to be both. The 'issue' here is based upon bad moral psychology. Even if Kant is right in thinking that reason demands that *accountable* people be governed by respect for the moral law, it may well be thoroughly rational for *Hobbots* to be governed by the desire to maximize their pleasures and minimize their pains or the desire to gratify their various inclinations and higher order desires.

Hobbots provide us with a start towards one possible crude model of the moral psychology of people who are concerned about morality and, perhaps, claim to have a conscience. We will just add a Butlerian Conscience to the other modules. I call the result a 'Butlerian Android,' or 'Butleroid' for short.

(Perhaps it would not be absurd to regard Plato's three-part 'soul' as an early ancestor of Butler's three-part psyche. The 'appetitive part,' as Plato calls it, is clearly similar to the Inclinations module. And Conscience seems to fulfill one of the jobs of 'reason' (Nous). The 'spirited part'—Thumos—seems a bit more problematic as an ancestor of Self-Love, or the Desire Resolver. In the Phadrus Plato pictures the Thumos as the Good Horse in contrast to the appetitive part—the Bad Horse—and Nous as the charioteer. In the Laws, Plato regards the Thumos with considerable suspicion. It is the residence of Macho vanity—the inclination to think of oneself as an important figure, a tragic 'hero,' or whatever.)

To be up-to-date, let's use a Hobbot with a 'Desire-Resolver' rather than one with a 'Self-Love' module, as our basic creature. And let's throw in some other higher order desires.

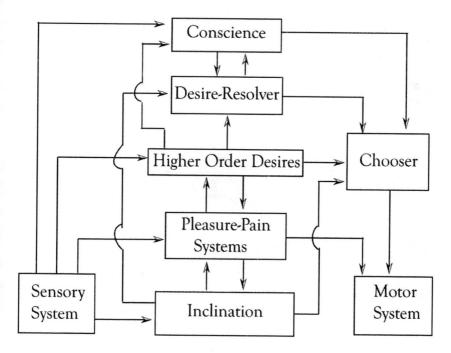

As I have said, the 'Conscience' here is based upon Butler's view of the matter. For Butler, Conscience is that particular kind of reflection which is involved in the appraisal of virtue and vice.[5] It includes both a cognitive and an appetitive element; more specifically it requires both sentiment and perception—heart and understanding. It involves "...both the discernment of what is right, and a disposition to regulate ourselves by it."[6]

The Desire-Resolver orders preferences in ways that reflect non-deliberate, basic, desires of whatever order. Hence, of course, the Desire-Resolver takes *moral* desires into consideration. It follows that in cases of conflict between the Desire-Resolver and Conscience the moral desires are not sufficiently strong to out-weigh non-moral desires. Nevertheless, Conscience sometimes wins in cases of conflict—the Chooser goes along with Conscience. It seems to me that realists in regard to morality, or at least those that are Platonists, should hold that the resulting behavior is rational and justifiable. In fact, by hypothesis, anyone who is morally accountable must to some extent have the idea (or feeling) that Conscience should win in such cases. Does this just mean their Conscience 'says' that Conscience should win? No doubt the Desire-Resolver would say that the Desire-Resolver should win. What, if anything, makes the claim of Conscience special?

At this point some Platonists may want to say that the Chooser itself should 'see' that Conscience ought to be sovereign over the Desire-Resolver. (Presumably these Platonists picture the Chooser as a little person who perceives how it ought to proceed. Does the Chooser have a little Conscience of its own? In general, the concept of a 'Chooser' is likely to give Platonists headaches. 'Free-will' is operative here.[7])

How should *naturalists* and *disenchanters* interpret the moral psychology of a Butleroid? They cannot regard the Conscience as a module that more or less accurately perceives, or constructs conceptions of, objective, non-naturalistic, moral facts. I presume Naturalists and Disenchanters take Conscience to be an internalized reflection, or rationalization, of 'folk-ethics'. (And, of course, on this view, folk-ethics does not include any genuine, objective, absolute, non-naturalistic moral truths.)

Let's spell this out a bit. According to naturalists and disenchanters, Butleroids do not have a *Conscience*; they have a 'Conscience'. This devise contains an internalized system of rules and values consciously or unconsciously designed and promulgated by a group or society to serve various complex, and perhaps conflicting, purposes. (Of course its possessor may have 'up dated' it a bit—subtracting some items and adding twists and quirks of her own.) It makes good sense for a group to design and implant such a system. But why on earth should a perceptive Butleroid who has any choice in the matter obey her 'conscience' at the expense of her Desire-Resolver? (Wouldn't a clear perception of this set-up, as seen from the naturalistic/disenchanting perspective, tend to undermine a resolve to be governed by 'Conscience'?)

High-minded, full-strength, Platonists think that *Conscience* (not 'Conscience') should dominate the Desire-Resolver. They may also hold that if the naturalists were right about the Butleroid's 'Conscience', then it would be preferable that the creature's Desire-Resolver be dominant. Given that a creature is not accountable, what is best for it is that it be healthy and happy—that its various desires be fulfilled over the long run. The Desire-Resolver is likely to be a better guide than 'Conscience' in this regard.

Naturalists (and everyone else for that matter) go astray if they think it's an objective fact that Butleroids should follow a policy of pure submission to the Desire-Resolver. It's a legitimate *subjective* claim for naturalists to make. I mean, a naturalist who happens to 'value' the resolution of desire can, of course, whole-heartedly approve of Butleroids following the pure desire-resolving policy. Notice that this involves a shift to non-realism. "Values", a naturalist of this sort can say, "are subjective, not objective."[8]

Suppose these people are right about 'Conscience'. A certain Butleroid named 'Nancy' belongs to a small and somewhat inept tribe. One day Nancy notices that her 'Conscience' is badly designed (i.e. doesn't do a good job of serving any of the purposes the inept tribe might reasonably wish it to serve). Is it an objective fact that she should, in this case, follow a policy of pure submission to her Desire-Resolver? Suppose the tribe has, to some extent, succeeded in getting her to want to be useful to her society. Given naturalism, why shouldn't she make a valiant effort to re-design her 'Conscience' and be guided by *it* (even, on occasion, in opposition to her Desire-Resolver)?

Notice that naturalists can deploy at least two, or perhaps even three, 'shoulds' (or 'oughts'). The first one is objective, and the last is subjective: (1) A creature 'should' do x in the sense that it would do x if it were operating properly ("The light should go on with the switch in this position."). This 'should' is certainly not a moral 'should.' It is not even ethical. (2) A creature 'should' do x, as judged by the 'values' of the naturalist. (Of course the naturalist must be prepared to admit that these 'values' are subjective.) In addition (3) naturalists may be able to hold that a creature 'should' do x, in the sense that given its beliefs and desires, this would be the 'best choice' as shown by decision theory.

Naturalists cannot regard it as an absolute objective fact that the Desire-Resolver should dominate Conscience, or that Conscience should dominate the Desire-Resolver. *Both* procedures make sense from the naturalistic point of view.[9] And, in fact, all possible 'mixes' of the two make equal sense. (Follow Conscience on Mondays, Wednesdays, and Fridays, and the Desire-Resolver on other days.) From the Naturalistic point of view, neither one outranks, or takes precedence over, the other. Consequently, there is no general naturalistic recipe for how Butleroids should assign utility values to possible outcomes. (Of course, when Conscience (as the naturalists view it) and the Desire-Resolver agree in their ranking of possible outcomes, there is no problem.)

Can naturalists hold that preference sets should be 'rational?' Well, they can like, and endorse, this arraignment. But I don't see how they can hold that, as an objective fact, this is how things should be.

Naturalists and disenchanters deny the existence of accountable people. Many moralists say *we* are accountable. In order to consider this issue we need to have a more precise idea of what sort of a creature an 'accountable person' is supposed to be. How would these people differ from those that are not accountable? The topic is murky and difficult, but (with the help of Plato, Anselm, Butler, and, of course, Kant) we can make a start. (For the remainder of this chapter, we more or less assume, or pretend, that we are accountable people.)

(1) To some extent at least, accountable people 'see', or figure out, what genuine goodness (virtue, uprightness, or whatever) requires of them.

(2) To some extent at least, they are capable of doing what goodness (in the sense just mentioned) requires of them *for its own sake* and not, for example, for the sake of the reputation they might gain thereby (pleasure, reward in the after-life, or whatever).[10]

(3) To some extent at least, they 'see', or postulate, that they ought to be good, and they *want* to be governed by this perception or postulate.

In (1) we do not insist that accountable people *believe* that they 'see', or have figured out, what genuine goodness requires of them. On the contrary, accountable creatures need not believe this. Thus, for example, Platonists can hold that some, if not all, disenchanters are accountable. Perhaps I should also point out again that accountable people needn't be *good* people. In fact, only accountable people can be genuinely wicked.

On Kant's view, as I understand it, accountable people who are bad deserve God's punishment. (I am not now thinking of the kinds of punishments the courts might impose in order to reduce crime, or parents might carry out in an attempt to modify a child's behavior.) I want to eliminate the purely retributive element in Kant's concept of 'accountability.' In part this is because I do not want to be committed to anything like Kantian supernatural 'free-will.' In fact, I want it to be possible for Butleroids, and 'accountable' people in general, to have nothing more than the naturalistic sort of 'free-will' Daniel Dennett describes in *Elbow Room*. Because of this, I am inclined to think that retributive punishment of Butleroids for the evil deeds they have done makes no moral sense. (It might make a kind of *aesthetic* sense. We like to see both good people and bad 'get what they deserve.') On the other hand, I think it might well be appropriate, at least in some cases, for Butleroids and accountable people in general to be made fully aware of the nature of their deeds, and of the motives, intentions, and action-guiding rules involved in their doing of those deeds. This awareness, of course, is likely to be quite painful.

The idea of 'real goodness' (or something more or less equivalent to it) clearly plays a crucial part in the analysis of accountability. But what is it? With what is it being contrasted? I take it that the sort of 'goodness' promulgated by a particular folk ethics may well be something quite distinct from this alleged 'real goodness'.

In regard to the content of goodness, let's stick to a few fairly obvious claims. Presumably a good person would be 'truthful' not just in the sense that she can usually be trusted not to tell lies, but also in the sense that she is committed to seeing things as they are and to a struggle against self-protective lies and blind-spots. Since the truth about the world and oneself can be quite grim, this will require courage. In addition, I imagine, a good person is perceptive and clear-headed about others and generally tries to be helpful to them or, at least, not harm them. She also tries to be fair (i.e. just) and respect the rights of others.[11]

The remainder of this chapter consists in discussions of various problems in regard to the view of moral psychology, and, in particular, of Butleroids sketched above. For the most part, naturalism and disenchantment drop out of sight.

The Bowl of Porridge

A good man and a bad one are lost in the woods. Both are very hungry. Luckily, they find a big bowl of hot porridge (with cream and sugar) in a hollow tree. The good man calls out (rather faintly) trying to find its owner; but there's no answer. "O.K.", he says to the bad man, "you eat your half, then I'll eat mine."

"Wait a minute," the bad man says, "that's not fair."

"Of course it is. What could be more fair that that?" the good man asks.

"But you *want* to go fifty-fifty" the bad man replies, "whereas I want the whole damn thing. If we split the difference, I should get three quarters and you one quarter."

The good man's mouth drops open. "You're crazy!" he says.

The bad man just laughs.

Something has gone wrong here, but what exactly? I want to make two points. First, even if the good man's strongest desire at the moment is that the porridge be divided fairly (i.e. fifty-fifty), the bad man's argument is a cheat. And second, the good man may have a very weak desire to be fair.

In regard to non-moral desires, the good man and the bad are presumably indistinguishable—each wants all the porridge. The good man's serious thinking about what should be done begins with recognition of this standoff. On this basis, and on a principle of fairness, he concludes that a fifty-fifty division is an appropriate compromise. Suppose he has a strong desire to be fair. That desire must be *irrelevant* in his calculations. Conscience cannot include its own (moral) desires in its calculations of what is fair. Imagine the good man, in his confusion, agreeing with the bad one.

"Alright, you eat three quarters and I'll eat the remainder."

"You're sure that's what you want?"

"Yes, yes... please get going!"

"But don't you see? If you just want a quarter of the porridge and I want it all, I should get about 87% and you about 13%. That's the fair division now."

The result is an absurd regress. The bad man is urging the good one to indulge in this absurdity.

Now suppose the good man has a weak desire to be fair. (His Chooser regularly favors conscience even when moral desires are weak.)

"Look," says the bad man, "which do you want more, to be fair, or to eat all the porridge?"

"Hmm.." says the good man in his confusion, "I guess I want to be fair; but, damn it, I'm just as *hungry* as you are!"

"Nevertheless your desire to be fair is the stronger of the two. Right?"

"Well, yes."

Once again the bad man is generating confusion. His question "which do you want more?" should strike us as ambiguous. On the one hand, it is a call for a decision ("Do you now propose to eat all the porridge yourself or is it your suggestion that we divide it fifty-fifty?") On the other, it seems to be an invitation to measure the relative strengths of two desires (whatever that may mean.)

The good man may be swindled into thinking like this: "I have come to the decision that we should go fifty-fifty, so I must have had a stronger prior desire to be fair than to eat all the porridge myself." Given that the good man is a Butleroid, the Platonistic analysis might well be that his decision springs from his perception that the fifty-fifty division is fair, plus his desire to be fair *however strong or weak that desire may be*. One can imagine the good man saying: "My desire to eat all the porridge is *much* stronger than my desire to be fair (alas); but I have decided, nevertheless, that we should go fifty-fifty." Is this absurd? On the supposition that it is true, must we hold that the good man is acting irrationally?

(If we think of a 'desire' as an internal condition—for instance the strength of the current in certain wires—then the idea of a sharp distinction between resolute judgments about what one should do and strong 'desires' seems to make sense. On the other hand, we might think of the matter like this: a judgment itself can generate a strong deliberate desire. But neither the Desire-Resolver nor Conscience can take the strengths of deliberate desires into consideration without falling into absurdity.)

Immoral People

By an 'immoral' person moralists presumably mean an accountable person who does things her Conscience tells her not to do. How are we to understand the moral psychology of such people?

Look again at the block-diagram for Butleroids. The diagram suggests at least two ways in which Conscience can be overcome. First, the immoral person might act from a non-deliberate desire (i.e. an inclination) and be acting contrary to both Conscience and the Desire-Resolver. Second, she might act from an inclination endorsed by the Desire-Resolver, but contrary to Conscience. Let's think about the second sort of immorality. The suggestion I want to make is that this sort of immorality does not entail irrationality. *Reason does not require accountable people to be really good.*

Consider a Butleroid caught in a conflict between Conscience and the Desire-Resolver. I think it makes sense—is understandable and reasonable—for the Butleroid to obey the urgings of the Desire-Resolver. This is not to say it would not make sense, would be incomprehensible, for her to obey her Conscience. I have already said that too would make sense. Both wicked people and saints can be fully rational. From the emerging at least somewhat enchantment-tolerating point of view, reason faces a 'dilemma': goodness is justifiable; but immorality is also justifiable when it is urged by the Desire-Resolver. Conflicts between Conscience and the Desire-Resolver cannot be resolved by pure reason.[12] We will think about this a bit more in the next Chapter.

Disenchanters too can, and should, say there is a form of 'wrong doing' that sometimes makes sense. The Desire-Resolver can urge a creature to violate local folk-ethics—i.e. to do something 'wrong' or 'bad'. Given the disenchanted view, it seems entirely justifiable for a creature to violate folk-ethics (and act against its 'Conscience') under these conditions.

The Good

Let's begin with *non*-accountable people. What is good with regard to them? In asking this, we are not concerned with what these creatures *think* is 'good', or what they *want*. We are asking what it is for them to 'do well'. Under what sort of conditions do things 'go well' for them? When can we say that one such creature is 'doing better' than it used to do, or than another such creature does? Under what conditions do they 'have it made'?

Most, if not all, sentient creatures have conflicting desires. To take an extreme example, consider a non-accountable 'self-hater'.

If the Self-Hate module urges a policy of minimal satisfaction of first-order desires, the creature might just annihilate himself at the first opportunity. To make things more interesting, let's have the module aim at maximizing pain, misery, and the frustration of first order desires over the long haul.

The Self-Hater

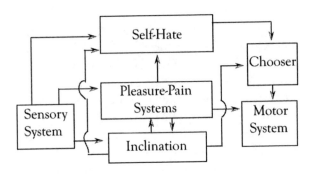

Wherein lies the Self-Hater's good? Here are three suggestions:

(1) The Self-Hater is doing well to the extent that he is fulfilling his inclinations (i.e. to the extent that he is acting as if he were governed by a Desire-Resolver and is lucky).

(2) The Self-Hater is doing well to the extent that he fulfills his policy of self-hatred (i.e. to the extent that he is frustrated, in pain, and so forth).

(3) There is no way the Self-Hater can do well so long as he remains a self-hater. Satisfaction of his inclinations entails frustration of his higher order desires, and visa versa

Many of us feel some inclination to accept (3). This inclination seems to rest upon the impression that it is *prima facie* good that a desire of whatever order be fulfilled. Higher order desires do not, *ipso facto*, count more (or less) than first-order desires. This would explain the fact (if it is a fact) that there is no happy solution to the conflict within the Self-Hater.

On the theory under consideration, Desire-Resolvers play a very special role. If a non-accountable person has such a module, then, by hypothesis, he cannot do better than to obey the dictates of that module. It urges his good. I want to raise just a hint of doubt about this view. The problem I have in mind concerns self-chosen higher order desires other than the desire to comply with one's Desire-resolver. Consider the following kind of creature:

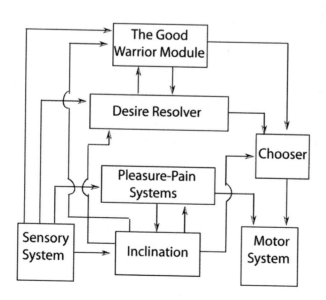

The 'Good Warrior' module is self-chosen. The Warrior has decided to have it and has installed it herself. (Don't ask me how this happened.) It urges her to fulfill a certain ideal self-image. As a consequence, it often urges the suppression of first order wants, needs, and so on.

The Warrior's Desire-Resolver urges the long-term satisfaction of her non-deliberate desires—both first order and higher order. Hence, I suppose, it sometimes endorses a first order desire rejected by the Good Warrior module, and, at other times it rejects desires endorsed by that module.

Imagine such a conflict between the Desire-Resolver and the Good Warrior module. Is it obviously best with respect to the Warrior that the Desire-Resolver should win? The argument on the other side would be that she is in the process of 'creating herself'. Desires that belong to her new, chosen self take precedence over 'natural' desires in consideration of what is best for her.

(On the other hand, suppose someone is more or less deliberately becoming more and more of a self-hater. Do we really want to say that self-hatred takes precedence over 'natural' desires in regard to what is best for such a person?)

Back to accountable people. On the assumption that we are such people and that we are Butleroids, wherein lies our good? In asking this we might be concerned about various things. Here are five distinct questions relevant to our worry:

(1) Under what conditions should we be said to *flourish*?
(2) What sort of general policy should we have, or try to have, in regard to decision-making, and, in particular, in regard to conflicts between Conscience and Desire-Resolver?
(3) What should be the ordering of our preferences in regard to our character and life?
(4) What sort of general character and life should we wish for those we love?
(5) Under what conditions should we say that so-and-so is 'doing better' than what's-his-name—that things are 'going better' for her?

Three simple answers to the first question come to mind:

(a) A person is flourishing if, and only if, she is having lots of fun (her life contains many diverse pleasures and few pains).
(b) A person is flourishing if and only if things are going as she wants them to go (i.e. she is unusually successful in gratifying her desires.)

(c) A person is flourishing if, and only if, she is good (virtuous, upright, etc.).

More complex answers can be formed by combining these simple answers. Thus, for example, we might add: (d) A person is flourishing if, and only if, things go as she wants them to go, *and she is good.*

Surely a bad person can have a long and happy life? He may experience many intense, enduring, and significant, pleasures. His pains may be few and mild. His genuine needs and desires may be largely fulfilled. (Of course some Supernaturalists will insist that he must eventually (after his death) suffer horrible torments; but it is not at all clear that we should believe this.)

Can a bad (i.e. wicked) person succeed in gratifying most of his strong desires and only be forced to frustrate a few? Can he, that is, have a gratifying life? By hypothesis, bad people are accountable. Accountable people, by definition, have some desire to be good. Hence, a morally bad person must have at least one frustrated desire. That is to say, a morally bad person cannot succeed in gratifying all of his desires. But then, who can? Surely the life of a bad person can be as gratifying a life as anyone can reasonably hope to have?

It is at least conceivable that there are people who have almost no inclination to be bad and also have such strong moral desires that the Desire-Resolver almost always urges them to be good. Bad people do not have this problem. On the contrary, their bad desires are likely to be strong, and their good desires weak. If they behaved as they should, their bad desires (e.g. the desire to humiliate subordinates) would be frustrated, and their lives would be less gratifying than they could be. In short, bad people can have happy and gratifying lives.

The next question is: Can bad people *flourish*; can they really 'have it made'? The straightforward, no nonsense, answer is that they can. A vile person can be healthy, sexy, rich, intelligent, happy, widely admired, and so on. What more could one want?[13] (The claim that a bad person can flourish is compatible with the theory that goodness is conducive to happiness—i.e. that a good person is more likely to be happy than a bad one. This is needed if one wants to use the hedonic paradox in defending virtue.[14])

Traditionally, Platonists have held that bad people are *ipso facto* defective. The idea is not just that such people misbehave. (Of course they do). The claim is that a bad person is in some way 'in bad shape'. It's as if he had a very serious, hidden, disease—his 'soul' is 'ill'. Somehow, it is not 'ultimately' in his interest to be bad (where this does not entail anything supernatural).

To a certain extent, this traditional picture may be right. Superficially, of course, it seems absurd to say bad people fall short of flourishing simply by virtue of being bad. But there is, I think, an important, though elusive, truth here.

Imagine a perceptive woman who genuinely loves a morally defective man. She sees, for example, that he has a habit of undermining and putting-down others. Nevertheless, somehow, she does not regard him as a devil. She sees him as a bit like a kid in some ways, and as self-absorbed. She denies that he is flourishing. On her view, he would be better off if he were a better man. Must this rather belittling view be mere self-defense on her part? I don't think so. Perhaps she wishes he were a better man simply because she loves him (i.e. out of concern for his well being).

Given that a bad person can be happy and can lead a gratifying life, and given that a bad person cannot really flourish, it would follow that flourishing is not just a matter of being happy or of having things go as one wishes.

Of course it wouldn't follow that we flourish just to the extent that we are good. In fact it seems clear that this is *false*. Imagine a good young woman who is miserable, and is in the process of dying. Many of her desires will never be fulfilled (leaving aside supernatural prospects of bliss). Should we say, nevertheless, that she is flourishing? The claim seems grotesque.

Perhaps flourishing requires goodness *and* a gratifying life. I think that we should stick with common sense and depart from and Socrates and Plato here.[15]

So much for question (1). Now let's tackle (2). What should be our policy in regard to Conscience and the resolution of desires? (We might think of this a problem faced by the 'Chooser'.) I will deal with this question in a rather mechanical and simplistic way because I think there is more to be gained than lost by this approach. Nevertheless we should be aware of the various departures from reality this induces. For example, in real life we operate in a sort of fog. We tend not to think about what would be the right thing to do. We deceive ourselves. Nor are we very clear about our real needs and desires.

Possible outcomes of actions can be scaled with respect to how well they would fulfill various desires. (There is a problem here when we take probabilities into account, as, of course, we must.) Just for the fun of it, let's suppose that actions acceptable from the point of view of the Desire-Resolver are assigned numbers between 0 and 10. Actions condemned by the Desire-Resolver get negative numbers between 0 and -10. Similarly, actions can be scaled with respect to how good or bad they would be from a moral point of view. Actions acceptable to Conscience get scores between 0 and 10; actions condemned by Conscience get scores between 0 and -10.

Here is a case: Andrea is trying to decide whether or not to tell a little lie. If she lies, she will score 2 on the Desire-Resolver scale and -1 on the Conscience scale. If she doesn't lie, she will score -2 on the Desire-Resolver scale, but 1 on the Conscience scale. Should she lie or not?

	Desire Resolver	Conscience
Lie	2	1
Don't Lie	− 2	− 1

(I'm assuming that if the *doing* of something is recommended by a given module with force n, then *not* doing it is condemned by that module with force -n, and visa versa. The sum of recommendations and condemnations in regard to an action is always zero.)

Andrea's conscience assigns a score of -1 to the lie. It is unacceptable from a moral point of view, but not horribly wrong. There is no commitment here to the idea that lying is always wrong. Perhaps in some circumstances it is obligatory. The assumption is that in this case Andrea judges that it would be morally wrong (but not *vile*) to lie. Presumably in making this judgment she has taken into consideration the fact that her Desire-Resolver urges her to lie.

What should she do? Still thinking of the problem in our simplistic and mechanical way, we might say that people (or their Choosers) tend to operate according to some fixed policy in deciding such matters. Here are five such policies:

The 'Purest' policy:
Whatever is done must be acceptable to Conscience. Given two or more morally acceptable options, choose one that has a maximal score from the point of view of the Desire-Resolver.

The 'D-R' policy:
Whatever is done must be acceptable to the Desire-Resolver. Given two or more such options, choose one that has a maximal score from the moral point of view.

Mixed policy A:
Do not do anything strongly rejected by the Desire-Resolver (e.g. that scores less than minus 7 on the desire-resolver's scale). Apart from this restriction, always do things acceptable to Conscience, and when there are two or more morally acceptable options, choose one that is maximally recommended by the Desire-Resolver (i.e. apart from the restriction described above, follow the 'purist' policy).

Mixed policy B:
Do not do anything Conscience *strongly* rejects. Apart from this restriction, just follow the 'D-R' policy.

Mixed policy C:
When Conscience and the Desire-Resolver assign different acceptability scores (i.e. positive scores) to different options, choose an option having the higher of the two scores. Otherwise, pick an option with a maximal score at random. This policy assumes a common scale for the pronouncements of Conscience and the Desire-Resolver.[16]

(Note: We have left out various policies open to Standard Hobbots—policies that neglect conscience altogether. Clearly these would also be options for Butleroids. We have also neglected policies regarding Conscience, Desire-Resolver, and Inclinations—tripartite policies.)

Our collection of policies adds some content to the idea that there are various degrees of wickedness (or, if you prefer, of goodness). A person governed by mixed policy C is, I should think, worse than a person governed by mixed policy B given the same set of desires; and both are worse than a person governed by the 'purest' policy.

In principle, a Platonist could hold that gratification and moral goodness are equally good. On this view, I suppose, we should follow mixed policy C. Some Platonists might even say that gratification is *better* than moral goodness. If this were correct, perhaps we should be governed by the 'D-R' policy.

The idea that goodness is better than gratification and better than a great surplus of pleasure over pain seems plausible. The 'purest' policy reflects this idea. (The 'D-R' policy and all 'mixed' policies appear to be recipes for moral mediocrity.) It is not absurd to think that accountable people should, at least, try not to become worse. Presumably, when Conscience and the Desire-Resolver conflict and we yield to the Desire-Resolver, we become worse.

Hence, one might think, Conscience should be dominant. As we will see in the next chapter, Anselm held something like this.

Conscience, some people will say, should dominate the Desire-Resolver (and, for that matter, Butlerian Self-love). This implies that the project of becoming good, or, at least, not becoming worse, should take precedence over the project of becoming happy, or fulfilling our inclinations and desires.

How should we picture the process of becoming good (or bad)? Look again at the block diagram for Butleroids. How can Conscience come to dominate the Desire-Resolver and all other desires in decision making? The diagram suggests two distinct sorts of transformation.

Transformation A:
The 'Chooser' persists in one fixed policy (something like mixed policy C). It measures the 'strength' of the input from the Desire-Resolver, Conscience, Inclination, and higher order desires, and does whatever is urged by the 'strongest'. (In case of a tie, it randomizes.) Given this fixed policy, one becomes good, if, somehow, the output from Conscience is strengthened sufficiently and/or the outputs from the Desire-Resolver and the various desires are sufficiently weakened. [17]

Transformation B:
The strengths of the outputs from conscience, the Desire-Resolver, and the various desires, remain more or less fixed. The person becomes a better person as the Chooser shifts to something like the 'purest' policy.

Of course our higher-order desires and our first-order inclinations wax and wane in strength. It is natural to suppose that a strengthening of the desire to be good (and thus of the desire to do what's right in particular situations) plays a large part in becoming a better person. (Is this strengthening supposed to be voluntary? Do bad people have a moral obligation to strengthen their desire to be good?)

On the other hand, we seem to experience inner conflicts naturally described as battles between desire and judgment ("I don't much *want* to share this porridge with you; but I believe I *should!*"). It's as if the Chooser sometimes decides to favor Conscience even though the Desire-Resolver and the other desires are opposed and would win out if the contest depended upon strength alone.

Why should Platonists choose between these two models of moral transformation? Perhaps both occur and some mix of the two is common. Thinking of the matter this way yields greater flexibility in describing how people may become better or worse.

Let me point out again how simplistic and deceptive these models and diagrams are. One of the few things in traditional Platonistic moral psychology that seems absolutely certain is that it is more or less impossible to become a really good person, or even to change much. Our discussion may have made it sound as though it might be done over a long weekend.

How could it be so difficult? Well for one thing, a Platonist might say, the human conscience doesn't work very well. We are not good at thinking about other people and ourselves properly, or 'seeing' what should be done. And it is very difficult to improve these skills. There is no algorithm for their performance. Furthermore, the Platonist might add, becoming good often seems an unnatural, unromantic, and rather grim process. Goodness is somehow attractive; but our own more or less immutable nature offers powerful objections to it.

We turn now to question (3) [page 152]. Consider a set of four simple, clear-cut options in regard to one's character and life. One can be good and happy, good but unhappy, happy but bad, or bad and unhappy. How should we rank these options?

	Happy	Unhappy
Good		
Bad		

According to Platonist theory, as we have been describing it, a thoroughly decent human being would want to be thoroughly good and thoroughly happy. Given a choice of lives, that would be her first choice.

Her second choice, surely, would be that she should be thoroughly good, but not happy.

Her third choice seems more problematic. Given that she is not going to be a good person, should she prefer that she be happy or that she be unhappy?

The idea that unhappiness can be remedial is beside the point. Of course, as traditional moralists have seen it, unhappiness can sometimes help one find the way towards goodness. But we are now supposing that she will not be good. Her present choice is between being happy or unhappy given this fact. Shouldn't she choose to be happy? I think Kant goes wrong here. He apparently holds that we should want our happiness to be directly proportional to our goodness. His theory is *retributive*. I reject this conception of preferable lives. If anything is objectively good, then surely happiness, gratification, perhaps even existence itself, are good. But then, *given that one is going to be wicked,* one does better if one is wicked and happy than if one is wicked and miserable.[18]

I am suggesting that the ordering of preferences should go like this:

	Happy	Unhappy
Good	1st	2ond
Bad	3ord	4th

Kant, presumably, would have it as follows:

	Happy	Unhappy
Good	1st	2ond
Bad	4th	3ord

Does the same ordering (the one I think Platonists should recommend) apply to our preferences in regard to other people? If Alice loved George properly, there is little doubt what her first choice would be. She would prefer him to be happy and good than that any of the other options should obtain. And, I think, she would rather he be wicked and happy than wicked and miserable (leaving aside the bad effects of his wickedness on others).

But these claims leave open the possibility that her preferences should go as follows:

	Happy	Unhappy
Good	1st	3ord
Bad	2ond	4th

Would love at its best prefer that George be good but unhappy, or happy but bad? It's a painful question. Nevertheless, perhaps our preferences for others should be the same as those we ought to have for ourselves.

One more puzzle about our good. There are, presumably, different degrees of wickedness, and different degrees of unhappiness. Given that Alice loves George properly, would she prefer that he suffer horribly and even that he die, than that he should become even a tiny bit more wicked? Suppose there is no life after death and Alice has no illusions in this regard. She does not think George will be rewarded in heaven.

Perhaps the story goes like this. George has been captured by a mad neurophysiologist. He will be tortured and killed unless he 'volunteers' to undergo surgery that will shift his Chooser from mixed policy B to the 'D-R' policy, and increase his intellectual laziness a bit. That's all there is to it.

The surgery really will make George a worse person, but not a lot worse, and not in a way likely to result in much harm to others. The alternative is dreadful. Perhaps, then, George's *Conscience* urges him to accept the surgery. After all, his continued existence counts. His animal pleasures count. The satisfaction of his desires of whatever order count. Conscience must weigh these things against the slight deterioration in his character. It seems fanatical to hold that torture and death are preferable to the least degree of moral decay in a person already far from perfect. I do not think love, or Conscience, would make such a claim.[19]

NOTES

1. David Sussman, one of my Kantian friends, calls the footnote in which this occurs "the footnote from Hell."

2. The observer in the picture is wearing dark glasses. This is to remind the reader that Naturalists and Platonists will 'see' the Butleroid in two radically different ways.

3. On Kant's view, moral obligation presupposes something noumenal—something 'outside' the empirical world—namely Kantian freedom of will. That's major league enchantment.

4. As mentioned in the previous chapter, Kant imagines a world in which the only rational creatures are unaccountable, and says, or seems to say, that such creatures are of no value in themselves—i.e. they do not 'count.' [*Critique of Judgment*, sec. 87, translated by J. H. Bernard, Hafner Press, New York, 1951, p. 300] On the other hand, in the *Groundwork of the Metaphysic of Morals*, ch. 2 [pp. 28-29 Second Edition] Kant says that the moral law holds, not only for human beings but for all *rational beings as such*—for every rational nature. I do not know how to reconcile these claims.

5. See Butler's *Sermons*, sermon ii, par. 5. Here Butler refers to conscience as a particular kind of reflection.

6. Butler's "Dissertation on the Nature of Virtue," par. 2.

7. For a *naturalistic* account of 'free-will', see Daniel Dennett's *Elbow Room*, A Bradford Book, The MIT Press, Cambridge, Mass., 1985. See also Book one Chapter V of Sidgwick's *The Methods of Ethics*. Here Sidgwick argues effectively that determinism is compatible with much of morality.

8. As I understand it, this is the view of David Gauthier. See, for example, his *Morals by Agreement*, Clarendon Press, Oxford, 1986, Ch. II, esp. pp. 21–38.

9. Many naturalists seem to deny this. See, for example, Gilbert Harman's, "Moral Relativism Defended", *The Philosophical Review*, Jan. 1975, pp. 3–22, and esp. p. 9.

10. Anselm says "... free choice is nothing other than a choice which is able to keep uprightness of will for the sake of this uprightness itself." [*Truth, Freedom, and Evil*, edited and translated by Jasper Hopkins and Herbert Richardson, Harper and Row, 1965, p. 127.] For a good exposition of Anselm's theory of ethics, see Jeffrey Brower's "Anselm on Ethics", in *The Cambridge Companion to Anselm*, Edited by Brian Davies and Brian Leftow, Cambridge University Press, 2004, pp. 222–256.

11. This is a pared-down, and in other ways slightly modified, version of the suggestions offered by Butler in his "Dissertation upon the Nature of Virtue", and by Richard Price in his *A Review of the Principal Questions in Morals*, Chapter VII. If one is a Platonist and believes that these claims are basic, one is well on the way to being an intuitionist. All that is needed in addition is the belief that at least some such claims are self-evident. Price is a paradigmatic intuitionist; and, as I read him, Butler is another.

12. Henry Sidgwick was tormented by this "contradiction in Ethics", or, more exactly, by the inability of Reason to resolve apparent conflicts between Conscience and Butlerian Self-Love. See the concluding chapter of his *The Methods of Ethics*.

13. Well, lots of things of course. One might, for instance, want to be of some use to other people, to create something worthwhile, or to acquire some desirable but difficult skill. (I know this sounds a bit 'high minded.')

14 According to 'the hedonic paradox' if one wants to be happy it is a mistake to aim at maximizing one's own happiness (or the satisfaction of one's desires). The idea is that happiness is best achieved by aiming at *something else*, for instance, the happiness of others, or artistic excellence.

15. Aristotle, at least sometimes, makes this departure from Socrates and Plato. Human eudaimonia (well being), he says, requires adequate health, food, and so on. See, for instance, *The Nicomachean Ethics*, Book 10, chapter, 8.

16. The basic idea in regard to these policies is to be found in Kant's discussion of possible 'fundamental maxims.' See his *Religion within the Boundaries of Mere Reason*, Book One, Sections I and II.

17. I believe Kant would say that this sort of person remains basically *bad*, in spite of the improvement in his behavior. On Kant's view, one's basic moral status is determined by one's 'fundamental maxim.' See, for instance, ibid., 6:58–59.

18. Plato's idea that punishment per se benefits a wicked person seems to me to make sense only if the person being punished *sees it* as punishment. In the context of an atheistic world-view, it is quite possible that neither the wicked person, nor those who love him, see his misery as punishment. Under these circumstances, and given that he is going to remain wicked, how is it *better* that he should be miserable?

19. There is danger of a slippery slope here. Ten successive episodes of the sort described might well make George a *much* worse person. Conscience must be on guard against repetitions of the mad neurophysiologist scenario.

The opposite sort of surgery—the kind that makes one a *better* person—also deserves consideration. If such surgery became possible, would we all have a moral obligation to undergo it?

CHAPTER FOURTEEN

Knaves or Fools

The idea that there is a sort of dualism in regard to basic, rational, objectives, or in regard to practical reason itself, has a long history. Many thoughtful people have held that it is entirely reasonable to try to be happy and also entirely reasonable to try to be good. The idea is that these are our two fundamental, rational, objectives.[1]

Anselm

Anselm employs this dualism in explaining the origin of moral evil. Prior to Satan's fall, there was no moral evil. Satan, like the other angels, had a 'will for happiness' (*voluntas beatitudinis*) and a 'will for rectitude' (justice—moral rightness—*voluntas rectitudinis*). On Anselm's view, both of these 'wills' are necessary prerequisites for moral wrongdoing.

How could Satan go wrong? As a high ranking angel, he lived, so to speak, in the presence of God. As a rational spirit, he was not tempted by physical frailties and desires. In spite of these advantages he managed to will something he should not have willed.

Anselm's answer is that there were basically only two things Satan could will: rectitude and happiness. Clearly, his will for rectitude could not lead him into wickedness. So it must have been his will for happiness.

> Teacher: So he sinned by willing something that pleased him and that he did not have and that he should not then have willed, but that could increase his happiness.
>
> Student: He could not sin in any other way.[2]

How could Satan think that attaining x (where x was something he should not have) would be conducive to his long-term happiness? How could he think he would escape punishment—pain—that would more than counter-balance the pleasure to be found in x? Of course, Anselm says, Satan knew that it would be appropriate for God to punish sin; but he did not, and could not, know what God would in fact do if someone sinned. It had never happened, and "God's judgments are a deep abyss and his ways inaccessible to us" [Rom. 11:33][3] Furthermore, there were good reasons for thinking that God would reconstitute a fallen Angel—not throw him out of heaven forever.[4] In short, it was reasonable for Satan to think that he could probably get away with it. (Anselm does not *say* this was reasonable; but it seems to be the upshot of what he says.) It really did look as if attaining x would be more conducive to Satan's long term happiness than not doing so. Satan was not acting irrationally.[5]

Suppose that Satan, under these conditions, had decided to forego x on moral grounds. Would that have been unreasonable, or irrational? I am confident that Anselm would regard this choice as at least equally rational and reasonable.

If Satan had lacked either his will for rectitude or his will for happiness, he could not have done anything morally wrong. Here is Anselm's argument for this conclusion. Suppose God had created Satan with only a will for happiness (i.e. as a sort of determined, spiritual, Hobbot). Such a creature, by nature, wills happiness to whatever degree he is able to conceive it. If he has an idea of God's happiness, he necessarily wants to be as happy as that—wants to be like God in this regard. This is an absurd, improper, and unattainable, ambition. But would it be morally wrong?

Teacher: ...he wills to be like God.

Student: Nothing is clearer.

Teacher: So what do you think, can the will to be like God be unjust?

Student: I cannot call it just, because he would want what does not befit him, nor unjust, because he would will it necessarily.[6]

Anselm adds that a Satan lacking a will for moral goodness could not be perfectly happy. "If in fact he wills what he cannot and ought not to be, he cannot be perfectly and worthily happy."[7]

What about the other alternative? Suppose Satan had a will for rectitude, but lacked a will for happiness.

Student: It must be exactly the same here as it was with the will for happiness.

Teacher: Then this angel would have a will that is neither moral nor immoral. For just as above there could not be an unjust will if he willed something unfitting, since he

could not not will it, so if he should will what is fitting, his will would not be just, since it was so given to him that he could not will otherwise.

Student: That is so.

Teacher: So neither by willing happiness alone nor by willing only that which befits its nature could that angel be called moral or immoral, because his will would be necessitated; on the other hand, if he neither can nor ought to be happy if he does not will and if his will is not morally good, God must harmonize the two wills in him such that he wills to be happy but wills it justly.[8]

Apparently, then, on Anselm's view:

(1) Only creatures that will *both* their own happiness *and* rectitude can be wicked.

(2) Only creatures of this dualistic sort can be *moral*. And

(3) In conflict cases, both wicked decisions and just decisions need not be irrational, or foolish. They can both make sense.

Butler

Butler describes conscience as follows:

... There is a superior principle of reflection or conscience in every man, which distinguishes between the internal principles of his heart, as well as his external actions: which passes judgment upon himself and them; pronounces determinately some actions to be in themselves just, right, good; others to be in themselves evil, wrong, unjust: which, without being consulted, without being advised with, magisterially exerts itself, and approves or condemns him the doer of them accordingly...

It is by this faculty, natural to man, that he is a moral agent, that he is a law to himself: by this faculty, I say, not to be considered merely as a principle in his heart, which is to have some influence as well as others; but considered as a faculty in kind and in nature supreme over all others, and which bears its own authority of being so.[9]

According to Butler, Shaftesbury was aware of our obligation to pursue our own happiness, but was oblivious to the authority of conscience. Butler offers something like the following argument for the authority of conscience.

Consider a skeptic in regard to religion, say Bertrand Russell, who simply does not see the perfect correlation between virtue and happiness (either in this life, or in the next). Shaftesbury presumably would declare the case to be "without remedy."[10] Butler draws a more radical conclusion. If conscience lacked authority—if we were not obliged by its dictates—Russell ought to act viciously when such a course is in his long-term interest. After all, it has been admitted that we have some obligation to seek happiness. In the absence of any competing obligation, we are obliged to do what is in our own interest. But the idea that Russell has an obligation to act viciously is absurd. Hence, we must admit that *conscience* has some authority too.

Does this admission clear up our problem? The result would seem to be that Russell may be caught between an obligation (stemming from the authority of self-love) to do a certain deed, x, and another obligation (stemming from the authority of conscience) not to do x. Merely admitting the authority of conscience does not by itself, provide the remedy Shaftesbury despaired of finding. Nevertheless, Butler says:

... to be under two contrary obligations, i.e. under none at all, would not be exactly the same, as to be under a formal obligation to be vicious, or to be in circumstances in which the constitution of man's nature plainly required that vice should be preferred.[11]

However, this is not Butler's final analysis of the situation.

... the obligation on the side of interest really does not remain. For the natural authority of the principle of reflection is an obligation the most near and intimate, the most certain and known: whereas the contrary obligation can at the most appear no more than probable; since no man can be *certain* in any circumstances that vice is in his interest in the present world, much less can he be certain against another and thus the certain obligation would entirely supersede and destroy the uncertain one; which yet would have been of real force without the former[12]

I think Butler may (understandably) have gone wrong here. Probabilistic prudential calculations can yield flat-out, non-probabilistic, conclusions. Given Russell's situation, he may *know for certain* what decision theory and self love would have him do. Self Love need not say he 'probably' should do such and so. Self Love may well say he *definitely* should do such and so, even though the outcome is uncertain.

In any case, why does Butler take this weak line in defending the claim that, in cases of conflict, Conscience should have the deciding vote? Why doesn't he just say (as he seems to imply elsewhere) that Conscience simply out-ranks Self Love—that it has *greater* authority? This is obviously a claim available to Platonists, and, perhaps to others.

Knaves or Fools

Some theists believe that God, in this life or the next, rewards good people with a degree of happiness exactly proportional to the good things they have done and punishes wicked people with pain and misery exactly proportional to the evil of the bad things they have done.[13] The idea of Karma is similar. Given knowledge of some such set-up, how could Conscience and Self-love come into irreconcilable conflict? If Conscience is opposed a certain deed, Self love will almost certainly come to oppose it too in order to reap the long-term reward for goodness and avoid the punishment for wickedness.

But, of course, this sort of belief is not universal. Many of us (including many theists) deny, or at least strongly doubt, that happiness and virtue are linked in this nice, straightforward, way. How should those of us who find ourselves in this state conduct our lives? Given that we want to be happy but also at least sometimes think that that we ought to try to be good, how should we proceed?

Some moralists say we are caught in a trap—condemned to be either wicked or stupid, knaves or fools, scoundrels or visionaries. Here, for instance, is Thomas Reid:

>...if we suppose a man to be an atheist in his belief, and, at the same time, by wrong judgment, to believe that virtue is contrary to his happiness upon the whole, this case, as Lord Shaftesbury justly observes, is without remedy. It will be impossible for the man to act so as not to contradict a leading principle of his nature. He must either sacrifice his happiness to virtue, or virtue to happiness; and is reduced to this miserable dilemma, whether it be best to be a fool or a knave. This shows the strong connection between morality and religion; as the last only can secure a man from the possibility of an apprehension that he may play the fool by doing his duty.[14]

Here is Kant on the same topic:

>...there must exist a being who rules the world according to reason and moral laws, and who has established, in the course of things to come, a state where the creature who has remained true to his nature and who has made himself worthy of happiness through morality will actually participate in this happiness. For otherwise all

subjectively necessary duties which I as a rational being am responsible for performing will lose their objective reality. Why should I make myself worthy of happiness through morality if there is no being who can give me this happiness? Hence without God I would have to be either a visionary or scoundrel.[15]

It seems plausible to say that in some cases of conflict, if one decides to go with self-love and reject the dictate of conscience, one is a scoundrel, at least for the moment. But is it necessarily foolish or visionary for a non-believer to reject the urging of self-love and go with her conscience? As I said in the preceding chapter, I think not.

If Self Love (or a Desire Resolver) urges us to do x, then we have good reason to do x. Doing x 'makes sense,' and is not stupid. As I see it, this is so even when Self Love is in conflict with one's Conscience. In cases of conflict between these two, I claim, one has 'good reason' to do x and, also, at the same time, 'good reason' not to do x.

So far as I can see, reason (in any ordinary sense) does not resolve the conflict.[16] But, if reason does not resolve the issue, what does? Platonists, at least, can hold that we somehow just 'see' that our conscience has greater authority than self love. We have come to a 'first principle' that has, and needs, no further grounding.[17]

NOTES

1. Daniel How mentions Butler, Reid, Price, and Dugald Stewart as people who held this view. It was the orthodox view at Harvard in the period between 1805 and 1861. See Howe's *The Unitarian Conscience*, Weslean University Press, Middletown, Connecicut, 1970, pp. 53-67.

2. *Anselm of Canterbury: The Major Works*, Edited by Brian Davies and Gillian Evans, Oxford University Press, 1998, "On the Fall of the Devil," Chapter 4, p. 202. Augustine held that there are two wills (*duas voluntates*) in us [See, for instance, Confessions, book VIII, Chapter X] I presume that Anselm was inspired by Augustine in this regard; but, I think, he modified Augustine's theory considerably. For Augustine's view, see James Wetzel's *Augustine and the Limits of Virtue*, Cambridge University Press, 1992, Chapters 4 and 5. Anselm's dualism of the will was further developed and modified by John Duns Scotus. See Allan Wolter's *The Philosophical Theology of John Duns Scotus*, Cornell University Press, Ithica, 1990, pp. 149-157. Scotus discusses two basic 'inclinations' of the will — an *affectio commodi* and an *affectio justitae*.

   My guess is that Butler was influenced by Augustine, Anselm or Scotus (or some combination of these) in this regard. Perhaps Kant was too.

3. Ibid. p. 226.

4. See ibid. p. 227.

5. Perhaps we should have some degree of belief (subjective probability) numbers here. Satan's conclusion might be more properly expressed in terms of expected values.

6. Ibid. Chapter 14, p. 215.

7. Ibid. p. 216. I do not see why a Hobbot-Angel would have to will something he must know is impossible. Why shouldn't he limit his ambition to the greatest happiness possible for *finite* spirits?

8. Ibid. p. 216.

9. Joseph Butler, *Fifteen Sermons Preached at the Rolls Chapel*, Sermon 2, par. 8.

10. Butler, Ibid., Preface, par. 26.

11. Ibid.

12. Ibid.

13. As I understand it, many Christians deny this. Some Christians, for instance, hold that God forgives the past wickedness of people who accept Jesus as their savior. Apparently, the idea is that these wicked people are *not* punished for their past wickedness.

14. Thomas Reid, *Essays on the Active Powers of Man*, Essay III, Part III.

15. Immanuel Kant, *Lectures on Philosophical Theology*, Second Part, First Section, [Moral Faith in God] Translated by Allen W. Wood and Gertrude M. Clark, Cornell University Press, Ithaca, 1978, p. 110.

16. In a very nice paper ("Is Ethics Rationally Required?", *Inquiry*, 47, pp. 1-19) Alison Hills argues that the 'dualism of reason' shows that neither a Kantian version of prudential law (i.e. something like the rule of self-love) nor Kantian moral law is required by reason. Hence, also, I am tempted to add, recent efforts by Kantian rational Constructivists and Contractarians of various stripes to ground morality, or, at least its central area, in reason or reasonableness, are fataly flawed.

17. Butler seems to be appealing to something like Platonistic 'intuition' on our part when he asks us to imagine a man rushing into almost certain ruin 'for the sake of a present gratification.' The case is supposed to show us that there is a 'disproportion' between the nature of man, and certain kinds of behavior. It presumably enables us to *see* that cool self-love has greater 'authority' than any particular passion. (See *Fifteen Sermons*, Sermon 2, pars. 10 and 11)

The Pirate

One respect in which Platonism in regard to morals strikes many of us as preferable to either form of disenchantment theory is that it is fully compatible with our strongest and clearest moral intuitions, and it interprets them in a straight-forward way. Disenchantment, in contrast, seems to compel us to abandon a good number of these intuitions, or reinterpret them in implausible ways.

In this chapter, we will consider one particular deed and our moral intuitions in regard to it.

The Pirate

Twenty elderly pirates are winding up their last voyage. They are nine leagues from land. On board are three Carib Native Americans the pirates have been using as guides. Now the pirates can sail to the nearest land and drop the Caribs off (as they have promised to do) or they can throw them overboard and be done with it. The eighteen-league round trip would mean, say, a five-hour delay in arriving back at their homeport. A man can have a lot of fun in five hours. Enough said; they feed the Caribs to the sharks.

Surely it is entirely possible that their Desire-Resolvers (or, if you prefer, their Self-Love modules) found the deed permissible? Let's assume this to be the case. The pirates don't feel terribly guilty about killing Native Americans. They are really looking forward to the parties back home. Furthermore, they need not be acting frivolously. Perhaps they have given careful consideration to what sort of people they want to be. They have decided to be bold and selfish. So what's the objection?

There are obvious *Platonistic* objections: Native Americans 'count'. Their lives 'matter'. It is objectively and absolutely a 'bad thing' that they have been killed in this cavalier fashion. The pirates are 'accountable', and must be at least dimly aware of these moral facts. What they have done is 'morally wrong'. They have violated their moral obligations.[1]

Disenchanters who reject God, karma, and so on, may well be stuck with the claim that the pirates had no binding moral obligations in this situation. Suppose this is the disenchanters view. We could then offer the following argument against the proposed disenchanted[2] approach to ethics:

Argument One
(1) If the disenchanted view were correct, it would be objectively permissible for the pirates to throw the Caribs overboard.
(2) It is objectively impermissible for the pirates to throw the Caribs overboard.
(3) Hence, the disenchanted view is incorrect.

Perhaps there are defenders of the disenchanted view who would reject premise (1).[3] Disenchanters who accept it can use it in the following counterattack on (2):

(1) If the disenchanted view is correct, it is objectively permissible for the pirates to throw the Caribs overboard.
(4) The disenchanted view is correct.
(5) Hence, it is objectively permissible for the pirates to throw the Caribs overboard [i.e. (2) is false].

There are two basic issues to be considered in regard to this pair of arguments: first, is (1) true? Second, on the supposition that (1) is true, which is more plausible, (2) or (4)? I want to suggest that (1) is true and that it is intellectually permissible to regard (2) as more plausible than (4). (Notice how weak this claim is.)

We begin with the defense of (1). On any disenchantment theory, the pirates cannot be accountable. One of the issues between Disenchanters and Platonists concerns accountability. If there are accountable creatures, natural or artificial, anywhere in the universe, then the disenchanted view in both of its principle forms is false.

How should Disenchanters interpret the pirates' moral psychology? Two crude hypotheses come to mind. (I am not saying Disenchanters must be crude. We only use these hypotheses to provide ourselves with rough, simplistic, models for moral psychology.) Perhaps the pirates should be seen as Hobbots. Or we might see them as 'Butleroids' torn between 'Conscience' and the resolution of their desires. Let's look at the first interpretation.

If the pirates are Determined Hobbots, there is a clear, non-ethical, sense in which they 'ought' to throw the Native Americans overboard. If they do not do so, there has been some sort of malfunction, or miscalculation. On the other hand, if the pirates are 'Free' Hobbots, it is certainly permissible for them to throw the Native Americans overboard. Rationality is all that counts here, and, we suppose, they are not acting irrationally. Either way, they are morally blameless. That is to say, genuine morality is simply not applicable to them.

Suppose they are Butleroids. As I said in Chapter Thirteen, disenchanters should hold that it is objectively acceptable for Butleroids to operate on a policy of dominant desire-resolution, or dominant 'Conscience' or, indeed, on any mix of the two that yields a rational set of preferences. Given that the pirates are Butleroids, and given an absence of supernatural factors, the disenchanted view should be that it is permissible for the pirates to throw the Caribs overboard.

What about premise (2)? Consider this possibility: the pirate captain stands for a moment looking the leader of the Caribs straight in the eye. Both faces are expressionless. He turns and walks a few paces along the deck and back again. "Aw shit, men", he says, "let's take 'em back to Tortuga."

This is a better scene. One has the feeling that in this version of the story the captain does the right thing. What's right about it? What exactly has happened?

Perhaps the captain feels a sort of respect for the Carib. In this light, murdering the man in order to get to a party doesn't make much sense. In addition, it seems quite possible that there has been a shift in the nature of the captain's reasoning. He has been trying to figure out what he really wants out of this situation (consulting his Desire-Resolver). Exchanging stares with the

Native American got him thinking in some other way. Perhaps he has suddenly seen the situation 'from outside'. His own wants, needs, desires, pleasures, and pains, are, for the moment, no longer central. His Conscience is in operation. To Platonists, this sort of shift may seem valuable in itself.

If the pirates had three horses on board, and were trying to decide whether to throw them to the sharks or take them back to the islands, the situation would not be fundamentally different. People who take morality seriously (nowadays) are likely to say it would be wrong to throw horses overboard in these circumstances. Horses, like people, 'count'. (Well, *don't they?*)

Platonism is plainly compatible with many, if not all, of our deepest and most serious moral 'intuitions'—not just intuitions about how fictional pirates should behave. These intuitions seem clear and precious—something we should hang onto if we can.

On the other hand, disenchanters do seem to be forced to say that it could be objectively permissible for the pirates to throw the Native Americans overboard (i.e. they must reject premise (2)). But there are at least two 'fall-back' positions available. Disenchanters might say:

(a) "It is true, for example, that the pirate captain should now throw the Caribs overboard; but it is also the case that *he should long ago have turned himself into the sort of person who shouldn't now throw the Caribs overboard.*" Or:

(b) "It is true that the pirate captain should now throw the Caribs overboard. Nevertheless, he like everyone else, should have been trained to value other people more than this."

What disenchanting grounds might be offered for these claims? The idea might be that people who have been trained, or have trained themselves, to value other humans as such, tend to have happier lives. The pirate would probably have been a happier man if he had received the proper moral training. Presumably he has always wanted to be happy. So, by his own lights, he would probably have been better off if he had gotten that training.

Obviously, this is an empirical claim. Do we have good evidence for its truth? And even if it is true, it is entirely possible that there should be people very much like us, except that they would *not* be happier thus trained.

Let's go back to our alternative story in which the pirate captain decides to spare the Caribs. According to more or less standard versions of morality, this may well be a rational decision for the captain to make. The Caribs 'count.' It is wrong to kill them for trivial reasons. To the extent that he spares the Caribs because that is the right thing to do, the captain's act is rational. Doing what is

right because it is right is *ipso facto* rational. It seems unlikely that disenchanters can take this line. Hence we may have another argument against that view:

Argument Two
(a) If the disenchanted view were correct, the captain would not be acting
    rationally in sparing the Caribs for the reasons given.
(b) The captain would be acting rationally in sparing the Caribs for the
    reasons given.
(c) Hence the disenchanted view is incorrect.

Is (a) true? Can disenchanters hold that the captain might be acting rationally in sparing the Native Americans, e.g. on the grounds that they 'count'?

Disenchanter: Well, I, for one, hold exactly that.
Platonist: How *can* you?
Disenchanter: Look, on *your* theory, the captain is an accountable person,
    right?
Platonist: Of course.
Disenchanter: That means, among other things, that he *wants* to be 'good'
    (in your queer sense of that term), he wants to respect creatures that
    'count.'
Platonist: Right.
Disenchanter: If the captain really wants to be 'good' (in your sense), the
    disenchanted view can't require me to deny it.
Platonist: I never thought it did.
Disenchanter: It's plainly reasonable to do what one wants, after due
    consideration. The captain really wants to be 'good' and has given the
    matter due consideration. Being 'good' requires him to spare the
    Caribs. Hence, he would be acting rationally in sparing the Caribs;
    QED.
Platonist: Hold it! Remember the assumption that the captain's Desire-
    Resolver urges him to throw the Caribs overboard.
Disenchanter: I remember.
Platonist: How, on your theory, can it be rational to act in way unaccept-
    able to the Desire-Resolver?
Disenchanter: Your question seems to show that you are making one of
    the common mistakes about the disenchanted view. You think disen-
    chanters have to say that we should be governed by the Desire-
    Resolver, or some other 'down-to-earth' desire or policy—any other
    procedure would be 'irrational'. But our view, or at least *mine*, is much

more liberal than this. If the captain really wants to be governed by his 'Conscience' (re-tooled any way you like) there is nothing irrational about his being governed in this way.

Platonist: How can you believe this? And besides, how does it clear up the captain's problem?

Disenchanter: It's obvious. The captain's desire to be 'good' in your sense presumably includes the desire that 'Conscience' should overrule the Desire-Resolver.

Platonist: Well...yes.

Disenchanter: That being the case, I think it is, at the very least, rationally permissible for him to be governed by 'Conscience'. Furthermore, I don't mind confessing that I myself favor, and endorse, values like respect for other people and so on. So I would *favor* the captain's decision to spare the Native Americans.

Platonist: Why on earth should you 'favor' *those* 'values'? (I hate these terms.)

Disenchanter: I'm simply confessing a personal preference. I like, and recommend, them. I don't say they're objectively, absolutely, right— although they do have some nice features.

Platonist: Good grief!

Disenchanter: Is that supposed to be an objection?

Platonist: Let me get this clear. You do *not* regard it as an objective fact that Native Americans 'count'?

Disenchanter: Of course not. It's a subjective matter. I *approve* of treating other human beings with a certain degree of respect and consideration.

Platonist: Consequently, you do not regard it as an objective fact that the pirate might well be acting rationally in sparing the Caribs?

Disenchanter: I *do!* Can't we agree about this? I think we should. I mean, I think we should agree that it's perfectly rational to follow a policy of submission to a carefully thought out 'Conscience.' Furthermore, it can be perfectly rational to follow a policy of submission to a Desire-Resolver.

Platonist: All right, both policies are *rational;* but only one of them is *morally permissible* for accountable people.

Disenchanter: Right. You've got it. Except, of course, that there's no such thing as 'moral permissibility', there are no 'accountable' people, no creatures 'count'—these are bogus properties.

Platonist: If you think these properties are bogus, how can you hold that the captain would have been rational in thinking that the Native

Americans 'count', or whatever? If that had been his reason for not throwing Caribs overboard, wouldn't he have been acting irrationally, on your view?

Disenchanter: Look. I don't believe that there is any such thing as a genuine 'haunted house,' right? Nevertheless, someone who *does* believe in such things has reason to avoid spending the night in one. It isn't *irrational* for him to do this.

Platonist: You can't think he has *good* reason to do it.

Disenchanter: Maybe not. But he has a reason. Let's try another case. Some people think that some places are genuinely 'holy.' I don't think there is any such property, so, of course I don't think there are any such places. This is compatible with my holding that believers have reason to feel a bit frightened, or whatever, when they are in a place they regard as 'holy.'

Platonist: Do you want to say that they have *good* reason to feel that way?

Disenchanter: They think they do. But in fact they don't. It's the same sort of case as the 'haunted house.' Nevertheless, I say again that these people are not acting irrationally. And that's the point I wanted to make about the captain.

Platonist: It looks as though you needn't hold that it would be foolish for the captain to spare the Caribs. But you seem committed to the view that a moral reason would not be a good reason for doing so. So much for Argument Two.[4] Let's talk about Argument One. Your disenchanted view commits you to the claim that the pirates may well have behaved rationally and properly in throwing the Indians overboard.

Disenchanter: You *agree* that such behavior could have been rational?

Platonist: Yes, Yes, There's no need to keep harping on that topic.

Disenchanter: Just checking.

Platonist: The issue now is whether it was *all right* for the pirates to murder the Caribs.

Disenchanter: I told you a minute ago, I strongly *disapprove* of that sort of thing.

Platonist: You're a nice, decent, sort of person. But your theory of morality is unacceptable.

Disenchanter: Thanks a lot. What don't you like about my theory?

Platonist: It can't explain the obvious *wrongness* of the pirate's behavior.

Disenchanter: From my point of view, an 'accountable' person is just someone who's dominant high-level desire is that he should operate on a policy of perfect compliance with his 'Conscience.'[5] Given that the captain is a person of this type, he is open to criticism if he allows the Caribs to be thrown to the sharks.

Platonist: But, on your view, an 'accountable' person could become *unaccountable* simply by developing a dominant desire to be governed by the Desire-Resolver. And, I take it, he would *not* be 'open to criticism' (as you put it) for the transformation.

Disenchanter: No, I guess not.

Platonist: I picture the captain as a person much like the rest of us. He has *conflicting* desires in regard to what sort of person to be—what sort of 'chooser-policy' to follow. To some extent, he would like to be a good man—one who acts in accordance with Conscience. On the other hand, perhaps, he would like to be a 'good pirate'—one who is bold, brave, and merciless to those who stand in his way.

Disenchanter: In that case, he isn't 'accountable' in my sense.

Platonist: Exactly. And yet we feel that he shouldn't have thrown the Caribs to the sharks.

The first argument against the disenchanted view is simply that Platonism better suits our moral 'intuitions' and our belief, or half-belief, that there are genuine moral properties. But, of course, compatibility between Platonism and these 'intuitions' and beliefs is not at all surprising. The obvious explanation is that there has been a long tradition of Platonism in our society. Our moral training is still heavily influenced by it. The interesting point (if it is true) is that the disenchanted view cannot exhibit equal compatibility.

Is there any objective, disenchantedly acceptable, sense in which the murder of the three Native Americans is a bad thing? The answer, I think, is 'no'. But an ersatz look-alike may be available. Disenchanters (and Platonists) may be interested in what would be objectively best relative to the group made up of the three Caribs and the twenty pirates. Is it objectively better for them (those twenty-three people as a patched together group) that three are killed and the others get to spend five extra hours at a party then that they all should live?

A Platonist answer might be that *everyone* is worse off. The Pirates have committed yet another vile deed, and acted against the (now feeble) voice of Conscience. That is to say, they have done further damage *to themselves*. And the Caribs have been murdered. Hence, these twenty-three people are in worse shape because of the deed.

Can disenchanters say anything like this? Perhaps they can. For example, there is plainly more *bodily harm* in the one course than in the other (three people destroyed versus a few extra hours of healthy exercise). This appears to be be an objective and naturalistically defensible measure of physical harm relative to the whole group. Furthermore, on the highly questionable assumption that an objective, naturalistically acceptable, scale of inter-personal pleasure and pain can be constructed, it seems at least half-way plausible that there is a greater long-term total surplus of pleasure over pain for the twenty three humans in sparing the Caribs than in killing them. This is because the three Native Americans may well live for a good number of years and make a substantial contribution to the total pool of pleasure. If by all such naturalistic measures it is better for the twenty-three that the Caribs be spared, then, surely, it is objectively better with respect to the twenty-three that the Caribs be spared.

Suppose something like this works. What good would it do? There is no disenchantedly acceptable reason why the pirates ought to do that which is objectively best relative to this patched together, artificial, group of twenty-three people. Presumably the pirates can do something which is objectively better *relative to their own sub-group* (viz. the twenty pirates), and each one can to something objectively better *relative to himself*.

Summary of Main Points

(1) Disenchanters cannot take it to be an absolute and objective fact that the Native Americans 'count', that their lives 'matter', that they have a 'right to life', and so on. These properties are of the sort that Disenchanters reject.

(2) Given a conflict within the pirate captain between Conscience and Desire-Resolver, Disenchanters cannot take it to be an absolute and objective fact that he ought to obey his conscience.

(3) Disenchanters cannot hold that it is absolutely and objectively better that the Native Americans should live than that the pirates should have five hours of fun.

These results, and others like them, give some of us reason to prefer Platonist theories of morality to a disenchanted view. Nevertheless, it is far from clear that they pose decisive problems for disenchantment theories. Disenchanters can, and should, admit (perhaps with a sigh) that their view conflicts with many of our strongest and clearest moral intuitions and beliefs.

NOTES

1. Clearly *Platonists* can make these claims; but what about *reductive* realists? This is less clear. As I will suggest in the next chapter, Reductionists may well be forced to reject some important and widespread moral and modal intuitions.

    I have been accused of being unrealistic in thinking that the pirates are, perhaps dimly, aware of the relevant moral facts. Maybe so. On the other hand, it's my story. The way I tell it, many of them were at one time fairly ordinary English (French, Spanish, or whatever) lads. Somehow, over the years, they've gone astray. Isn't life like that sometimes?

2. From here on in this discussion, by a 'disenchanter' I mean a 'non-supernaturalistic disenchanter.' The long phrase, repeated over and over again, gets tiresome.

3. But on what grounds? I can't think of any good disenchanter reasons for rejecting premise (1).

4. At this point, the Platonist could have offered a revised version of Argument Two. (a') If the disenchanted view were correct, the captain would not have had *good* reason to spare the Caribs. (b') But the captain *did* have good reason to spare them. (c') Hence the disenchanted view is incorrect.

5. This particular Disenchanter seems to have his own notion of 'accountability.' According to the view I have recommended, an accountable person's desire to be good may be deeply buried and far from 'dominant.'

CHAPTER SIXTEEN

Reductive Realism

A reductive theory of morality must be able to reduce *all* of the moral properties, relations, or whatever, that it accepts as legitimate. If, for instance, it admits the existence of intrinsically valuable creatures, then it must be able at least to sketch a reduction of this kind of value. I will assume that the things to be reduced include properties of individual actions, properties of people, laws, and so on. More specifically, I will assume that a plausible reductive theory must, at least, be able to provide a reduction of 'being morally right,' 'being morally wrong,' and 'having a moral obligation' to do, or not do, something.

There are various kinds of reduction. I will only consider three: reduction via sameness of meaning, reduction via Kripkian identity, and reduction via 'constitution.' In the next section of this chapter I sketch the first two and ignore the third.

Sameness of Meaning

Suppose someone claims that 'Such and so is morally right' *just means* 'Such and so is conducive to the general happiness.'

What might be said in opposition to this claim?

Consider these two propositions:

[A] It is morally right to do what is conducive to the general happiness.
[B] It is conducive to the general happiness to do what is conducive to the general happiness.

Here is an argument:

(1) Proposition A is informative, and important if true.
(2) Proposition B is less informative and a lot less important (but obviously true).

(3) If 'is morally right' just meant 'is conducive to the general happiness,' then A and B would be equivalent in meaning.

(4) If A and B were equivalent in meaning, then they would be equally informative and important and the same in truth value.

(5) Hence 'is morally right' doesn't just mean 'is conducive to the general happiness.'

This argument assumes that terms belonging to the same language and having exactly the same meaning can be substituted one for the other in any statement without a change in the meaning of the statement.

Divine Command Theory

Obviously, objections of roughly the sort offered above are applicable to many, if not all, 'sameness of meaning' theories of moral rightness. Here is another one that is relevant to our present topic:

[C] It is morally right to do what God commands.

[D] God commands us to do what God commands.

Now the argument:

(1) Proposition C is informative, and important if true.

(2) Proposition D is either trivial or absurd.

(3) If 'is morally right' just meant 'is commanded by God,' then C and D would be equivalent in meaning.

(4) If C and D were equivalent in meaning, then they would be equally informative, and equally important or absurd.

(5) Hence 'is morally right' doesn't just mean 'is commanded by God.'

This sort of argument has often been made against reductionists.[1] Richard Whately (1787–1863) says:

... the sacred writers always speak of God as just and good, and his command as right and reasonable.

Now all this would have been quite unmeaning if Man had no idea of what is good or bad in itself, and meant by those words merely what is commanded or forbidden by God. For, then, to say that God's commands are just and good, would be only saying that his commands are his commands. If man had not been originally endowed by his Maker with any power of distinguishing between moral good and evil, or with any preference of the one to the other, then it would be mere trifling to speak of the divine goodness; since it would be merely saying that "God is what He is,"–which is no more than might be said of any being in the universe. [2]

The arguments seem decisive.[3] Of course this is not very surprising. Exact sameness of meaning between different terms is, at best, uncommon. Let's move on to a more promising form of reduction.

Kripkian Identity

One of the many important and interesting items in Saul Kripke's *Naming and Necessity* is the idea that some identity claims state necessary truths that are only known (by creatures like us) *a posteriori*. Thus for instance, scientists could not have discovered that gold is the element having atomic number 79 by 'conceptual analysis.' It took lots of experimentation. Nevertheless, if Kripke is right, what they discovered is (and always was) a *necessary* truth. The identity is *metaphysically* necessary—not *logically*, or *epistemically* necessary with respect to us—and not an a priori truth.

Why should we think that the result is a necessary truth? Kripke basis his claim, in part, on the idea that terms like 'gold' and 'the element having atomic number 79' are *rigid designators*. The term 'gold' designates the same metal in all possible worlds (that is to say, all *metaphysically* possible worlds), and the phrase 'the element having atomic number 79' designates the same element in all those worlds. Hence, if there is a world in which the term and the phrase designate the same stuff, then they both designate that stuff in all possible worlds (i.e. they *necessarily* designate the same stuff).

Kripke's exposition of these matters opens the way for a new, and more plausible, formulation of some, if not all, reductive moral theories. One can hold, for example, that, necessarily, the property of being commanded by God and the property of being morally right are one and the same. One can hold this while admitting that 'is morally right' and 'is commanded by God' are not synonyms.

In spite of this refinement, some of the traditional Platonistic objections to the Divine Command theory still seem applicable. I will briefly describe two such lines of thought.

Essentialist Objections

The property of 'being morally wrong' (or 'being morally right') as applied to individual actions typically seems to yield necessary truths. The wrongness (or rightness) of any particular, actual, deed seems to be one of its *essential* features.

Think again of the pirates who murdered the Native Americans. We are inclined to think that any possible world in which they do that very deed, to those people, in the same context, for the same reasons, and so on, would be one in which the deed is morally wrong. Its moral wrongness is not *contingent*.

But, according to the Divine Command theory, this is not so. God could have brought it about that, in this particular case, killing those innocent people for trivial reasons is morally right. That is to say, there are possible worlds in which God does this. In those worlds, the pirates do the right thing in deciding to kill the Native Americans in order to have a bit more fun back home. Those of us who find this conclusion unacceptable can regard this as a reason for rejecting the Divine Command theory.

Nevertheless, technically speaking, the objection is not, as it stands, decisive. Theological reductionists can say that necessity is a matter of convention, and that they too accept the convention that moral properties are essential features of some individual acts.[4] Presumably the pirates' deed is an act of this sort. Given this convention, the Divine Command theorist could deny that there are any possible worlds in which the pirates' deed is morally right. In fact, given this convention, God *cannot* make that individual deed morally right. Presumably this is compatible with the Divine Command theory.

Platonists should resist conventionalist accounts of this necessity. They should, I think, hold that it is irreducibly metaphysical. The act is fully individuated by its *non*-moral properties. Its moral wrongness supervenes on those properties. What we 'see' (or postulate) is a brute, metaphysical, fact. Necessarily, any killing that had exactly those subvenient features would be morally wrong. This appears to be incompatible with the Divine Command theory and, if true, counts against it.

A similar essentialist argument can be given in regard to general moral truths. It is morally wrong to kill innocent people for trivial reasons.[5] Many of us take this to be a necessary truth. But the Divine Command theory seems to entail that this general truth is contingent. God could have abstained from making this sort of killing morally wrong. He could have made it morally permissible instead. This consequence strikes many of us as grotesque, and constitutes an objection to the theory.

Problems about Moral Obligation

Why should we do what God commands? Reductive Divine Command theorists cannot say that we should do it because it is morally right—because we owe everything to God, and so on. They must not, when pressed, start making irreducible moral claims. What they must do is provide some *non-moral* source of obligation.

Paley does exactly this:

> Let it be remembered, that to be obliged, 'is to be urged by a violent motive, resulting from the command of another.' And then let it be asked why am I obliged to keep my word? And the answer will be, because I am 'urged to do so by a violent motive,' (namely, the expectation of being after this life rewarded, if I do, or punished for it, if I do not) 'resulting from the command of another,' (namely, of God). This solution goes to the bottom of the subject, as no farther question can reasonably be asked.
>
> Therefore, private happiness is our motive, and the will of God our rule. [6]

This may be an excellent answer for theistic Hobbots. But many of us (presumably *not* theistic Hobbots) find it unsatisfactory.

Whately puts the opposing view forcefully. He begins by inviting us to ask ordinary believers why we should obey God. Is it a matter of prudence, or a matter of legitimate entitlement?

> They will doubtless answer that we *ought* to obey the divine commands as a point of duty, and not merely on the ground of expediency; that God is not only powerful, but good; and that conformity to his will is a thing right in itself, and should be practiced, not through mere fear of punishment, or hope of reward, but *because* it is *right*.
>
> Now this proves (Whately continues) that they must be sensible that there is in the human mind some notion of such a thing as Duty, and of things being right or wrong in their own nature. For, when any persons submit to the will of another merely because it is their interest, or because they dare not resist, we never speak of this submission as a matter of *duty*, but merely of prudence. If robbers were to seize you and carry you off as a slave, threatening you with death if you offered to resist or to escape, you might think it *advisable* to submit, if you saw that resistance would be hopeless; but you would not think yourself bound in duty to do so.[7]

Here is a related line of thought. Suppose that moral obligation simply *is* the sort of violent motivation Paley describes. In that case, one might think, the gravity of the obligation varies with the degree of violence. If we are threatened with horrible, long-lasting, torture for our disobedience, then we have a *very strong* obligation to comply with the command. On the other hand, if the threat is a frown or two, the obligation doesn't amount to much. I think it is fairly clear that this is an absurd view. The gravity of the moral obligation not to do x, seems to vary with the degree of wrongness we perceive, or should perceive, in doing x. The degree of punishment we will actually receive for doing x seems more or less irrelevant.

At first sight anyway, the stark Platonistic theory seems preferable. We are obliged to do what is right simply because it is right. Its rightness is itself the basis of our obligation to do it.[8] The fact that Divine Command theorists seem to be stuck with something less satisfactory counts against the Divine Command theory in any form (conceptual identity, Kripkian identity, or constitutivity).

Naturalistic Reduction

David Brink defends a naturalistic form of reductive realism in regard to moral facts and properties. I say this in spite of the fact that he describes his view as 'non-reductive.' (By a 'reductive' naturalistic view, he may mean the view that moral facts and properties are conceptually one and the same as certain natural facts and properties.) His official view is that moral facts and properties are either one and the same as natural facts and properties (even though the relevant terms are not synonymous) or they are 'constituted' by (instantiated by, realized by, composed of) natural facts and properties, but are not one and the same as those facts and properties. He writes:

> Ethical naturalism claims that moral facts are nothing more than familiar facts about the natural, including social, world. I shall gloss this as the claim that moral facts *are* natural and social scientific (e.g., social, psychological, economic, and biological) facts. To understand the import of this claim, we should distinguish between the 'is' of *identity* and the 'is' of *constitution*. Because 'are' can represent the 'is' of identity or the 'is' of constitution, naturalism can be construed as claiming either that moral facts and properties are identical with natural and social scientific facts and properties or that moral facts and properties are constituted by, but not identical with, natural and social scientific facts and properties.[9]

I have the impression that Brink uses the term 'constitutivity' in a technical sense—something a bit different from our ordinary notion.[10] This is suggested by his claim that identity implies constitution. That is to say, if property A is one and the same as property B, then property A is 'constituted by' property B.[11] This seems incompatible with the ordinary sense of the term. Identity is *symmetric*. Necessarily, if A is one and the same thing as B, then B is one and the same thing as A. On the other hand, 'constitutivity,' in any ordinary sense, is *anti*-symmetric. If A is constituted by B (i.e. B constitutes A), then B is *not* constituted by A (i.e. A does *not* constitute B). Given that certain particles arraigned in a certain way at time t constitute a certain table, it follows that, at time t, that table does *not* constitute those particles. To take another case, water, we say, is H_2O. And, of course, H_2O is water. They are one and the same thing. Furthermore, water consists of H_2O. It is made up (mostly) of H_2O

molecules. But H_2O is not made up of water. Water does not 'constitute' H_2O in any ordinary sense. Identity does not imply constitutivity.

Identity is also *reflexive*. Mark Twain was Mark Twain. But do we really want to say that Mark Twain was constituted by Mark Twain, that Mark Twain was made up of Mark Twain, and so on? Again, identity does not imply constitutivity.

[What about the converse claim? Does constitutivity imply identity? If A is constituted by B, does it follow that A and B are one and the same thing? Presumably not. This is an important feature of 'constitutivity' in Brink's sense, and, I think, in the ordinary sense.]

Brink thinks that moral properties are constituted by naturalistically acceptable properties, but he is inclined to think that they are not one and the same as those properties. He, somewhat hesitantly, offers two arguments for this view.

The first of these is the following:

If G actually composes or realizes F, but F can be, or could have been, realized differently, then G constitutes, but is not identical with, F. For instance, a table is constituted by, but not identical with, a particular arrangement of microphysical particles, since the table could survive certain changes in its particles or their arrangement. Similarly, moral properties are constituted by, but not identical with, natural properties if, though actually constituted or realized by natural properties, moral properties can be or could have been realized by properties not studied by the natural or social sciences. Moral properties may well be constituted by natural properties; they may be nothing over and above organized combinations of natural and social scientific properties. But if moral properties, though actually constituted by natural properties, could have been realized by some properties that are not natural—say, by supernatural properties of a divine being—then moral properties are not necessarily natural properties. Though constituted by natural properties, moral properties, on this counterfactual assumption, cannot be identical with natural properties.[12]

Here is more or less the same argument in shortened form:

For a moral property to be identical with a natural property, they must be necessarily identical. But it may seem that moral properties, even though actually realized by natural properties, could have been realized by properties that are not natural, for instance, supernatural properties. If so, moral properties are not necessarily natural properties and so cannot be identical with natural properties.[13]

The line of thought is based in part on the idea that if A and B are one and the same thing (or property), then A and B are *necessarily* one and the same thing (or property), and the closely related idea that true identity claims expressed by means of rigid designators are necessary truths.[14] Roughly speaking a 'rigid designator' is a term that designates the same thing (individual, property, or whatever) in every possible world.[15] Suppose, for instance, that 'conducive to the general happiness' rigidly designates a naturalistically acceptable property in the actual world and that 'morally right' rigidly designates that same property in the actual world. In that case, both of these phrases must designate that same property in any world in which either of them designates anything. That is to say, being morally right and being conducive to the general happiness are *necessarily* one and the same thing.

But now suppose that there are possible worlds in which something like Paley's theory of morality is correct. In those worlds, there is a God, and moral rightness is one and the same thing as being in accord with God's will. Furthermore, we presume, in some of those worlds, being conducive to the general happiness is not always morally right, since God sometimes commands behavior that is not conducive to the general happiness.[16] If there is one such world, then, being morally right and being conducive to the general happiness are not necessarily one and the same. But then, following Kripke, they cannot be one and the same even in the actual world.

Should this line of thought persuade everyone that being morally right cannot, in fact, be identical with being conducive to the general happiness? I think not.

Consider Jones, who holds that 'morally right' and 'conducive to the general happiness' are rigid designators, and that they designate one and the same property in the actual world. Suppose that Jones is a Kripkian about these things. In that case, Jones should hold that there is *no* possible world in which moral rightness is something other than being conducive to the general happiness. Consequentially, Jones should reject the idea that there are possible worlds in which the Divine Command theory is true and God commands something contrary to the maximization of general happiness. Jones should hold that this is metaphysically *impossible.*

The second line of argument has to do with 'multiple realizability.'

A plausible claim about a variety of property types and tokens (properties and property instances) is that they could have been realized in a variety of different ways. Functionalist theories of mind, for example, are based partly on this kind of claim about the one-many relationship between mental states and physical systems .... A similar claim seems plausible about moral properties. For example, both the property of injustice and particular instances of injustice, in whatever social and economic conditions they are actually realized, could have been realized by a variety of somewhat different configurations of social and economic properties and property instances. Moral properties could have been realized by an indefinite and perhaps infinite number of sets of natural properties. If we deny that identity is a relation that can hold between relata that are indefinitely or infinitely disjunctive—say, because we insist that identity holds only between genuine properties and we deny that disjunctive properties are genuine properties...—then the multiple realizability of moral properties provides us with a reason for resisting the identification of moral and natural properties.[17]

This argument too is given in a shortened form.

... the fact that moral properties can be realized by an indefinite and perhaps infinite number of combinations of natural properties provides another reason for resisting the identification of moral and natural properties, if we assume that identity is a relation that cannot hold between relata that are indefinitely or infinitely disjunctive.[18]

Obviously, this sort of argument is not applicable to reductionist theories of the form 'A is just B', where A is a moral property and B is a *non-disjunctive* non-moral property. Consider, again, the theory that being morally right is just the property of being something that has been commanded by God. Here, we are not offered a disjunction of properties. Of course God might command a lot of different things. Do these things *constitute* being commanded by God? If so, then, I suppose, by the transitivity of constitution, these things constitute moral rightness. But this view seems wrongheaded. Surely Divine Command theorists should say that the things God commands are simply things that have the property of having been commanded by God. They do not *constitute* his commanding them. Hence, they need not be thought to constitute moral rightness.

Similarly, the theory that moral rightness is constituted by the property of being conducive to the general happiness does not appear to offer us a disjunction of non-moral properties. Of course lots of different acts, policies, practices, or whatever, are conducive to the general happiness. But do these various things constitute being conducive to the general happiness? It would be better to say that they *have the property* of being conducive the general happiness, but do not constitute that property.

In the quotation above, Brink apparently offers 'injustice' as a moral property that is, or might well be, constituted by a variety of different 'configurations of social and economic properties and property instances.' He clearly says that injustice is, or might well by, *realized* by these various properties and property instances.

As a possible alternative view, consider John Stuart Mill's theory that an injustice is a violation of some specific individual's rights.[19] A present-day follower of Mill might say that injustice is *constituted* by such a violation. Is there a disjunctive array of properties here? As I understand it, Mill does not think so. On his view, there is one particular property that makes various kinds of deeds, laws, and so on, unjust. (Of course, if Mill wants to provide a *naturalistic* account of injustice, he will have to get rid of the reference to 'rights.' Having a 'right', in the relevant sense, is plainly a moral property. Mill thinks that 'having a right' to x is having a valid claim on society to be protected in possession of x. [20] But 'validity,' in this sense, may mean something like 'legitimate,' and designate another moral property; so we may still be some distance from a naturalistic reduction.)

My point is simply that a *non*-disjunctive naturalistic account of injustice is, in principle, compatible with acknowledgment of a wide variety (perhaps an indefinite, or infinite, variety) of kinds of injustice.

If A is constituted (in Brink's sense) by some naturalistically acceptable property, or by some infinite or indefinite disjunction of naturalistically acceptable properties, then A itself is thereby, to this extent, rendered naturalistically acceptable. In this regard, showing that some moral property is constituted by some non-moral property, or by some disjunct of non-moral properties, is like showing that some moral property is one and the same thing as some non-moral property. Consequently, some of the same objections may be applicable.

Suppose that moral rightness is constituted by, but not one and the same thing as, 'being something that God commands.' It would still follow, I think, that God could make it the case that it was morally right to kill innocent people for trivial reasons. Brink's constitutivity seems to be like identity in this regard. But this is an unacceptable consequence. So far as I can see, the Divine Command theory in it's 'constitutional' form has just as much difficulty in dealing with essentialist objections as it does in its 'identity' form.

Some, if not all, *naturalistic* constitutional theories seem to be open to similar objections. Consider the theory that moral wrongness is constituted by the property of being detrimental to the general happiness. On this view the killing of an innocent person for trivial reasons is made wrong by the fact that it diminishes, or tends to diminish, the general happiness. If killing innocent people for trivial reasons was, or tended to be, conducive to the general happiness, then it would not be morally wrong, and might even be morally obligatory. But then, it would seem, the wrongness of one person killing another for trivial reasons is a contingent matter.

Suppose we were vastly outnumbered by hidden supernatural diabolical creatures who spend much of their time watching us. They are delighted by what they regard as our vile behavior, and depressed by what they regard as our goodness. (They make videotapes, so to speak, of particularly vicious human deeds for public viewing by their diabolical friends.) In worlds of this sort, one human killing another for trivial reasons generates, or tends to generate, a huge wave of diabolical pleasure—pleasure that vastly outweighs the pain that such killings tend to produce. Hence, according to the theory we are considering, in those worlds a killing of this kind is not morally wrong—in fact it may well be morally right. (The diabolical creatures *think* it is wrong for us humans to kill innocent people for trivial reasons. They do not take their own nasty supernatural pleasures and pains into consideration in arriving at this conclusion.) Hence, on this view, it is not a necessary truth that we should not kill innocent people for trivial reasons. I take this conclusion to be counter-intuitive, and offer it as an objection to the naturalistic constitutional theory that led us to it.

Similarly, we have reason to suspect that a naturalistic constitutional theory of *moral obligation* will violate our moral intuitions.

Mill's theory of obligation, perhaps with a few minor modifications, is available to naturalists. As I understand it, he holds that moral obligation is primarily grounded in the 'ultimate sanction' of morality. The ultimate sanction is "... a feeling in our own mind; a pain, more or less intense, attendant on violation of duty..."[21] The 'binding force' of moral obligation

> ...consists in the existence of a mass of feeling which must be broken through in order to do what violates our standard of right, and which, if we do nevertheless violate that standard, will probably have to be encountered afterwards in the form of remorse. Whatever theory we have of the nature or origin of conscience, this is what essentially constitutes it.[22]

This is not radically different from Paley's account of obligation. Some of the Platonistic objections to Paley's theory can be made applicable to a constitutional reading of the theory Mill offers.

Imagine a society in which people have been trained to feel guilty about not supporting slavery. When, for instance, these people contemplate helping a slave escape they know they will feel terribly guilty if they do it.[23] On a natural reading of Mill's theory, such people have an *obligation* not to aid the escape. This is counter-intuitive. (My guess is that Mill would say that the obligation isn't *moral*, since slavery is morally wrong.)

As is the case with Paley's theory of obligation, it would seem that on Mill's theory the strength of a moral obligation to do D ought to vary in accordance with the strength of the bad feelings one would have if one did D. On Mill's view, this is a matter of training and instinct. Thus, apparently, someone might come to have a very strong moral obligation not to burp in public, and a very weak obligation not to break the bones of innocent people. (It all depends on one's training.) But this seems quite wrong, and to provide another objection to the theory.

Mill himself imagines someone thinking that, on his (Mill's) view we could, apparently, get rid of a moral obligation by getting rid of the associated pangs of conscience. (Perhaps a psychologist could do this for us.)

...if a person is able to say to himself, "That which is restraining me and which is called my conscience is only a feeling in my own mind," he may possibly draw the conclusion that when the feeling ceases the obligation ceases, and that if he find the feeling inconvenient, he may disregard it and endeavor to get rid of it.[24]

Some of us, at this point, hope that Mill is going to say that a moral obligation *cannot* be gotten rid of in this way. But he does not. In fact, it looks as though his theory actually does have this unfortunate consequence.[25]

A person who was desperately anxious to escape all moral obligations could, no doubt, do so by having himself or herself transformed into a brute. In fact, if I am right, a person could escape all genuine moral obligations by being transformed into a Hobbot. Why isn't this consequence of my theory just as objectionable as the similar apparent consequence of Mill's view? Well, there is, at least, one important difference. Hobbots and brutes have no notion of genuine moral rightness and wrongness. Transformation into a brute or a Hobbot would, so to speak, make one 'blind' in regard to these properties. On a traditional (Platonistic) view of obligation, perception that a certain act is morally wrong carries with it a prima facie obligation not to do it.[26] On the other hand, if one simply cannot 'see' these properties, one has no genuine moral obligations. Getting rid of the pangs that go with a guilty conscience need not have this effect. Amputation of the pangs, it would seem, might well leave one fully aware of genuine moral rightness and wrongness, and thus aware of some moral obligations.

There is something a bit mysterious about this traditional view of moral obligation. How does the perception that a certain act is morally wrong 'carry with it' an obligation not to do it? Reductive accounts of obligation dispel the mystery. This may be a positive feature of those accounts. On the other hand, it may be a defect. Perhaps there really are genuine moral obligations and they really are mysterious in some way. If so, this feature is lost in most, if not all, reductive theories

Paley's story of his work on morality is interesting in this regard.

When I first turned my thoughts to moral speculations, an air of mystery seemed to hang over the whole subject; which arose, I believe, from hence—that I supposed, with many authors whom I had read, that to be obliged to do a thing, was very different from being induced only to do it; and that the obligation to practice virtue, to do what is right, just, &c. was quite another thing, and of another kind, than the obligation which a soldier is under to obey his officer, a servant his master, or any of the civil and ordinary obligations of human life. Whereas, from what has been said it appears, that moral obligation is like all other obligations; and that all obligation is nothing more than an inducement of sufficient strength, and resulting, in some way, from the command of another.[27]

From a Platonistic point of view, Paley was nearer the truth when he found moral obligation mysterious and different from the ordinary (prudential) obligations of a soldier to obey his officer, and so on.

In this chapter there has been no argument offered against reductive accounts of morality in general.[28] We only considered arguments against specific versions of two relatively simple reductive theories. I do not regard these arguments as conclusive refutations of even these theories. Obviously they do not refute reductive accounts in general; but they do, I think, call our attention to possible weak spots in any reductive theory of morality.

NOTES

1. Prior gives examples from Shaftesbury, Hutcheson, Price, Whately, and Sidgwick. See Prior's *Logic and the Basis of Ethics*, pp. 95–107. It is *not*, as many people seem to think, a form of argument invented by G. E. Moore.

2. Richard Whately, *Introductory Lessons on Morals, and Christian Evidences*, Cambridge, John Bartlett, 1857, p. 7.

3. One might have Quineian objections to the argument's employment of 'exact sameness of meaning;' but then these objections could themselves be used against the claim that 'is morally right' means exactly the same thing as 'is commanded by God'.

4. See my discussion of the Essentialist Argument in Appendix B.

5. I hope it is clear that I am not suggesting that it is morally permissible to kill people provided one has a fairly compelling reason for doing so—for instance, one thinks, that killing someone is the only way to impress the other members of one's gang. I have offered an absurdly permissive version of the rule in order to maximize its intuitive plausibility.

6. William Paley, *The Principles of Moral Philosophy*, Book II, Chapter III, quoted from *British Moralists*, Vol. II, Edited by L.A. Selby-Bigge, Dover Publications, Inc., New York, p. 359. There are some nice comments on this matter in Prior's *Logic and the Basis of Ethics*, pp. 100–101.

7. Richard Whately, op. cit. p. 8.

8. This is one of the central ideas in H. A. Prichard's well known paper "Does Moral Philosophy Rest on a Mistake?," *Mind*, New Series. No. 81, January 1912, pp. 21–37.

9. David O. Brink, *Moral Realism and the Foundations of Ethics*, Cambridge University Press, Cambridge, 1989, pp. 156–157.

10. For a discussion of identity and constitutivity, see my "Constitutivity and Identity", *Noûs* 5 (1971), pp. 313–319, reprinted in *Material Constitution*, edited by Michael Rea, Rowman & Littlefield Publishers, Lanhan, 1997.

11. Op Cit. p. 157.

12. Ibid. pp.157–158. In a footnote to p. 158, Brink points out that theists need not hold the Divine Command theory. They might, for instance be 'theological objectivists'. "...if theological objectivism is true, we will not think that moral properties consist in properties

of divine will even in those worlds in which God exists and commands all and only morally correct actions." ('Theological objectivism' is the view that ".. if God were to exist, she would command all and only good or morally correct actions *because* these actions are good or right prior to and independently of God's will and because God herself is good.")

13. Ibid. p. 177.

14. See Saul Kripke's *Naming and Necessity*, Harvard University Press, Cambridge Massachusetts, 1972, pp. 3–5.

15. See ibid. p. 48.

16. I am not saying that God does this in the *actual* world. My claim is only that, according to the Divine Command theory, God *could* command things not conducive to the general happiness. That is to say, there are 'possible worlds' in which he issues such commands.

17. Brink, op. cit. pp. 158–159.

18. Ibid.

19. See John Stuart Mill's, *Utilitarianism*, Hackett publishing Company, Indianapolis, 1979, p. 49.

20. See *Utilitarianism*, op. cit. p. 52.

21. Ibid. p. 27.

22. Ibid. p. 28.

23. Huck Finn feels guilty about helping Jim escape.

24. Ibid. p. 29.

25. For a bit more on Mill's theory of moral obligation, see appendix D.

26. I believe it was David Ross who gave the idea of prima facie obligations importance in ethics.

27. William Paley, op. cit., pp. 359–360.

28. One traditional, general, argument goes as follows. The enterprise of working out a *naturalistic* reduction of ethics seems misguided from the outset. Ethics is not a putative predictive science. Ethics is concerned with how things *ought* to be, what is really *important*, and so on. It is not in the business of developing predictive laws and theories.

CHAPTER SEVENTEEN

Superfluous Explanation

Both reductive and non-reductive moral realists are confronted by the apparent fact that moral theory yields only superfluous explanations and predictions—predictions we are already able to make, explanations of events we can already explain, without the help of moral theory.

Last Tuesday Babs set fire to her cat, Chester, just for the fun of it. She used lighter fluid and a match.

Assuming that Babs is not insane and that she 'knows better,' I take it most of us would agree that this is a fairly clear-cut case of a bad deed—if there are such things. She shouldn't have done it. It isn't right.

Alice saw it happen. She was parking her car, and happened to look into the back yard just as Babs did it. She was horrified. By the time she had gotten herself out of the car and around to the patio, it was too late to save the cat. Afterwards she told Harry that what she saw right off—the thing that sickened her—was the absolute wrongness of what Babs was doing.

Gilbert Harman calls this sort of thing a 'moral observation'. Alice didn't reason it out. She is saying what she saw. Harman, in effect, asks whether the moral observation was brought about, at least in part, by the moral wrongness of Babs' deed, or did Alice see the deed this way because of her 'moral' upbringing.[1]

Of course there is widespread *belief* in 'moral wrongness'. This is a naturalistically acceptable (and explicable) fact. There is also widespread belief in ghosts. Some people make 'ghost observations' (i.e. 'see ghosts'); but it doesn't follow that there *are* ghosts. It seems likely that the vast majority of 'ghost' observers think that the actual presence of a ghost plays a crucial part in the best explanation of their experience. Given that a real ghost would be a supernatural entity, naturalists must deny this or abandon naturalism. On the other hand, surely, many if not all encounters with 'ghosts' are better explained without the invocation of anything supernatural.

In some sense of 'possible', it seems possible that moral properties should play a crucial part in the operation of the world. This could happen in either one of at least two quite different ways: (1) *Irreducible*, Platonistic, moral properties might appear, for example, in every optimal set of scientific laws applicable to our world; or (2) moral properties might turn out to be perfectly respectable natural properties (via discovered identities or constitution relations).

Another possibility is that moral properties are, in fact, simply not relevant to how the world works in this scientific sort of way—they add nothing to our explanatory-predictive power. (This looks like a fairly good bet.)[2]

Suppose moral properties are not crucial to a scientific understanding of how the actual world works. Suppose they yield no gain in our ability to predict the course of events. This would open up the way for an attack on Platonism in regard to morals:

(1) *Real* properties play a part in least one optimal set of scientific laws applicable to our world.
(2) Moral properties play no part in any optimal set of scientific laws applicable to our world. (The view that they *do*, is a form of *supernaturalism*.)
(3) Hence these alleged properties are bogus.

Even the beginning of an analysis of these claims takes us into very deep waters.

Supernaturalism, Mechanism, and Platonism

What, exactly, is 'supernaturalism'? Let's define it as the theory that *'mechanism'* is false because any optimal set of laws proper to physics is regularly, or at least occasionally, 'violated' by irreducible psychological, moral, aesthetic, or religious factors. (I'll try to say what 'mechanism' is in a moment.) Thus, for example, spirits work countless miracles in our brains, or there tends to be a lot more light around really good people than in the vicinity of those who are bad.

Of course it is conceivable that photons should be generated by goodness and swallowed up by wickedness. More than that, it seems metaphysically possible. In possible worlds of this sort, we might say, physics yields an 'incomplete' account of its own domain. A full account of how these worlds work physically would have to deal with moral goodness and moral evil and this, we suppose, takes us 'outside' of physics.

What is 'mechanism'? Basically it is composed of the following two doctrines: (a) if a physical event, E1 is caused by another event, E2, then E2 itself is a physical event. (Or, failing that, there is, at least, some physical event, E3, such that E3 'embodies' E2, and E3 causes E1). (b) If one physical event causes another, then there is some causal law of physics covering the transaction. There is an optional third doctrine: (c) If a physical event, E1, causes another event, E2, then E2 itself (or it's embodiment) is a physical event.[3] I call this optional because it eliminates the possibility that physical events cause disembodied mental events, and it is not clear that mechanists are required to go that far.

Mechanism is, among other things, a rejection of supernaturalism (and visa versa); but it is not equivalent to Naturalism Naturalists need not be mechanists. Thus, for example, a good Naturalist might reject mechanism because she thinks there is substantial evidence that irreducible biological events sometimes have physical effects ('*vitalism*').

It seems possible that mechanism is correct. (There are, at least, possible mechanistic worlds that look much like ours—that contain, or seem to contain, stars, people, wild-flowers, and so on.)

People who accept mechanism are also likely to hold that physics is optimally predictive. A demon examining our world (from 'outside') who knew all there was to know about what was going on so far as a perfected physics is concerned, could not extend the range of her predictive powers in regard to this world by learning any other science (or, for that matter, any other discipline—say theology or economics). (So far as I can see, this doctrine about prediction is not entailed by mechanism.) Can one coherently accept both of these doctrines (mechanism, and the optimality of physics as a predictor of physical events) plus Platonism in regard to morals? I think so.

Let me try to clarify the notion of a 'superfluous' explanatory or predictive system by means of an example.

A 'hoak' is a complex individual made up of an oak-tree and the nearest horse. 'hoakology' is the study of hoaks. The 'size' of a hoak sometimes varies rapidly, and is measured by the distance between the center of gravity of the oak and of the horse. So long as there is at least one horse, the number of hoaks and the number of oak-trees is one and the same. Some horses are components of more than one hoak. At the present time, every oak is a component of a hoak; but some horses are not. When an oak-tree dies, or is destroyed, a hoak ceases to exist. When a horse that is part of a hoak dies, the hoak almost always undergoes an abrupt change in size. Hoaks tend to be much larger in some geographical regions than in others. Hoakologists (if they existed) would try to understand this, and other peculiar facts about hoaks.

I take it we should be absolute objectivists in regard to this domain. If there is a very small hoak in a certain field, then this is a hoakalogical fact—not a matter of opinion.

Should we be realists about these things? A proper answer to this question would tell us at least as much about the intended meaning of 'realism' as about hoaks.

Clearly we did not create all the millions of hoaks that have existed on our planet—we did not invent them or conjure them into existence. Neither they themselves nor the empirical facts about them depend upon our beliefs, conventions, practices, or whatever. In this sense they are real enough.

So far as I know, I am the inventor of the concept 'hoak'. I made up the crucial 'grammatical' rules (e.g. that so long as there is at least one horse, the death of an oak-tree is the end of a hoak.). These admissions in no way undermine realism in regard to hoaks themselves. (People produced the concept 'quark'; but quarks may be real for all of that.)

One is tempted to say that hoakological data doesn't explain anything. In a sense this is true. Nevertheless, hoaks are clearly involved in complex causal processes. People climb and ride them. Birds build nests in them. They could easily play a part in causal explanations. ("I was awakened by the hoof-beats of a rapidly changing hoak.")

The real defect of hoakology is that it is essentially superfluous so far as explanation and prediction are concerned. Hoakological information can be resolved into information about horses and information about oak-trees. If we want to understand our world, we need to know about horses (even those that are not hoak parts, if there are any) and oak-trees. Suppose a certain body of Hoakological information, B, yields certain predictions and explanations. I take it that a resolution of this information into information about horses and oaks yields all of the predictions yielded by B, and permits us to explain everything explained by B at least equally well.

Given our knowledge of humans and hoaks, we know that if George punched one he may well have gotten an injured hand, or a kick. Given that George punched a hoak, we know (by reduction of hoak-talk to plant and animal talk) that George punched an oak or a horse. From what we know of humans, horses and oaks we can equally well predict the injured hand, or kick.

Consider Aesthetics. Of course aesthetic properties and relations yield useful predictions and explanations. It would be misleading to say that these properties and relations are 'inert'—don't do anything. The delicacy and grace of a drawing can sometimes stop our chatter and lower our blood pressure. Nevertheless, surely naturalists are onto something when they claim that aesthetic properties and relations have no place in our over-all, scientific, depiction of the world. Given that there are such things as 'aesthetic observations', why are we reluctant to give this domain a place among the sciences?

The answer, I think, is that aesthetic predictions and explanations are, or appear to be, superfluous. Aesthetic properties and relations 'supervene' on non-aesthetic properties and relations like color, distribution in space, pitch, and various features of human psychology and cultural history. Any understanding of aesthetic matters requires some understanding of these underlying realms. But then, we are inclined to think, these domains generate all the predictions, and can be used to explain all the naturalistically admissible phenomena that can be explained in terms of aesthetics.

Is moral theory superfluous so far as scientific explanation and prediction are concerned? That is to say, are there 'sciences' (in a broad sense) that (a) moral theorists must admit are prerequisites for an adequate understanding of the world and that (b) render moral explanations and predictions superfluous?

In regard to our scientific understanding of the world, we seem to be committed to physics, chemistry, biology, psychology, and perhaps even sociology. So the question is, given our data in these and related areas, do alleged moral 'facts' yield any *additional* explanatory or predictive power?

Back to Babs. It seems to me that non-moral psychological facts, sociological facts, and so on, yield no explanation of the moral wrongness of her deed. Nor do they yield the prediction that Alice would perceive this wrongness, or that the perception would sicken her. So there appears to be a sense in which moral properties yield predictions not available from psychology and so on.

But this is question begging. What we want to know is whether moral theory can generate explanations and predictions of things *strict naturalists* would like to predict and explain. For example, we would like an explanation of Alice's sudden sick-feeling and of her 'moral observation' (viz. her immediate, irresistible, impression that Babs' setting fire to the cat was 'morally vile'). The answer seems obvious. Sociology, history, psychology, and biology can in combination provide powerful and persuasive explanations of these things. Alice's background may have been such as to leave her disoriented when confronted by violent, sadistic, 'irrational' deeds. Her 'moral judgment' is probably the product of her internalization of her society's 'folk ethics' as interpreted by her parents.

I think realists (including Platonists) should grant all this. That is to say, I think they themselves should say that moral explanations and predictions are probably superfluous (from a scientific point of view).

What Platonists (and, no doubt, others) ought to deny is that scientific respectability is the only legitimate criterion of what we should regard as real.

Relevant Papers

Gilbert Harman, "Ethics and Observation", in *Essays on Moral Realism*, Edited by Geoffrey Sayre-McCord, Cornell University Press, Ithaca, N.Y., 1988,

Chapter 6; Reprinted from Harman's *The Nature of Morality*, New York: Oxford University Press, 1977, Chapter One.

Nicholas L. Sturgeon, "Moral Explanations", in the Sayre-McCord book, Chapter 10.

Geoffrey Sayre-McCord, "Moral Theory and Explanatory Impotence", Ibid.

NOTES

1. Harman tells a similar cat-burning story. See *The Nature of Morality*, Oxford University Press, New York, 1977, p. 4.

2. Colin McGinn writes: "It is really a condition of adequacy on any account of goodness that causal powers *not* be conferred on it." *Ethics, Evil, and Fiction*, Clarendon Press, Oxford, 1997, p. 17.

3. See Terence Horgan's "Supervenient Qualia", *The Philosophical Review*, Vol. XCVI, No. 4 (October 1987), pp. 491–520, especially pp. 500–501.

CHAPTER EIGHTEEN

Moral Zombies

Since at least early in the twentieth century, most moral realists—including Platonists—have insisted that moral properties are in some sense 'dependent upon' non-moral properties. Thus, for instance, Moore, in replying to C. D. Broad's puzzlement about 'non-natural' properties, writes:

> ...I should never have thought of suggesting that goodness was 'non-natural,' unless I had supposed that it was 'derivative' in the sense that, whenever a thing is good (in the sense in question) its goodness (in Mr. Broad's words) 'depends on the presence of certain non-ethical characteristics' possessed by the thing in question: I have always supposed that it did so 'depend,' in the sense that, if a thing is good (in my sense), then that it is so *follows* from the fact that it possesses certain natural intrinsic properties, which are such that from the fact that it is good it does *not* follow conversely that it has those properties.[1]

In effect, Moore holds that the moral realm 'supervenes' (in some sense) on the non-moral. Most, if not all, Platonists would agree. But Frank Jackson has recently argued that supervenient moral properties are one and the same as properties at the subvenient level. That is to say, those supervenient properties are necessarily reducible to non-moral properties. This, if true, would constitute a serious problem for Platonism. In fact, if Jackson's line of thought is correct, Platonists seem to be compelled to give up the idea that Platonistic moral properties supervene on non-moral properties or give up Platonism.

Two Kinds of Supervenience

Suppose we have two families of properties, namely A-type properties and B-type properties. These families are built up in the following way, We begin with some basic, primitive, properties and then add all their 'nons', and all the permissible conjuncts and disjuncts of those primitive properties. Thus, for instance, in the 'moral' family we might have just 'good,' 'non-good', and the trivial disjunctive property 'good or non-good.' In the 'non-moral' family we might have just two basic properties, namely 'tall' and 'thin', plus their 'nons,' plus all the permissible disjuncts, and conjuncts, 'tall and thin', 'tall and non-thin,' 'either non-tall or non-thin' and so on. Here's the basic picture:

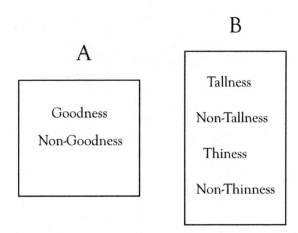

A claim that the A-type properties 'supervene' on the B-type properties means roughly that any individual's B properties determine that individual's A properties.

Here is one way of making this more precise.[2]

> A *weakly supervenes* on B if and only if necessarily for any x and y if x and y share all properties in B then x and y share all properties in A.[3]

In terms of 'possible worlds' this means, for instance, that if, in some possible world, W1, there is a person who is tall, thin, and good, then any other person in W1 who is tall and thin is also good. Perhaps these are the only good people in W1.

The weak supervenience of the A properties on the B properties, and the fact that in W1 everyone who is tall and thin is good, does not rule out there being another possible world, W2, in which exactly the reverse is true. Thus, in W2 it may be the case that anyone who is tall and thin is NON-good.

Platonists, like other realists in regard to moral properties, typically want something stronger than weak supervenience. Their idea is that moral properties are *determined* by non-moral properties. If moral goodness supervenes (in the realist's sense) on being tall and thin, then *necessarily* anyone who is tall and thin is a good person. That is to say, *in every possible world,* the tall and thin people (if there are any) are good. What they want is what Kim calls 'strong supervenience.'

A *strongly supervenes* on B if, and only if, necessarily, for each x and each property F in A, if x has F, then there is a property G in B such that x has G, and *necessarily* if any y has G, it has F.
Strong supervenience is equivalent to 'global supervenience.'[4]

A *globally supervenes* on B if, and only if, worlds that are indiscernible with respect to B are also indiscernible with respect to A.

Suppose that moral goodness strongly supervenes on traits in the B box. In that case, if Jones is morally good there must be some trait in the B box (saying being tall and thin) such that Jones has that trait, and, necessarily, every entity that has that trait is morally good. That is to say, for instance, Jones is tall and thin, and necessarily (i.e. in every 'possible world') any entity that is tall and thin is morally good.

Why Might We Want Such a Notion?

Consider again the wickedness of the pirates' deed described in Chapter Fifteen. It seems natural to suppose that this wickedness is 'derivative from' certain non-moral properties of the deed—the relevant psychological, biological, physical, culinary, aesthetic, sociological, theological, or whatever, facts of the case. It is, some of us feel, necessarily the case that, given those facts, the pirates did something wicked (i.e. vile, very bad). Furthermore, we want to say that *any possible* deed that had exactly those non-moral properties would be wicked.

Apparently, among other things, we want to rule out the possibility of any sort of 'moral inversion.' Thus, for instance we want to rule out creatures exactly like our pirates in every non-moral way, who threw some Native Americans' overboard in exactly the same way, in the same sociological, etc. etc. sort of context, but, in doing so, did what was morally obligatory. We are inclined to think no such pirates are *possible*.

Moral Zombies

Do we want to say that there might be creatures exactly like our pirates in all non-moral respects, doing their deed in circumstances physically, biologically, psychologically, sociologically, and so on, exactly like the circumstances of our pirates, but such that genuine morality is simply not applicable to them? Might there be *moral zombies?*[5]

If it were reasonably clear that we are not moral zombies and also that such zombies are metaphysically possible, this would provide a nice argument for the irreducibility of moral properties to non-moral properties. After all, the pirate captain's zombie twin would have all of the captain's non-moral properties, and, the non-moral context in which the zombie did his deeds would be exactly like the non-moral context in which the captain operated. Like our pirate, the zombie twin would throw the Native Americans overboard. And yet, he would not be wicked—would not be not guilty of any bad deed. Hence our captain's wickedness could not to be reducible to any configuration of non-moral properties.

In spite of this possible advantage, I think most, if not all, Platonists would (and should) deny the metaphysical possibility of moral zombies. Given that we have genuine moral properties, it seems absurd to suppose that there could be entities exactly like us in all non-moral respects but *lacking* our moral properties. This, it seems to me, is the line Platonists should take.

Notice however, that, in effect, the disenchanters see *us* as 'moral zombies.' And I have claimed that we cannot know for certain that the disenchanters are wrong. So aren't I forced to say that moral zombies are possible— i.e. that there are possible worlds in which we (or our exact counterparts) have no genuine positive moral properties?

Daisy, the moral   Rose, the
Zombie   Accountable Woman

Two Kinds of Epistemic Possibility

Epistemic possibility (sense A): A proposition, P, is epistemically possible relative to someone, S, at time *t*, if and only if, for all S knows at *t*, P is true.

It seems fairly clear that, in this sense, moral zombies are epistemically possible. Certainly I, at least, do not know for sure that they do not exist, since I

I do not know for sure that I am not one myself. I think we are all in this position. Of course this kind of epistemic possibility does not imply metaphysical possibility. There are, presumably, lots of metaphysically necessary truths that might be false for all any of us now know. The mere fact that moral zombies are epistemically possible in sense A, does not force us to the conclusion that they are metaphysically possible.

Epistemic possibility (sense B): A proposition, P, is epistemically possible (relative to us) if and only if, it is not the case that we can know a priori that not P.[6]

For instance, it is epistemically possible in this sense that the sky should be green rather than blue. We do not, and cannot, know a priori that it is blue rather than green.

From now on I will use 'epistemically possible' in sense B. (Sense A is of no real use to us for present purposes.)

Are moral zombies epistemically possible? Of course disenchanters will say 'yes' since they think *we* are moral zombies. Perhaps Platonists should agree. Do we know a priori that we have moral properties and that moral properties supervene on natural properties, and, consequently, that our alleged zombie duplicates are impossible? Perhaps not.

According to my view of these matters, there are three distinct objective classes of 'possible worlds' that form a nested series.[7] All of these worlds are epistemically possible so far as we are concerned. But only some of them are metaphysically possible. Many epistemically possible worlds are metaphysically impossible. A further restriction on the metaphysically possible worlds takes us to the naturally possible worlds (alias the 'physically' or 'nomically' possible worlds). These are the worlds that have the same natural laws as those in the real world—our world.

Platonists who hold that the moral realm supervenes on the non-moral, and also admit that moral zombies are genuinely possible, not just epistemically (i.e. 'logically') possible, seem to be caught in a bind. If we have genuine moral properties, and yet we have zombie duplicates in some possible worlds, then, it would seem, the moral realm does *not* strongly supervene on the non-moral.

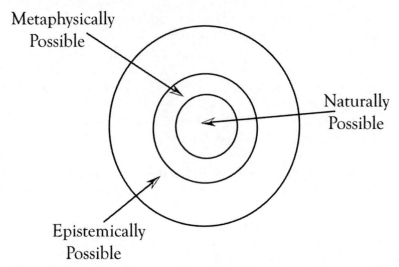

Metaphysically
Possible

Naturally
Possible

Epistemically
Possible

So far as I can see, there is only one feasible avenue of escape. These Platonists should hold that moral zombies are *epistemically* possible, but not *metaphysically* possible. The supervenience of the moral on the non-moral is strong *metaphysical* supervenience, not strong *epistemic* supervenience.

My suggestion is, then, that Platonists should accept strong metaphysical supervenience of the moral on the non-moral, namely:

It is metaphysically necessary that for every x and every moral property, F, if x has F, then there is a non-moral property, G, such that x has G and it is metaphysically necessary that if any y has G it has F.

But they should reject the corresponding formulation in terms of *epistemic* necessity.

Chalmers's Objections to the Triad

Clearly I am committed to the view that metaphysically possible worlds, epistemically possible worlds, and naturally possible worlds form three distinct classes of worlds. David Chalmers argues that there is no such triad.[8] On his view, there are basically just two kinds of possible worlds, namely 'logically possible' worlds and naturally possible worlds. I take it that 'logically possible' worlds are what I am calling 'epistemically possible worlds.'[9] Here are some of his arguments.[10]

'Metaphysical necessities' [as distinct from epistemic necessities H.C.] will put constraints on the space of possible worlds that are brute and inexplicable. It may be reasonable to countenance brute, inexplicable facts about *our* world, but the existence of such facts about the space of possible worlds would be quite bizarre. The realm of the possible (as opposed to the realm of the natural) has no room for this sort of arbitrary constraint.[11]

I think Platonists should bite this bullet. They should hold that it is a brute metaphysical fact that there are no metaphysically possible worlds containing moral zombies. (Even if it is conceivable that God does not exist, it might, nevertheless, be a brute metaphysical fact that there is no metaphysically possible world in which God does not exist.)

> The position cannot be supported by analogy, as no analogies are available.[12]

The position, I take it, is the claim that standard zombies are 'logically' (i.e. epistemically) possible, but not *metaphysically* possible. My suggestion is that Platonists should hold exactly this in regard to *moral* zombies. That is to say, moral zombies constitute at least one analogy.

> ...if some worlds are logically possible but metaphysicalliy impossible, it seems we could never know it. By assumption the information is not available *apriori*, and *a posteriori* information only tells us about *our* world. This can serve to locate our world in the space of possible worlds, but it is hard to see how it could give information about the extent of that space. Any claims about the added constraints of metaphysical possibility would seem to be a matter of arbitrary stipulation. [13]

It seems to me that we *don't* know that there are genuine moral properties. We don't know for a fact that the disenchanters are wrong. How could we ever come to know this? Hence, it would seem, we don't know, and couldn't know, whether there are metaphysically possible worlds containing moral Zombies, or, for that matter, whether there are metaphysically possible worlds containing people with genuine positive moral properties. Of course, given our existence, at least one of these two things must be the case: either we are not moral Zombies and moral Zombies exactly like us in all non-moral ways are impossible or we are moral Zombies and creatures exactly like us in all non-moral ways but having genuine positive moral properties are impossible. These two potential impossibilities do not seem to be *logical* (epistemic) impossibilities; and they seem stronger than natural impossibilities. In fact, they look like potential *metaphysical* impossibilities.

> ...we would...have *three* objective classes of possible worlds: logically [i.e. epistemically, H.C.] possible worlds, metaphysically possible worlds, and naturally possible worlds. We have good reason to believe in the first and the last of these classes, but we have very little reason to believe in a third, distinct class as a metaphysical given. [14]

Platonists may well reply that the plausibility of the claim that moral Zombies are epistemically possible conjoined with the equally plausible claim that the moral realm strongly supervenes on the non-moral gives us good reason to believe that metaphysical possibility is something distinct from epistemic possibility.

Those of us who hold that there are genuine moral properties, and that the moral realm supervenes metaphysically on the non-moral, and yet admit that moral zombies are logically (i.e. epistemically) possible, must hold that there are epistemically possible moral zombie worlds that are not metaphysically possible. Chalmers, in effect, asks why God couldn't have made the world that way.

> Presumably it is in God's powers, when creating the world, to do anything that is logically possible. Yet the advocate of metaphysical necessity must say either the possibility is coherent, but God could not have created it, or God could have created it, but it is nevertheless metaphysically impossible. The first is quite unjustified, and the second is entirely arbitrary.[15]

As I have said, epistemic possibility is, presumably, epistemic possibility relative to 'us.' Perhaps some things that are epistemically possible relative to us are not epistemically possible relative to God. Imagine a tribe of English speakers living at a time when it was epistemically possible, so far as they were concerned, that gold should be some happy mix of earth, air, fire, and water. Does it follow that God should have been able to create 'gold' (in their sense of the term) that was a mix of earth, air, fire, and water? Perhaps not. Perhaps the term 'gold,' as those people used it, had an 'indexical' element. They may have fixed the reference of the term by pointing to some good samples of gold and somehow indicating that the term was to refer to stuff that in its innermost composition had the same features that made *those samples* malleable, heavy, rust-proof, shinny, and so on.[16] In this way, the referent of the term may have been fixed even though the actual, hidden, inner, nature of gold was not known to them—definitely not something they knew a priori. Nevertheless, presumably, God could have seen that by 'gold' they meant *gold*, and he knew that, necessarily, gold is not made up of earth, air, fire, and water. Hence, he knew that it was impossible for him to make gold according to their recipe. That is to say, he knew that something that was epistemically possible (with respect to those people) was not, in fact, *metaphysically* possible, and, I suppose, not even *epistemically* possible with respect to his own language and thought. Presumably, prior to the creation of the physical universe (so to speak), God knew that gold, if it were to exist at all, would have to have atomic number 79.

Similarly, from our point of view, it may be epistemically possible that cats don't really 'count,' and also epistemically possible that they do. Nevertheless,

God may have always (timelessly) known that if there were to be any *cats*, they would have to 'count.' He *could not* create *cats* that don't 'count.' His knowledge of this was a priori.

How is this possible? Perhaps it is just an ultimate moral fact (and thus, so to speak, part of the structure of God's 'thinking') that 'counting' strongly supervenes on sentience. Cats are, by nature, sentient. Hence, God knows a priori, that if there are to be any cats they must 'count'.

I still haven't answered the question I imagine Chalmers asking. If moral zombie 'humans' are *logically* (i.e. epistemically) *possible*, at least from our point of view, why can't God create a few? My suggestion is that this may be something like the situation in regard to gold and cats. The idea is that it may just be an ultimate moral fact that genuine moral accountability strongly supervenes on the non-moral properties of entities like us. Knowledge of this fact guides God's 'thinking' on these matters. Thus, God may 'see' that it is metaphysically, and perhaps epistemically, impossible (given his way of 'thinking') for him to create moral zombie humans. From his perspective, a 'moral zombie human' may be something like 'genuine gold composed of earth, air, fire, and water.'

Does Strong Supervenience Entail Reducibility?

In his 1983 paper "Concepts of supervenience" Jaegwon Kim argued that if A strongly supervenes on B then every A property has a *necessary coextension* in B.[17] Frank Jackson's argument that, given global supervenience (or, equivalently, strong supervenience) of the ethical on the non-ethical, every ethical property is a 'descriptive' property, goes further.[18] Jackson describes the conclusion he aims to provide as follows:

> ...You will have before you a schematic account of the meaning of ethical ascriptions and sentences in purely descriptive terms. In other words, I will be defending a version of what is often called definitional or analytical naturalism.[19]

Here is Jackson's argument (with a minor modification). Consider a simple statement, E, about how things are ethically.[20]

> ...each world at which E is true will have some descriptive nature: ethical nature without descriptive nature is impossible (an evil act, for example, must involve death or pain or...). And, for each such world, there will be a sentence containing only descriptive terms that gives that nature in full. Now let w_1, w_2, etc. be the worlds where E is true, and let D_1, D_2, etc. be purely descriptive sentences true at w_1, w_2, etc., respectively, which give the full descriptive nature of w_1, w_2, etc. Then the disjunction of D_1, D_2, etc., will also be a purely descriptive sentence, call it D. But then E entails and is entailed by D. For every world where E is true is a world where one or other of

the D_i is true, so E entails D. Moreover, every world where one or the other of the D_i are true is a world where E is true, as otherwise we would have a violation of [strong supervenience H.C.]: we would have descriptively exactly alike worlds differing in ethical nature. Therefore, D entails E. The same line of argument can be applied *mutatis mutandis* to ethical and descriptive predicates and open sentences: for any ethical predicate there is [a purely descriptive] one that is necessarily co-extensive with it.

It follows that ethical properties are descriptive properties. For it is a consequence of the way the ethical supervenes on the descriptive that any claim about how things are made in ethical vocabulary makes no distinctions among the possibilities that cannot in principle be made in purely descriptive vocabulary."[21]

Clearly the descriptive property that is necessarily co-extensive with a given moral property is a disjunctive property. It is the property of having some 'descriptive' (i.e. non-ethical) property D_1, or D_2, or .... and so on.

My guess is that the same pattern of argument could be used to argue that 'holiness' is a non-religious property. It is plausible to suppose that holiness (if there really is such a thing) supervenes on non-religious properties of people, places, and so on. Presumably then, in regard to each and every possible world, God knows which people, places, and so on, if any, are holy, and also knows the non-religious properties upon which that holiness supervenes. But then there must be an infinite, non-religious, disjunctive property, which is coextensive with holiness across all the possible worlds. Must we conclude that holiness is just that disjunctive non-religious property?

Suppose that there is such a disjunctive property. It seems to me that holiness is *essentially* a religious property. It *cannot* turn out to be a non-religious property. If that disjunctive non-religious property is all there is to it, then there is no such thing as *real* holiness. Non-reductive realists in regard to holiness should insist that this disjunctive property is not *holiness itself*. It is, so to speak, the shadow that holiness casts in the non-religious domain. And, of course, those who claim that there is, in fact, no such thing as holiness should agree with these realists. That is to say, they too should insist that the alleged, non-religious, disjunctive property is not holiness itself.

Obviously, some of us have good reason to hope that there is something wrong with Jackson's line of thought; but what could it be?

One possibility is that there are no such things as genuine disjunctive properties. D. M. Armstrong offers various arguments against such properties. Here are three of his arguments:

(1) Armstrong points out that if a and b both have a certain genuine property, G, then a and b are '*identical*' in that respect. He then says:

Suppose *a* has property P but lacks Q, while *b* has Q but lacks P. It seems laughable to conclude from these premises that *a* and *b* are identical in some respect. Yet both have the "property" P *or* Q.[22]

Unfortunately, I am not at all confident that the claim is laughable.[23] Why shouldn't we say that *a* and *b* are identical in that they both have the P *or* Q 'property'? The 'property' seems fishy in some way; but aren't *a* and *b* exactly alike in having this fishy 'property'?

(2)   According to Armstrong, if we know that *a* has property P, then we can know *a priori* that *a* has the property of being P *or* Q, where Q is any property whatsoever. Hence, he says,

... we can know *a priori* that the particular, *a*, will have an indefinite number of disjunctive properties: at least as many as there are properties. But an *a priori* proof that an object has certain properties should be taken as an argument for saying that it has not got those properties. For what, and how many, properties a thing has is not to be determined *a priori*..[24]

How is this supposed to work? Perhaps Armstrong is assuming that P itself is known a priori to be one of *a*'s properties. For, after all, if we do not know this a priori then we do not know *a priori*, that *a* has the property of being, say, P *or asthmatic*.

(3) Armstrong endorses, or seems to endorse, the 'natural assumption' that the genuine properties of things are linked to the causal powers of those things. Given this:

[s]uppose, again, that *a* has property P but lacks Q. The predicate 'P ∨ Q' applies to *a*. Nevertheless, when *a* acts, it will surely act only in virtue of being P. Its *being P or Q* will add no power to its arm. This suggests that *being P or Q* is not a property.[25]

If, as I have suggested, moral properties are causally 'superfluous,' then, while they are in a sense linked to the causal powers of things, they are not linked in such a way as to make them scientifically respectable.[26] Hence, those of us who take moral properties to be genuine, grade A, properties, should be cautious about accepting the 'natural assumption' here. One suspects that the assumption is intended to rule out superfluous properties as well as those not linked to causal powers. Caution and suspicion prevent me from using Armstrong's third argument in attacking disjunctive properties.

A distinction drawn by Jerry Fodor might be helpful. Fodor points out that there is an important difference between *closed disjunctions* and *open multiple realizations*.[27] Being jade is a disjunctive property. This is because jade (as it turns out) *just is* jadeite or nephrite. That's all there is to it. In any metaphysically possible world, if there is jade, then that jade is either jadeite or nephrite. On the other hand, Fodor says, the property of being a pain is *disjunctively realized* differently in different possible worlds. In some such worlds, there are, for instance, *silicon-based* pains.[28] Fodor holds that closed disjunctive properties are not 'projectible.' That is to say, there cannot be genuine scientific laws based on such properties.

> By assumption, if P is the closed disjunction $F \vee G$, then it is metaphysically necessary that the properties a thing has qua P are either properties it has qua F or properties it has qua G; and, of course, this includes projectible properties inter alia. That's why, if being jade really is a closed disjunctive property (if being jade is just being jadeite or nephrite) then *of course* there are no laws about being jade "as such"; all the jade laws are ipso facto either jadeite laws or nephrite laws.[29]

Similarly, it seems to me, if the property of being morally wrong were, say, the closed disjunctive property of being either a deliberate production of pain, or a deliberate production of false belief (as some intuitionists might hold), then the property of being morally wrong would not, "as such" (i.e. 'directly') give accountable people prima facie reason to avoid doing deeds that had that property. The fact that D is morally wrong, would, I suppose, give accountable people reason to believe that D has one or both of the properties that would, in themselves, give one a prima facie moral reason not to do D. But that's not enough to do the trick. Closed disjunctive properties, I suggest, cannot be genuine, direct, 'moral reason generators.'

But, it would seem, the property of being morally wrong *does* directly, and in itself, give accountable creatures reason not to do a deed that has that property. Hence, we might conclude, prima facie moral wrongness cannot be a closed disjunctive property.

Traditionally, of course, moral goodness was regarded as a simple property, hence not a disjunctive property. Perhaps this is the line Platonists should take. Simplicity is compatible with multiple realizations. There may be metaphysically possible worlds in which there are kinds of moral goodness (and moral evil) that we cannot imagine.

Let me try one last, quick, line of attack. Consider the sentence 'Babs is morally blameworthy.' That sentence is true in regard to every metaphysically possible world in which Babs has at least one of the possible configurations of non-moral properties upon which moral blameworthiness supervenes. And, in every possible world in which she lacks all such configurations, she is *not* morally blameworthy.

Should we hold, then, that 'Babs is morally blameworthy' *just means* that Babs has at least one of those relevant configurations of 'descriptive' properties? If this were all we meant, then moral zombies would be *epistemically impossible*. The very idea would be absurd. Nevertheless, I assume, moral zombies *are* epistemically possible (from our point of view). Hence, if I am right, we do *not* mean (or do not always mean) what Jackson would have us mean.[30]

NOTES

1.. *The Philosophy of G. E. Moore*, Edited by Paul Arthur Schilpp, Open Court, La sale, Illinois, 1942, p. 588.

2. Jaegwon Kim is the principal expert in these matters. On this topic, I more or less just repeat portions of Kim's *Supervenience and Mind*, Cambridge University Press, 1993.

3.. Ibid. p. 58.

4. For a proof, see Kim's *Supervenience and Mind*, p. 69.

5. A *standard* 'zombie' is, of course, just like us, except that he or she is not *conscious*. Suppose that only conscious entities can have genuine moral properties. Would it follow that standard zombies are also *moral* zombies? No, it would not. Standard zombies, by hypothesis, are not *psychologically* exactly like us since they are not conscious.

   For a defense of standard zombies see David Chalmers' *The Conscious Mind*, Oxford University Press, 1996. For a blistering attack on the very idea of such creatures, see Dennett's "The Unimagined Preposterousness of Zombies: Commentary on Moody, Flanagan, and Polger," [Chapter 10 of Dennett's *Brainchildren*, The MIT Press, Cambridge, Massachusetts, 1998]. Hilary Putnam offers a somewhat different attack on standard Zombies ['automatic sweethearts']. See *the threefold cord: mind, body, and world*, Columbia University Press, New York, 1999, pp. 73–91.

6. This definition is, in part, based on Soames' discussion of the topic in *Reference and Description*, p. 83. Tim McCarthy forced me to abandon an earlier, more confused and confusing definition.

7. Suppose I know a priori that I exist. It would follow that it is not epistemically possible that I do not exist. Nevertheless, my non-existence would be *metaphysically* possible. There are lots of possible worlds in which I do not exist. As a result, it would not be the case that all metaphysically possible worlds are also epistemically possible worlds. The relevant worlds would not be nicely nested.

   In *Naming and Necessity* Kripke offers alleged examples of contingent a priori truths. Soames argues that Kripke's examples fail to do the job. But then Soames offers examples of his own. [See *The Age of Meaning*, ch. 16.] I am not sure that these examples work, and, for now, I am assuming, or pretending, that they fail. If there are such cases, then either the definition of 'epistemic possibility' will have to be made more complex or the idea that all metaphysically possible worlds are epistemically possible will have to be abandoned.

8. David J. Chalmers, *Op Cit*, pp. 137–138.

9. Scott Soames makes the same assumption. See *Reference and Description*, p. 243.

10. A closely related line of thought in Chalmers's book is a defense of what Scott Soames calls 'ambitious two-dimensionalism.' Given his rejection of the triad, Chalmers needs

something like this. I find Soames' attack on Chalmers's view persuasive. See *Reference and Description, the Case against Two-Dimensionalism*, Princeton University Press, Princeton and Oxford, 2005.

11. Chalmers, ibid. p. 137.

12. Ibid.

13. Ibid..

14. Chalmers refers to *standard* zombies here; but his claim seems equally applicable to moral zombies.

15. Ibid. p. 138.

16. I am here relying on something like the Kripke-Putnum theory of the meaning of natural kind terms, as emended by Tim McCarthy. [See his *Ratical Interpritation and Indeterminacy*, Oxford University Press, 2002. Note especially page 128.] The somewhat shocking idea that what is logically possible from God's point of view may be different than what is logically possible from our perspective was suggested to me by McCarthy in conversation.

17. See Kim's *Supervenience and Mind*, Cambridge University Press, Cambridge, 1993, Chapter 4, pp. 7071.

18. See Frank Jackson's, *From Metaphysics to Ethics*, Oxford University Press, 1997.

19. Ibid. p. 113. Jackson is a 'Two-Dimensionalist' like Chalmers, and, as with Chalmers, his view comes under attack in Soames's *Reference and Description.*

20. The 'modification' is that I have introduced the term 'simple' here. I do so in order to eliminate statements like "There have been at least one hundred evil acts or tea-drinking is common." [Jackson's example]. A statement, E, is 'simple' if and only if: "(a) E is framed in ethical terms and descriptive terms; (b) every world at which E is true has some ethical nature; and (c) for all w and w^*, if E is true at w and false at w^*, then w and w^* differ ethically." Ibid. p. 122.

21. Ibid. pp. 122–123.

22. See D. M. Armstrong, A *Theory of Universals*, Vol. II of *Uiversals and Scientific Realism*, Cambridge University Press, Cambridge, 1978, p. 20.

23. Perhaps it deserves a smile.

24. Ibid.

25. Ibid.

26. It is clear that Armstrong himself would have us exclude Platonistic moral properties from our 'world-hypothesis'. See his *Nominalism and Realism*, Vol. I, Chapter 12.

27. See Jerry Fodor, *In Critical Condition*, The MIT Press, Cambridge, Mass. 1998, pp. 9–23.

28. Ibid. p. 13.

29. Ibid. p. 18.

30. Fodor argues that at least some alleged open disjunctive properties are 'gerrymandered.' I think he is right about this, and I suspect that Jackson's reductive disjuncts have this defect. Unfortunately, I don't see how to spell out this additional objection.

Epistemic Problems

There are no special epistemic problems in regard to the sociological, anthropological, and psychological aspects of morality. Human groups develop rules of conduct, values, standards for judging character, and so on. People have moral beliefs, feelings of guilt, and so on. Knowledge of these things is no more problematic than knowledge of currently popular games or knowledge of the religious beliefs held by the members of various tribes.

On the other hand, Platonism in regard to genuine morality (the domain rejected by disenchanters as bogus) seems to generate epistemic embarrassments. Here it is like Platonism in regard to mathematics.[1]

To begin with, do we know for sure that all non-Platonistic theories of morality are false? If we do not, then we cannot know for sure that some Platonistic theory is correct. Some forms of the disenchanted view seem quite plausible. Is there conclusive, or fairly conclusive, evidence against them? I don't know of any. On the other hand, do we know for sure that all forms of Platonism in regard to morality are false? If not, then we cannot know for sure that some form of the disenchanted view is correct. The situation seems to be one that is common in philosophy. There are various incompatible 'big pictures' such that there is, at least as yet, no conclusive proof, no decisive evidence, for, or against any of them. In some cases it seems quite likely that there will never be any such proof or evidence.

The embarrassment just mentioned applies more or less equally to all meta-ethical theories. But Platonism in regard to morality has, or seems to have, specific, more severe, epistemic problems than some of the other theories. For instance, as noted in Chapter Twelve, some Platonists claim that mice, cats, porcupines, and so on, 'count.' Others say they don't, or that this is an indeterminate matter (metaphysically indeterminate, not just epistemically indeterminate). According to at least some Platonists, this is not a matter of opinion. It's a matter of brute fact. But how could we find out who is right? How are we to know? Some people have strong 'intuitions' about 'counting.'

But why should we trust those intuitions, especially given the fact that people on both sides of the issue apparently have equally strong intuitions?

Suppose that cats 'count.' What sort of property is this? In part, I think, the idea is that cats have certain natural properties such that accountable people who are aware of those properties in cats should treat cats as, at least to some extent, 'ends in themselves' rather than as mere things (or something like that). That is to say, cats have properties that generate certain duties in accountable people. They deserve a certain amount of respect.[2] To some extent, perhaps, they have a right to conduct their own lives in their own way. If this is more or less right, then the alleged 'brute fact' is, in part, that those natural properties in an entity generate those duties in us.

In addition, the idea may be that cats have 'intrinsic value.' Each cat is, in some sense, 'valuable in itself.' Other things being equal, it is objectively a 'good thing' that the cat actually exists and flourishes. I don't mean it is a good thing for us. The idea seems to be that, other things being equal, the universe is made better by the fact that this cat exists and leads a happy life. Presumably, this would be so even if there were no rational creatures at all. That is to say the 'value' of cats is not somehow dependent upon their being valued by creatures like us.

These claims strike some of us, at least sometimes, as unclear and odd.

Here is another example. According to some Platonists, Conscience has more 'authority' than Self-Love. According to others, they are equally authoritative. What sort of 'authority' is in question here? Again, this is supposed to be a matter of brute fact. But how could we ever arrive at the truth? In both of these cases (a) it is not perfectly clear what is being claimed—the property in question seems a bit elusive and 'queer', and (b) it is not clear how we could become aware of the property in question. Might we not have the same experiences no matter which of the options was in fact the case?

Platonists have offered various epistemic theories. I will mention just two. One theory is that our own faculties, our reason, and our feelings perhaps, enable us to work these things out. The other is that something like perception is involved. We 'see' things in the light of the Good (Plato). The imagery of the 'perceptive' theory strongly suggests some sort of *causal* process.

Hume tells us that reason cannot supply the ultimate ends of human actions. Those ends, he thinks, are generated by our sentiments and affections. Why do we hate pain? We just do, that's all. Reason, he thinks, is concerned with truth and falsity. It discloses things as they are in themselves. Taste, on the other hand adds to, or subtracts from, the world 'gilding or staining all natural objects' with 'colors' generated by sentiment.[3] This view is compatible with a disenchanted theory of morality. What are the (rough, metaphoric) Platonistic alternatives? Here are two:

First Alternative (Perceptive Platonism): Sentient creatures 'gild' and 'stain' the world in various ways. The resultant 'coloration' is subjective or a social construct. But there are also real 'colors' out there in the world, and our Conscience has the ability to 'see' at least some of them. Thus, for instance, we 'see' that people are intrinsically, and objectively, valuable.

Second Alternative (NonPerceptive Platonism): There are real 'colors' there in the world; but, alas, we have no ability to 'see' them. Our Conscience is blind. Thus we have to *figure out* what those colors might be.

How might someone come to see that people 'count' in a Platonistic sense? The process might start with one person. Suppose that Paul falls madly in love with Susan. He thinks, or half thinks, he now sees how *admirable*, and *important*, Susan is. She adds value to the world by her presence. Sometimes he suspects that these thoughts are exaggerated. Nevertheless, he finds himself thinking this way. Most of the time it seems to him that this is not madness, not something subjective, that his love for Susan enables him to see things about her that are just plain true. She is admirable, important, and objectively valuable, in ways that are difficult to explain to those who don't see these things in her.

Given that Susan really is admirable, important, and objectively valuable in roughly the way that Paul thinks she is, we might want to say that he has perceived things about her, come to know things about her, that most of us don't see.[4]

Of course there is another way of viewing the matter. Paul has a lover's illusions about Susan. She is 'important' only to Paul and others who love her—it's subjective. He is in love with an ordinary, unimportant, person who has no objective value.

Let's look at another example of someone coming to see an alleged moral fact. Suppose that Paul has told Susan a lie. He told her that he had worked on a ranch down near Amarillo Texas for several years. Why did he tell her this? He did it, more or less, as a kind of joke, and, perhaps, to impress her. Now he overhears Susan telling one of her friends that he (Paul) lived in Texas for a while. He is embarrassed. He has deliberately made Susan believe something false. It dawns on him that the lie was childish and may show lack of respect for Susan, and, perhaps, for himself. He should have told her the truth.

In the cases described, Paul perceives an alleged moral truth. He sees, or seems to see, that someone, or some act, has a moral property. It seems natural to suppose that, in general, K's perception that item O has property P requires some sort of causal relation between K and O, and between K and P.[5] The question I now want to raise is whether or not the moral property was causally relevant to the perception. More precisely, I am interested in *counterfactual dependence*. Counterfactual dependence is a sufficient condition for some kinds of causation.[6] If Paul's lie had not been morally wrong, would Paul nevertheless have seen it as wrong?

In many, if not all, ordinary cases of veridical perception, the perception is counterfactually dependent upon the presence of the perceived property. Suppose, for instance, that Susan feels the warmth of her cup of coffee. Of course it is the heat of the coffee and the cup that she is detecting. If the coffee had been cold, she would not have felt any warmth.

Suppose that Susan lacked value. There are, at least, two kinds of case here.

Case One: We are talking about ordinary evaluations of people. In this sense, some people are wonderful, make the world a better place to be in and so on, others aren't. The difference is, more or less, observable. Suppose that Susan was not a valuable person in this sense. Suppose she was pretty much worthless. People who know her at all well know this. Would Paul have noticed? He might have. That is to say, his perception of her value might well be counterfactually dependent upon her not being 'worthless' in this sense.

Case Two: We are talking about the metaphysical status of moral properties. We are being asked to suppose that Susan didn't have the alleged objective property of 'being intrinsically valuable.' Perhaps the Disenchanters are right. Suppose there is no such thing. We are not being asked to suppose that she looked, or acted, differently in any way. Would Paul have noticed this absence? The answer seems obvious. There would have been no observable difference. He would have 'seen' her as being objectively valuable whether or not she, or anyone else, actually had any such property.

Suppose that Paul's lie had not been morally wrong. Would he nevertheless have seen it as wrong? Again there are, at least, two kinds of cases:

Case One: When we speak of the possibility of the lie not being morally wrong, what we have in mind is the possibility of the context of the lie, Paul's intention and so on, being such as to make the lie morally permissible or even obligatory. Perhaps, then, we are to imagine something like this: Paul and Susan have a mutual friend who says that he (the mutual friend) grew up near Amarillo Texas. He has begged Paul to back him up on this—tell people that he (Paul) knew him there. Apparently, his life depends on the credibility of this story. Paul has promised to do what he can. That is why he told the lie. Given this background, why should Paul 'come to see' that he had done something morally wrong in lying to Susan? Presumably, he would know that he had a good (moral) reason for doing it. Apparently, then, his perception is counterfactually dependent upon the lie actually being wrong.

Case Two: When we speak of the possibility of the lie not being morally wrong, what we have in mind is that there might be no such thing as genuine, objective moral wrongness. Perhaps the Disenchanters are right. Suppose there is no such thing.[7] If this were the case, would Paul still have 'come to see' that he had done the wrong thing? One cannot 'come to see' something that is false, or nonsensical. But, I suggest, things might well seem exactly the same to Paul whether or not there is such a thing as genuine moral wrongness. Why should Paul think anything different? On this reading of the question, Paul's 'perception' is *not* counterfactually dependent upon the lie being morally wrong.

Technically, the fact that there is a sense in which these Platonistic moral perceptions seem not to be counterfactually dependent on the relevant Platonistic property need not worry a Platonist. Causal relations can occur without counterfactual dependence.[8]

Suppose that a demon has implanted a devise in Susan's head that makes her feel warmth in a cup of coffee when the coffee is *not* warm. If her coffee *is* warm, the device doesn't do anything at all; her heat detection system works in the normal way. When she has a cup of warm coffee in her hand and feels warmth, is she perceiving the warmth of the coffee? Is the feeling of warmth caused by the heat in the coffee? Clearly it is. Nevertheless, counterfactual dependence is absent. She would have had the same heat sensations, and formed the same heat beliefs, if the coffee had been cold.

There is at least one important difference between this implantation case and the Case Two examples. In the implantation case, something is rigged up to *intervene* and *prohibit* Susan's perception that her coffee isn't hot. There is no intervention or prohibition in the Case Two examples. Can there be a causal link where there is no counterfactual dependence and no intervention or prohibition in the counterfactual cases?

In the Case Two examples, it looks as though *exactly the same* 'perceptive' process occurs with, or without, the Platonistic property. But, if this is so, that property plays no part in the process. It seems causally *irrelevant*. This should worry a Platonist.

Technical worry: Counterfactual dependence is usually spelled out in terms of *metaphysical* possibilities. But, when we suppose that there might not, in fact, be any genuine moral wrongness, we are supposing something that, as at least some Platonists see it, is not metaphysically possible (i.e. that things might be just as they appear to be now in the actual world, but minus any genuine moral wrongness.). In fact, we are supposing a kind of moral zombie-hood. This 'possibility' may well be epistemically and logically possible, but *metaphysically impossible*. Perhaps, then, those zombie worlds cannot properly be offered as evidence for the causal irrelevance of moral properties. The 'evidence' may be question begging.

In any case, I am not suggesting that we should rule out the possibility that some people's Platonistic 'perceptions' *are* counterfactually dependent upon the presence of the perceived Platonistic property. The theory doesn't look very plausible; but perhaps there are people who are, somehow, Platonistic property detectors. How do they do it? It might be one of those things we couldn't understand even if it were explained to us by angels.[9] On the other hand, there might be no explanation. It just happens—the correlation is a brute fact. These are possibilities; but I think we should be hesitant in accepting either of them as the truth. It would be preferable to have a comprehensible account of putative moral knowledge.

Non-perceptive Platonism might be thought to provide such an account. On this view, we have to figure out the appropriate Platonistic moral properties of things.

How might the project start? Utilitarianism suggests one possible answer. Suppose we are creatures more or less like Butleroids. We seek happiness, and, to some extent, whatever we regard as moral goodness. What sorts of people, deeds, policies, and so on should we take to be morally good or morally bad? What is morally right and what is wrong? An obvious suggestion is that we should provisionally take maximization of everyone's happiness as our standard in developing our idea of what is morally right and what is morally wrong, as well as our idea of what a 'good person' or a 'bad person' would be like, what 'rights' are, and so on.

Happiness might be thought of in terms of long-term PMP maximization, or in terms of the long-term satisfaction of our desires. For our present purposes, let's stick with PMP scores. They are easier to manage.[10]

Where is the Platonism? So far nothing has been said that should offend a naturalistic Disenchanter. We seem to be considering a suggestion in regard to a social engineering project.

Here is some Platonism. Suppose that a Platonist recommends the following hypothesis: *General Happiness is in fact the ultimate moral standard.* This is not offered as a hypothesis about folk ethics, and not as a way of organizing certain kinds of sociological data. Nor is it offered simply as a possible goal in social engineering—the development of a workable 'morality' for a given society. The suggestion is that this is the one and only correct standard for generating objectively correct moral rules, values, rights, virtues, and so on. Accepting this claim is, presumably, acceptance of a Platonistic belief, or, at least, acceptance of a Platonistic working hypothesis. The Platonism is in the content of the claim; but no Platonistic intuition or perception of the truth of the claim is required for its acceptance.[11]

It might be helpful to consider another moral hypothesis. Consider the suggestion that *a deed is morally acceptable if, and only if, the total PMP (Pleasure Minus Pain) score of the consequences of the deed, taking everyone into account, is equal to or greater than the total PMP score of the consequences of each of the feasible alternatives to it.* If 'moral acceptability' is understood as a Platonistic property (i.e. as an objective, irreducible, moral property) then the content of this hypothesis is Platonistic. But, so far as I can see, that Platonistic hypothesis could be accepted as our working hypothesis, without any of us having a genuine Platonistic intuition of its truth.

There remains a problem about the referents of the moral terms in our Platonistic hypotheses. When we say something about such and so being 'moral acceptable,' to what property are we referring? At the present time, the Causal Theory of Reference (in one form or another) is held by many tough-minded philosophers.[12] According to a simple (and simplistic) version of the theory, the referent of a term is determined by a causal chain linking the speaker's use of the term to the individual, property, or whatever, referred to. If Susan says that her coffee is hot, the referent of the word 'hot' is presumably determined by a causal chain linking her use of the term to (physical) heat.

Is there any such causal linkage between Platonistic use of the term 'moral acceptability' and Platonistic moral acceptability? If there were no such thing as Platonistic acceptability, would we still be able to use the term in this way? There doesn't seem to be any counterfactual dependence here. Must we conclude that talk about 'Platonistic moral acceptability' is meaningless nonsense?

The simple version of the Causal Theory is no threat to Platonism because that version is clearly false. We can refer to things even though there is no causal chain linking us to them. For instance, we can speak of stars beyond the range of possible causal interaction with us. We can wonder weather there are any such stars. If there are such stars, then we have successfully referred to them. Similarly, we can speak of possible properties that will never have any effect upon us.

According to a more sophisticated version of the Causal Theory, the referent of a term is determined by a causal chain linking the speaker's use of the term to the individual, property, or whatever, referred to, *or by a description of the individual, property, or whatever, in terms which are themselves so linked to the things they denote.*[13]

Thus, presumably, we can speak of stars beyond our limits of possible interaction because we can speak of stars, and limits of interaction, and because we are causally linked to some stars and some 'limits of interaction.' (Are we also thus linked to 'possibility'?) But why should we be confined to just two semantic levels? Why, for instance, shouldn't we be permitted to use terms, s1, s2, ... and so on, referring to properties that can be described in terms, t1, t2 and so on, referring to properties to which our uses of t1, t2, and so on, are causally linked?

The basic question here is whether we can refer to, and think about, Platonistic moral properties even though we are not causally linked to them. An obvious suggestion is that we can do it via descriptions of those properties. What we want are descriptions that 'single out' the properties, or would do so if there were such properties.

It is possible that some Platonistic moral terms can be defined by means of others. Thus it may be that 'X is good' (in the Platonistic sense) can be taken to mean that it would be morally appropriate for anyone who was aware of X's non-moral properties to desire X.[14] But even if all Platonistic terms could be defined in this way, that would not solve our present problem. The question is how can we refer to *any* such properties? Definitions of Platonistic terms by means of other Platonistic terms leave us just where we started, so to speak.

Traditionally, intuitionists (and thus some Platonists) have held that most, if not all, basic Platonistic moral properties are 'simple', and consequently unanalyzable.[15] Assuming this to be correct, we should not hope to find analytic definitions of such properties.

Consider the following argument pattern:

(1) We have the concept of property P.
(2) P is a simple property.
(3) If P is a simple property, one can only acquire a concept of P by acquaintance with P itself.[16]
(4) We can only be acquainted with properties that actually exist (i.e. that are such that there is something that actually has the property).
(5) Therefore, P actually exists.[17]

This pattern would generate nice arguments for the existence of Platonistic moral properties provided that (a) at least some such properties are simple, (b) we have concepts of these properties, and (c) the pattern does its job correctly.

However, I suspect that premise (3) is not true. For one thing, the notion of a 'simple' property is questionable. More relevant to our present topic is the possibility that we can sometimes acquire the concept of a simple property, not by acquaintance, but by means of an identifying description. I have already mentioned the possibility that this might be done for Platonistic 'goodness' by means of the concept of Platonistic 'moral propriety.' Assuming that Platonistic goodness is a simple property and that someone could know (perhaps by acquaintance) what Platonistic moral propriety is without knowing what Platonistic goodness is, such a person could, perhaps, acquire the later concept by means of a description that invokes the former.

Can it be done without using Platonistic moral terms? I think it can, if we are permissive about what kind of descriptions are allowed.

Imagine a tribe of Hobbots who have a well-developed folk-ethics, but, up to this time, have had no notion of Platonistic morality. Now some of them are beginning to turn into Butleroids. They are developing a Conscience, and the idea of Platonistic morality is beginning to emerge among them. They try to explain this new idea to the others. That is to say, they try to describe some alleged Platonistic moral properties using non-Platonistic terms.

"Maybe," one of them says, "there are things I ought to do, even though something else would give me more pleasure minus pain, or do a better job of satisfying my desires. Maybe it's just an objective fact, independent of our conventions and practices, that one should do this sort of thing. Maybe it's a fact like a fact of physics or math that one should do it." Of course the Hobbots think the Butleroid/Hobbot is misusing a relativistic prudential 'ought.' She seems to be saying, "Maybe there are some prudent deeds (relative to me) that aren't prudent (relative to me)." Suppose someone points this out to her.

"Yes, you are right," she says, "I'm stretching the language. The idea is that there may be something *like* an ordinary 'ought' here, only not linked to hedonic payoff for me and not a matter of satisfying my desires. It's like a (prudential) 'ought' in that reason seems to say 'do it.' But, as you point out, it's not something I (prudentially) ought to do."[18] (Of course most, if not all, of the Hobbots have no idea what she is talking about.)

Here is another case. "Maybe" the Buttleroid/Hobbot says, "there are norms that are not made up and enforced by society. This other kind of 'norm' is something like a law of nature. It's just 'there' in the world, independently of us." Many of the Hobbots think that her thinking apparatus has gotten scrambled.

Perhaps she should have begun with something more straightforward. Of course all the Hobbots have some acquaintance with pain, misery, tragic loss, or whatever. Philosophically sophisticated Hobbots take some if not all occurrences of these things to be *subjectively* bad, and/or bad *relative to* the suffering Hobbot and, we assume, relative to those who love that Hobbot. The new line of thought might be that this sort of pain, misery, and so on is *just plain* bad— objectively, and absolutely bad. It might also be suggested that this new kind of 'badness' is a simple, unanylizible, irreducible property of some, if not all, pains, and so on. (The technical terms here are, of course, understood by philosophically sophisticated Hobbots.)

Given that the property described actually exists, the description could be used to 'fix the reference' of a new (Platonistic) term.[19] ("Let's call this property 'Platonistic badness,'" the baptizer says.)

The description, and the new term, can also be used (or at least mentioned) by those who want to deny that there is any such property. It isn't just for believers. Anti-Platonistic Hobbots can say "There is no such property as 'badness' in this alleged new sense."

The Butleroid/Hobbot case was introduced, primarily, to help us with the problem as to whether Platonism in regard to morality requires perceptions of Platonistic moral facts. More specifically, could Hobbots turn into Platonistic Butleroids without having any causal linkage to Platonistic moral properties? I have suggested that they could develop descriptions of Platonistic moral properties without using Platonistic terms, and that those descriptions could be used to fix the reference of Platonistic moral terms (if those properties actually exist). In addition, the descriptions, or terms, could be used in formulating Platonistic beliefs.

Let's assume that the 'non-perceptive' view is the Platonist's best bet. I suggest this not because I believe it, but as a sort of 'worst case' strategy. The idea is to suppose that there really are crushing objections to perceptive Platonism and then see whether Platonism can, nevertheless, be defended.

> Disenchanter: We now have several strong reasons for rejecting Platonism in regard to morality. For one thing, according to Unperceptive Platonism, we are supposed to believe various independent things each one of which seems to be based on shear conjecture. Suppose that there were just three crucial claims in the theory, and that each one is subjectively probable (for me) to degree 0.6. In that case, the subjective probability of the whole theory would be 0.6 times 0.6 times 0.6. That is to say 0.216, and dropping like a rock.
>
> Platonist: What makes you think the various doctrines of the theory are independent?
>
> Disenchanter: What makes you think they are not?

Platonist: Nothing. Your argument does seem to give us a reason to keep the basic doctrine fairly simple.

Disenchanter: Here's another objection. Platonistic moral properties sound *very* queer. I 'ought' to do such and so where the 'ought' is like a prudential 'ought' except that it has nothing to do with my pleasures and pains, or with the satisfaction of my desires. That's like something a lot like a bicycle, except that it doesn't have wheels, or pedals, or a place to sit.

Platonist: It's an analogy, as in talk about God.

Disenchanter: Oh. *That's* a big help.

Platonist: Furthermore, the strangeness of that particular description is due, at least in part, to the fact that a moral property is being described from outside the moral realm. Any other objections?

Disenchanter: Here's another problem. Unperceptive Platonists admit that we have no causal linkage to Platonistic moral properties. How then are we supposed to construct a full-scale Platonistic moral theory? How, for example, are we going to decide whether or not eating meat is wicked? Your project is a wild goose chase. People have tinkered with it, on and off, for several thousand years, and gotten nowhere.

Platonist: On the contrary. We now know, for example, that all kinds of people everywhere 'count.'

Disenchanter: It's not very surprising that people should insist that people 'count'. It would be a lot more surprising if they figured out that rocks 'count', and people *don't*.

Platonist: Your choice of examples shows that you *know* that rocks don't 'count,' or, at least, don't 'count' as much as people.

Disenchanter: I cannot help noticing that you are talking as if we had moral knowledge. Aren't Unperceptive Platonists supposed to hold that we don't know any moral facts?

Platonist: Of course we know lots of things about folk-morality.

Disenchanter: Sorry, I meant to be talking about Platonist moral claims.

Platonist: Technically, you are right. It's hard to see how it could be a matter of knowledge. Nevertheless, Non-Perceptive Platonists (as I prefer to call them) are allowed to use 'know' in a loose and popular sense— like everyone else.

Disenchanter: Are you ready for objection number...... Sorry, I've lost count.

Platonist: So have I.

Disenchanter: Anyway, I thought the strongest argument for Platonism was that it is compatible with our deepest and strongest moral intuitions, whereas reductionist and disenchanting theories are not. Are we now being told that those 'intuitions' are not required? We do not 'see,' for instance, that people 'count'?

Platonist: If by an 'intuition' you mean a mysterious kind of perception, then you are right. One can be a Platonist and yet not believe in such intuitions.

Disenchanter: Does that mean we can forget about our 'deep and important' intuitions?

Platonist: No. It just means that we should look at them differently. They are postulates—hypotheses that we humans have developed over the centuries, that seem to force themselves upon us, and that some of us provisionally accept.

Disenchanter: Accept as true?

Platonist: Yes. Accept as part of our working hypothesis in regard to morality.

Disenchanter: I think you are talking about something subjective.

Platonist: You think that our seeing people as ends in themselves rather than as means to our own gratification is just another way of coloring the world, like loving tapioca pudding.

Disenchanter: I do not. It's much more serious for us. We regard this sort of thing as *absolutely* serious—a crucial part of what makes our lives meaningful rather than frivolous and empty. Even people who love tapioca pudding would probably insist on the difference. But that doesn't make valuing people objectively and absolutely right.

Platonist: Haven't you more or less admitted it?

Disenchanter: For reasons that are perfectly understandable, we can take some values with a kind of seriousness we cannot apply to others. This is just a fact about us. There could be rational creatures who valued chunks of rock as 'ends in themselves', and took the property of being spherical with absolute seriousness.

Platonist: And, on your view, a Conscience that urges the valuing of people is no nearer the moral truth, than is a module that urges sphericity.

Disenchanter: Right! But don't gloss over what, for me, is crucial. You and I can take the idea of valuing others with total seriousness, as a kind of *basic* value in our lives—we just *can't* do that with sphericity. It makes sense for our 'Conscience' to urge the one, and not the other.

Platonist: Oh I get the picture all right. What I object to is your idea that the legitimacy of a basic value depends upon nothing more than a creature's ability to take it seriously. You've got the cart before the horse. We can't take sphericity seriously because it seems clear to us that 'Maximize sphericity' isn't a basic moral principle.

Disenchanter: As a Non-Perceptive Platonist, how do you know? Why can't it be?

Platonist: I am relying on various strongly held intuitions. For instance, I don't think we could have a basic moral obligation that we could never discover—never work out together. It wouldn't be fair. It wouldn't make sense.

Disenchanter: We are going around in a circle. In effect I am asking you to justify your reliance on any such intuition.

Platonist: We have nothing else to go on.

NOTES

1. For a discussion of the epistemic embarrassments apparently generated by Platonism in regard to mathematics see Paul Benaracerraf's important paper "Mathematical truth", *Journal of Philosophy*, 70 (1973): pp. 661–680; reprinted in *Philosophy of Mathematics*, edited by Paul Benacerraf and Hilary Putnam, second edition, Cambridge University Press, 1983, pp. 403–420.

2. When I said things like this to my late friend and colleague Charles Caton, he used to say, "What is *that* supposed to mean?" It wasn't, and still isn't, easy to explain. On one such occasion, he said, "I love my dogs; but I don't *respect* them." I think he was implying that I was misusing the word.

3. David Hume, *An Inquiry Concerning the Principles of Morals*, The Library of Liberal Arts, Bobbs-Merrill, pp. 111–112.

4. Thomas Nagel suggests that it is difficult for people to honestly accept the idea that they themselves are objectively worthless. If this is correct, then it would seem to provide another way of coming to see that at least one person (namely oneself) has objective value. See Thomas Nagel's *The Last Word*, Oxford University Press, Oxford, 1997, pp. 121–122.

5. Benacerraf writes: "I favor a causal account of knowledge on which for X to know that S is true requires some causal relation to obtain between X and the referents of the names, predicates, and quantifiers of S. I believe in addition in a causal theory of *reference*, thus making the link to my saying knowingly that S *doubly* causal." op. cit. p. 412. I think causal theories of perception are more plausible than causal theories of knowledge in general.

6. See Ned Hall's "Causation and the Price of Transitivity", *The Journal of Philosophy*, April 2000, pp. 1982–22.

7. How would this go in the 'possible world' language? If the Platonists are right, there *aren't* any metaphysically possible worlds in which there are people physically and mentally exactly like us, but lacking Platonistic moral properties. Conversely, if there is one such

world, then there are no Platonistic moral properties in any metaphysically possible world. It can't be a *contingent* matter. Presumably, genuine moral properties supervene on non-moral properties. How then can a Platonist 'suppose' that there could be two worlds identical in all non-moral properties, such that genuine moral properties exist in one but not in the other? Perhaps what one needs to do this trick are two *epistemically* possible worlds such that only one of them is metaphysically possible. The suggestion is that we humans cannot know for certain (a priori or a posteriori) which one that is.

8. See *the Journal of Philosophy*, Vol. XCVII, Number 4, April 2000.

9. Colin McGinn holds that moral properties are non-causal. Nevertheless, he holds, we have ethical (i.e. moral) knowledge. "It comes naturally to us on the basis of our innate endowment." [p. 60] The fact that we do not, and probably cannot, understand how this works, should not lead us to lead us to doubt its existence. (See his *Ethics Evil and Fiction*, pp. 57–60.]

10. As a start towards a possible refinement in the theory, we might stipulate that pleasure in one's own or someone else's pain or wickedness, and pain in the contemplation of one's own or someone else's pleasure or goodness, do not count. This refinement would get rid of the problem caused by crowds of demons who relish our wickedness (Chapter Sixteen). The stipulation presumably expresses another Platonistic belief or 'intuition'.

11. Henry Sidgwick infers the truth of the Utilitarian principle from two 'self evident' 'rational intuitions' (a) "...the good of any one individual is of no more importance, from the point of view (if I may say so) of the Universe, than the good of any other; unless, that is, there are special grounds for believing that more good is likely to be realized in the one case than the other." And (b) "I am bound to aim at good generally— so far as it is attainable by my efforts—not merely at a particular part of it." [*The Methods of Ethics*, Macmillan and Co. London, 1913, p. 382.] "Accordingly, I find that I arrive, in my search for really clear and certain ethical intuitions, at the fundamental principle of Utilitarianism." [*Ibid.* p. 387.] Of course Disenchanters reject both (a) and (b). They deny the existence of any absolute 'good' and that we are 'bound' by morality.

12. See, for instance, Michael Devitt and Kim Sterelny's *Language and Reality*, The MIT Press, Cambridge, Mass. 1987.

13. Hilary Putnam appears to have this formulation of the causal theory in mind when he spells out one of the premises in his 'Brain in a Vat' argument. See Hilary Putnam, *Reason, Truth and History*, Cambridge University Press, Cambridge, 1981, pp. 16–17.

14. This is a slightly modified version of a suggestion made by C. D. Broad in his *Five Types of Ethical Theory*, p. 283.

15. In his Introduction to David Ross's *The Right and the Good*, Philip Sratton-Lake argues against Ross's theory that basic moral properties are simple. [See pp. xvi–xxiii.]

16. I am using the term 'acquaintance' in roughly the way Bertrand Russell used it in *The Problems of Philosophy*, Oxford University Press, Oxford, 1959, Chapter V.

17. This argument occurred to me while I was reading Barry Stroud's *The Quest for Reality*, Oxford University Press, Oxford, 1999. Perhaps there was some causal relation here.

18. Why does reason seem to say, "Do it!"? I don't know.

19. For a discussion of 'fixing the reference,' see Saul A. Kripke, *Naming and Necessity*, Harvard University Press, Cambridge, Massachusetts, 1972, pp. 53–60 and elsewhere.

Conclusions

It is important to remember that I have said nothing about many of the various kinds of moral non-realism on the market. So far as this book is concerned, there may be a wonderful kind of non-realism, semi-realism, or whatever, that satisfies our deepest and best moral and modal intuitions and avoids all the apparent difficulties.[1] This book has for the most part confined itself to the conflict and contrast between Platonism in regard to morals on the one hand and disenchantment or reductionism on the other.

Disenchanters and Platonists agree that the principles of 'genuine morality' are putatively absolute, objective, and not man-made. They also agree that some, if not all, allegedly genuine moral properties are 'queer', at least in the sense that they are, or would be if they existed, irreducible to natural or theological properties. Disenchanters offer these things as objections to Platonism and genuine morality.

Platonism is incompatible with naturalism. I regard this as a serious worry. If, as it turns out, naturalism finds no real threat in consciousness, intentionality, numbers, meaning, or any other non-moral sort of thing, then, perhaps, we should regard moral Platonism as unacceptable. It may not be strong enough to stand alone against naturalism. But this is not, I think, our present situation. Naturalism has not yet blown away all legitimate non-moral opposition.

I wish I had managed to make the idea of genuine morality clearer.[2] But, hopefully, the Hobbots have been helpful. They show us what it would be like for there to be rational, social, creatures *totally lacking* in genuine morality even though they might have a well established and well designed system of folk ethics.[3] To the extent that we see what is missing in this regard, we see what genuine morality is supposed to be, and thus what the basic disagreement between Disenchanters and Platonists is all about.

Chapters seven and eight point towards a negative conclusion. It looks as though game theory, decision theory, and computer simulations of the interactions of rational agents are not going to prove that rational social creatures should be truly moral. This is a rapidly changing area of investigation, and there may well be some surprising discoveries yet to be made. Nevertheless, it seems fairly clear that dissembling, cheating, swindling, back-stabbing, and so on, are sometimes decidedly advantageous, and that adequate models of rational competitive social interaction will reflect this.

On a more positive note, it is a mistake to think that if a disenchanted view of human nature were correct (if, for instance, we were, more or less, Hobbots) stable, cooperative, social life would be impossible. Computer models of Hobbot-like social interaction seem to show that long periods of cooperative stability can occur.

I take Hobbots to suggest that a creature can be rational without having any genuine morality, or genuine moral obligations. This topic was discussed in Chapter Nine. One of the ways in which Hobbots are rational is that they can have good reason to do what they do. More specifically, they can have strictly *agent-relative* reasons for doing what they do. Rationalism—the idea that rationality itself requires one to have agent-neutral practical reasons and thus requires one to be moral—appears to be false. Conceivably, creatures that have agent-neutral practical reasons are thereby committed to morality; but rationality *per se* does not require one to have agent-neutral practical reasons; nor, I think, does reasonableness (in any ordinary sense of the term).

Reductive theorists in regard to morality are realists about morality; but, by hypothesis, they do not regard moral properties as irreducible, 'queer', or 'mysterious' (Paley). In Chapter Sixteen we looked at some objections to the views of some Reductionists. In Chapter Eighteen I offered criticisms of Frank Jackson's argument for reduction. Not too surprisingly, I think my objections and criticisms have some weight. Platonism, as I keep saying, fits our moral and modal intuitions better than either naturalistic or theological reductionism, and, for that matter, better than either form of disenchantment. Furthermore, it is compatible with both genuine and full-scale morality. This is a substantial plus since genuine full-scale morality seems very plausible to many of us.

At various places in the book I have suggested that being moral is not more (or less) rational than being governed by cool self-love or the resolution of desire. Practical reason is thus potentially divided against itself. I have also repeatedly claimed that we are sometimes confronted by what seem to be conflicts between morality and the pursuit of happiness. In regard to cases like these, Henry Sidgwick says:

> ... practical reason, being divided against itself, would cease to be a motive on either side; the conflict would have to be decided by the comparative preponderance of one or other of two groups of non-rational impulses.[4]

I don't think this is true. In cases of this sort, we have to make a choice, and, as Sidgwick suggests, *reason* does not favor either option over the other. But the outcome need not be decided by a preponderance of non-rational impulses. It could be left as a brute decision as to what sort of person we wish to be, and, perhaps, actually *try* to be. Furthermore, at least on the Platonist view, we may somehow 'see' that genuine morality has a stronger claim on us than does our happiness, or the resolution of our desires. A person who 'sees' this is, perhaps, more perceptive than one who does not; but this does not make the perceiver more *rational*. Chapter Fourteen provided some discussion of this sort of choice.

Incidentally, Platonists typically do not, and probably should not, hold that moral obligation is basically grounded in the sort of choice just mentioned. On the typical Platonistic view, it is not the case that we have an obligation to be good because we have made a fundamental choice to try to be that sort of person, or because this is a crucial part of our 'self-conception.' On the contrary, the decision to try to be a good person is typically thought to be grounded, at least in part, in the perception that we *ought* to be good—that this choice, this effort, and this way of viewing ourselves, are themselves morally obligatory.[5]

It would be nice to be able to say, truthfully, that one of our contending theories of meta-ethics has been shown to be true, or, for that matter, false; but we have arrived at no such definitive conclusion.

As far as I know, neither of the two kinds of disenchantment theory is demonstrably true, or demonstrably false. However, I think I have provided some evidence that both kinds of theory commit one to serious departures from common, deep, and serious, modal and moral intuitions. For instance, in Chapter Fifteen, I pointed out that many of us (perhaps *most* of us) would feel quite strongly that the pirate captain should have obeyed his Conscience, and not his Desire Resolver. Furthermore, at least some of us would hold that this is an absolute realist-type fact. Disenchanters cannot take this line. Disenchanters cannot hold that (as a flat-out fact) it is better that the Native Americans should live than that the pirates should have five hours of fun. This, I take it, counts against disenchantment.

Thin rationalism has the advantage of offering some account of what sort of people we should be (not always altogether nice) and how we should make our decisions. On the other hand, it commits us to Realism, and, I suspect, Platonism, in regard to rationality. Some people would regard this as a disadvantage.

If there were some way in which total disenchanters could offer us recommendations, or, at least, suggestions about how to live, without falling into

Realism, this would seem to provide a more widely acceptable form of disenchantment, since it would combine both an escape from Realism and the provision of something like guidance.

I think this combination is fairly plausible. Decision theory, game theory, and so on, need not be taken to reveal the true nature of rational behavior. They could be read as doing no more than what they obviously do, namely provide procedures that tend to maximize our 'pay off' in the long run. If that's what one wants, then one might consider these procedures. No more need be said.

Total disenchantment enables one to avoid not only Realism in regard to practical rationality but also, of course, Realism in regard to morality.

On a more theoretical level, total disenchantment is compatible with hardcore naturalism (scientism and physicalism). This is, as I have suggested, an advantage. In addition, acceptance of total disenchantment may well generate a sense of liberation in some people.

Given that we do not know, and perhaps can never know, whether or not one of our two possible kinds of disenchantment is correct, one might think that we should not 'accept' disenchantment of either kind. But this does not follow. By 'accept' I mean 'accept as one's working hypothesis,' or, more dramatically, 'accept as a basis upon which to construct one's life.' It is sometimes intellectually (and morally) permissible to 'accept' (in this sense) a theory we think is *probably false*. Thus, for instance, one might be confronted by just three mutually exclusive, and conjointly exhaustive, theories, T1, T2, and T3, such that one's 'degree of belief' (as Frank Ramsey calls it) for the three are T1 = 0.36, T2 = 0.34, and T3 = 0.3. In such a case, it would make perfectly good sense to accept T1 as one's working hypothesis, even though, one's degree of belief that it is false is 0.64.

There is something a bit odd, or questionable, about accepting a theory you think has a more likely competitor. Consider a person—let's call her 'Smith'—who has read the whole book up to this point. Pretend that, miraculously, the only meta-ethical options she finds at all plausible are those we have been considering. Her 'degree of belief' in subjectivism, social relativism, and all the other theories we have neglected, is close to zero. On the other hand, she finds Disenchantment a lot more plausible than the claim that some realist theory of morality is the winner. Among realist theories, she finds Platonism no more or less likely than either one of the reductive theories. And she finds both forms of Disenchantment equally plausible.

To fill in some rough numbers, her 'degree of belief' tree for meta-ethics looks something like this:

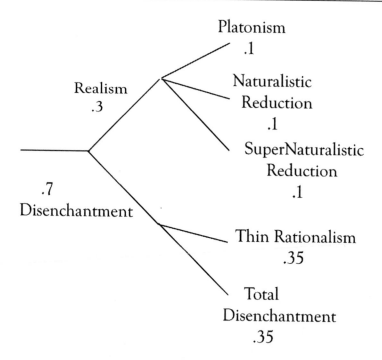

Platonism
.1

Naturalistic
Reduction
.1

SuperNaturalistic
Reduction
.1

Realism
.3

.7
Disenchantment

Thin Rationalism
.35

Total
Disenchantment
.35

Given this set-up, it would be very odd for Smith to accept Platonism as her working hypothesis—to live by, or try to live by, a moral code she believes only makes sense if Platonism is correct, and to teach her children to live this way. Why would she do these things? We want some justification, or, at least, an explanation. Perhaps *morally* her behavior is admirable; but *intellectually*, it looks strange. It would make more sense for Smith to accept Disenchantment. This choice might be regarded as lamentable from a moral point of view, but it seems more reasonable.

From a moral point of view, one might think that acceptance of Disenchantment must always be a wicked deed. But surely we can imagine cases in which this acceptance is morally permissible? Suppose, for instance, that Smith accepts it because it seems to her more likely to be true than any feasible alternative. She has thought long and hard about the issues. And, as a matter of fact, she finds Platonism more attractive. She *wishes* Platonism were true; but, alas, it seems false to her. Given this perception of the matter, and given her commitment to truth, she accepts Disenchantment. Isn't this permissible—perhaps even praiseworthy?[6]

If Smith claims to *know* that Disenchantment is true, then, I think, she goes too far. What Smith can do, so to speak, is *bet* that Platonism is false and

Disenchantment true. She can accept Disenchantment as her working hypothesis.

Here is another case. Jones is like Smith in dismissing out of hand all the meta-ethical theories we have neglected; but, unlike Smith, she finds Disenchantment theory much less plausible than Realism. Furthermore, Jones was somewhat moved by my reasons for finding Total Disenchantment more attractive than Thin Rationalism. Nevertheless, as she sees it, these two are not much different in regard to their degree of plausibility. According to her, I was more persuasive in arguing that there is a better case for Platonism than for either form of Reduction. In fact, she thinks that Supernaturalistic Reductionism is nearly out of the running. As a result, Jones says her Degree of Belief Tree looks something like the following:

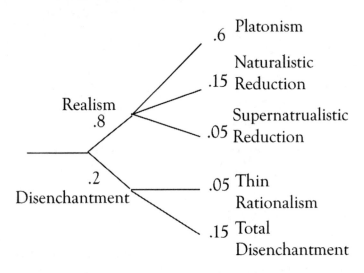

Platonism, on Jones' view, is far and away the most plausible of all particular meta-ethical theories. In fact she finds it much more plausible than that some form of Disenchantment is correct (0.6 as opposed to 0.2).

Assuming this Degree of Belief Tree, would it be morally and intellectually permissible for her to accept Platonism? One might think she has no choice. Nevertheless, I think she does have a choice. Couldn't she think that Platonism was a fairly good bet, but choose to live as though some form of Disenchantment theory was correct?

Suppose that Jones does accept Platonism. How could she be justified in doing so? Many of us find the idea of full-scale morality appealing. We would like it to be true. Surely this is an intellectually and morally permissible attitude? Platonism is compatible with full-scale morality. In fact, a well thought out, defensible, form of full-scale morality may require Platonism in regard to at least some moral properties. As we have seen, naturalistic and theistic forms of reductionism seem incompatible with some of the characteristic claims of full-scale morality. In particular, this seems to be the case in regard to the claim that morality trumps prudence. Disenchantment theories certainly make no such claim. Platonism may well be the full-scale moralist's only real option. Thus, some of us may have reason to *hope* that Platonism is correct—to *wish* it were true. But this is not, in itself, enough to make acceptance of it morally and intellectual permissible. Many of us would like to have at least a temporary life after death in which we come to understand things better, we live out some of our unfulfilled plans, we resolve at least some of our old unresolved problems and relationships. Furthermore, many of us have deceased loved ones we would like to think still exist and are happy. We thus have good reason to wish that there were a life after death. But, it seems to me, this does not justify our believing that there is such a life, nor does it make it permissible for us to accept this belief as our working hypothesis.

On the other hand, there is danger of falling into absurdity when we try to apply this reasoning to full-scale morality. It would be foolish to refuse acceptance of full-scale morality on the grounds that this acceptance would be morally wrong (according to full-scale morality). By a kind of contagion, a similar absurdity seems applicable to acceptance of Platonism. If full-scale morality more or less requires Platonism, and we are aware of this fact, then our refusal to accept Platonism (and, consequently, full-scale morality) on the grounds that it violates a duty imposed by full-scale morality seems absurd.

Jones is, so to speak, willing to bet that Platonism is true. I assume that her degree of belief is principally based on her feeling that there really is such a thing as full scale, genuine morality—that people really 'count', and so on. It isn't just a matter of her *wanting* these things to be true. She knows that she may well be wrong; but she has decided to trust these intuitions. Presumably she thinks it very likely that full-scale morality requires Platonism, and this line of thought is the basis of her having a fairly high degree of belief in Platonism.

If Jones is bothered by the fact that, by her own reckoning, she has a forty percent chance of being wrong, she can remind herself that, if she *is* wrong, it is very unlikely that she (or anyone else) will ever find out. How could she (or they)? Suppose a being she takes to be an angel lands on her front porch and gives her the news. Even so, it might be a trick. Maybe it's Satan in his old angel outfit.

NOTES

1. Of course my guess is that there is no such thing.

2. See 'Key Terms' at the end of the book for a brief and not very helpful effort in this direction.

3. As I have said, the fact that they totally lack genuine morality is compatible with their having some genuine moral properties. Perhaps, for instance, they 'count' and ought to be treated with respect by accountable people.

4. Henry Sidgwick, *The Methods of Ethics*, Macmillan and Co., London, 1913, p. 508. (Next to last paragraph of the book)

5. This seems to leave the grounds of moral obligation a matter of mysterious brute fact. Disenchanters, and reducers, understandably, take this to be a serious objection to the Platonistic view of moral obligation. For a sophisticated attack on 'realist' conceptions of moral obligation, see Christine Korsgaard's *The Sources of Normativity*, Cambridge University Press, 1996, pp. 28–48.

6. She runs into absurdity if she sees this as a moral matter. I assume she thinks she is just indulging her love of truth.

Appendix A   Nagel

In *The Possibility of Altruism*, Thomas Nagel contended that we commonly make choices *not* grounded in present desires, but grounded in the bare fact that we are *going to have* certain desires. He supported this allegation with an interesting case:

> Suppose that for no reason having to do with the future, I conceive now a desire to become a policeman on my 35th birthday. If I do not believe that the desire will persist, or that any circumstances then obtaining will provide me with reason for being or becoming a policeman, is it possible to maintain nevertheless that the desire itself gives me reason to do what will promote its realization? It would be extremely peculiar if anyone allowed himself to be moved to action by such a desire, or regarded it as anything but a nervous symptom to be looked on with suspicion and got rid of as soon as possible. In general, no one wants anything future in this way, without a reason derived from the expectation of a reason.[12]

It seems to me that Nagel had forgotten an important feature of desire. We desire a state of affairs *against a background of presupposed conditions*. If Brutus wants to see the emperor when he gets to Rome, we should not suppose that he wants to see the emperor *no matter what may then be the case*. Presumably he would not want to see an emperor who had just become a homicidal maniac. It is also to be noted that x may be a presupposed condition of some desired state of affairs even though x itself is not desired. Brutus may wish the emperor would go mad—even though his not having done so is one of the background conditions of Brutus' desire to see him.

When one wants to be a policeman, I suggest, one wants to be a policeman on the understanding that one will be a policeman who wants to be a policeman. Similarly, when one wants to get a drink of water, one wants to get the drink given that one will still want it when one gets it. This is not to say that one wants to want the water, or wants to want to be a policeman.

A child's desire to be a member of the police force in the remote future is usually poor evidence that one of the presuppositions of that desire will be fulfilled, namely, the presupposition that, in the remote future, he or she will still want to be a member of the force. On the other hand, my desire for water is excellent evidence that I will want the water when, finally, I get it.

How does this apply to Nagel's case? Suppose that it is now 2008. Alice wants to be a policeman when she gets to be 35. Let's call this present (2008) desire 'D_1'. In addition, it will be the case on Alice's 35th birthday that she will want to be a policeman (right then). Call this fact 'F_1'. Suppose that Alice now (2008) decides to send for a correspondence course in police work. That seems a reasonable thing to do. But what reason does she have for doing it? Is it D_1 or F_1 that provides her with a reason? In his book, Nagel tries, in effect, to answer this question. Given F_1, he thinks, it would be reasonable to send for the course, even in the absence of D_1. But it would be mad to send for the course in an attempt to provide for the satisfaction of D_1 if it were known that F_1 was not a fact. Hence, he concludes, it must be F_1 rather than D_1 that provides a reason to send for the course (and to want to send for the course).

It is easy to confuse these two things: 1) the facts that give Alice reason to send for the course, and 2) Alice's reason for sending for the course (or for wanting to send for it). Roughly speaking, the facts that make it reasonable for someone to act on a desire are the facts that warrant the conclusion that the object of the desire can be achieved, and that this achievement would be desirable, and that the background conditions of the desire will be forthcoming. Brutus *thinks* he *has reason* to seek admission to the palace. He thinks, for example, that the emperor has been hinting that he would be willing to see Brutus. Brutus *wants* to be admitted to the palace because he wants to see the emperor and he thinks there is some chance that this will be permitted. He does not just *think* (i.e. hazard the opinion) that he has *his reasons* for wanting admission to the palace.

It may well be that one of the facts that make it reasonable for Alice to send for the course is some fact that warrants the conclusion that she will want to be a policeman on her 35th birthday. But it does not follow that this fact, or F_1 itself, is Alice's *reason* for sending for the course (or for wanting to send for the course). For all that has been said, that reason may be that she has a desire (*now*—in 2008) to be a policeman when she gets to be 35, and she thinks this act will promote the satisfaction of that desire.

"But", Nagel may say, "How can *this* desire be part of her reason for sending for the course? If she knew that she was fated to have no desire to be a policeman, she would not send for it!" That, I suppose, is true; but not because her present desire to be a policeman when she gets to be 35 is no part of the reason behind her decision to send for the course. It is rather because, in seeing that the desire to be a policeman when she gets to be 35 will not last until she is 35, she would also see that one of the *presuppositions* of her present desire is fated to fail.

NOTES

1.   Thomas Nagel, *The Possibility of Altruism*, Clarendon Press, Oxford, 1970, pp. 43–44.

APPENDIX B   CUDWORTH

Ralph Cudworth (1617–1688), one of the 'Cambridge Platonists', rejects all accounts of moral goodness and moral evil, justice and injustice, that make these things entirely 'thetical.'¹According to theories of this stamp, things that are morally good or morally bad, just or unjust, are not so 'naturally' (i.e. realistically) and immutably. Their being morally good or morally bad, just or unjust is grounded in nothing more than human will, or divine command. Among his examples of philosophers who take the first approach (i.e. ground these things in *human* will), Cudworth lists Protagoras, Democritus, Aristippus², Pyrrho, Epicurus, and Hobbes. Presumably, all these people believe

> ...that good and evil, just and unjust (are) not naturally and immutably so, but (are made so) by human laws and appointment.³

> ...the vulgar generally look no higher for the original of moral good and evil, just and unjust, than the codes and pandects, the tables and laws of their country and religion, so there have not wanted pretended philosophers in all ages who have asserted nothing to be good and evil, just and unjust, φυσει και ακινητοσῐ'naturally and immutably;' but that all these things were θετικα, νομιμα, ψηφισματωδηⅢ'positive, arbitrary and factitious only.'⁴

Notice that Cudworth speaks of things being '*naturally*' just, and so on. Of course he is not endorsing *naturalism*. In fact when he says that something is 'naturally' just he is asserting *Platonistic realism* in regard to the justice of that thing—i.e. a kind of *non*-naturalism.

There are many passages in Hobbes that might lead one to believe he accepts the 'human laws' version of the thetic theory. For example, he writes:

> The desires and other passions of man, are in themselves no sin. No more are the actions, that proceed from those passions, till they know a law that forbids them: which till laws be made they cannot know: nor can any law be made, till they have agreed upon the person that shall make it.⁵

And again:

> To this war of every man, against every man, this also is consequent; that nothing can be unjust. The notions of right and wrong, justice and injustice have there no place. Where there is no common power, there is no law: where no law, no injustice.⁶

(So far as I can see, there is no incompatibility in holding both (1) that our fundamental obligation is to do whatever reason requires of us and also

(2) that moral right and wrong, justice and injustice, derive from human convention or will. It seems fairly clear that Hobbes was a reductionist, or Disenchanter, in regard to the *moral* domain. But was he, or was he not, a nonreductive realist with respect to what reason requires of us? I do not know the answer to this question.)

Equally abhorrent to Cudworth is the *theological* version of the thetic theory. Philosophers and theologians of this species claim

> ...that there is nothing absolutely, intrinsically, and naturally good and evil, just and unjust, antecedently to any positive command or prohibition of God; but that the arbitrary will and pleasure of God (that is, an omnipotent Being devoid of all essential and natural justice), by its commands and prohibitions, is the first and only rule and measure thereof. Whence it follows unavoidably, that nothing can be imagined so grossly wicked, or so foully unjust or dishonest, but if it were supposed to be commanded by this omnipotent Deity, must needs upon that hypothesis forthwith become holy, just, and righteous.[7]

In this group Cudworth places Ockham, Petrus Alliacus, Andreas de Novo Castro, Joannes Szydlovius, and many others whose names he does not think 'fit to mention'.[8] (It is reasonable to assume he is thinking of some Calvinists.) In addition, of course, there is Descartes.[9] I have the impression that Descartes is Cudworth's primary opponent here.

There are, then, a large number of

> ...philosophers and theologers that seemingly and verbally acknowledge such things as moral good and evil, just and unjust, that contend notwithstanding that these are not φύσει 'by nature,' but θέσι, 'institution,' and that there is nothing naturally or immutably just or unjust...[10]

In this formulation Cudworth's opponents are taken to accept two distinct claims: (1) There are things which are morally good, or morally bad, just, or unjust. (2) Things which are morally good, morally bad, just, or unjust are *thetically* rather than *naturally* and *immutably* so. The second claim commits thetic theorists to the proposition that for any item, x, such that x is just or unjust, morally good or morally evil, there is some act of will that makes x just or unjust, morally good or morally evil. In order to refute his opponents, Cudworth must either show that *nothing* is morally good or bad, just or unjust (obviously he doesn't want to do that) or demonstrate that there is at least one item, x, such that x is just or unjust, morally good or morally evil, but such that no act of will (human or divine) makes this so. (Of course he would like to show that are many such items.) Cudworth's actual strategy against thetic theorists is difficult to follow. My impression is that he is offering at least one of the following three distinct lines of thought.

The *Bold* Argument:

(1) Nothing is thetical.

(2) But some things are morally good, morally evil, just or unjust.

(3) Hence, moral goodness, moral evil, and so forth are not thetical.

The *Essentialist* Argument:

(1) Each thing has the nature it has, not thetically, but naturally and immutably; i.e. *essentially.*

(2) The moral status of a deed (or a disposition), D, is part of its nature.

(3) Hence, if D has a moral status, it is not a *thetical* fact that D has this moral status.

The *Disjunctive* Argument:

(1) Given that there is some deed, D, which is morally good, morally evil, or whatever, D has this moral status, either (a) by nature and immutably, or (b) thetically, by some act of will.

(2) If D has a particular moral status by nature and immutably, then the thetic theory is false.

(3) If D has a particular moral status by virtue of an act of will, then it must, under these circumstances, be naturally and immutably morally good to conform to this will in these circumstances and thus again the thetic theory is false.

(4) Hence, given that there is some deed, D, which is morally good, morally evil, or whatever, the thetic theory is false.

(If Cudworth only intends one of these, my guess would be that it is the third. The text often seems to invite this interpretation.)

Cudworth himself expresses the upshot of his attack as follows:

...if there be any thing at all good or evil, just or unjust, there must of necessity be δικαιον φυσικον και ακινητον,' something naturally and immutably good and just.'[11]

And:

...upon supposition that there is any thing really just or unjust, *debitum* or *illicitum,* 'due or unlawful,' there must of necessity be something so both naturally and immutably, which no law, decree, will, nor custom can alter.[12]

And again at greater length:

...the result of all that we have hitherto said is this, that the intelligible natures and essences of things are neither arbitrary nor fantastical, that is, neither alterable by any will whatsoever, nor changeable by opinion; and therefore every thing is necessarily and immutably to science and knowledge what it is, whether absolutely or relatively, to all minds and intellects in the world. So that if moral good and evil, just and unjust, signify any reality, either absolute or relative, in the things so denominated, as they must have some certain natures, which are the actions or souls of men, they are neither alterable by mere will nor opinion.[13]

In this last passage, as in many other places, it is not entirely clear whether Cudworth is talking about particular, individual, deed-tokens and disposition-tokens (e.g. Alice's abrupt departure from the party and George's hair-triggered temper), or about deed-*types*, disposition-*types*, and so on (e.g. abrupt departures from parties and hair-triggered tempers). My guess is that often when he seems to be talking about particulars he is actually thinking of types.

Exposition and Assessment of the Bold Argument

Cudworth's main line of argument (whatever that turns out to be) certainly begins with a defense of the claim that 'things' are what they are by virtue of their natures. Thus, for example:

...things are white by whiteness...triangular by triangularity...like by likeness...that is, by such certain natures of their own. Neither can Omnipotence itself (to speak with reverence) by mere will make a thing white ...without whiteness... that is, without such certain natures, whether we consider them as qualities in the objects without us according to the Peripatetical philosophy, or as certain dispositions of parts in respect of magnitude, figure, site and motion, which beget those sensations or phantasms of white... in us. Or, to instance in geometrical figures, Omnipotence itself cannot by mere will make a body triangular, without having the nature of a triangle in it; that is, without having three angles equal to two right ones, nor circular without the nature of a circle; that is, without having a circumference equidistant every where from the center or middle point. Or lastly, to instance in things relative only; omnipotent will cannot make things like or equal to another, without the natures of likeness and equality. The reason whereof is plain, because all these things imply a manifest contradiction; that things should be what they are not.[14]

From this innocuous beginning, Cudworth, somehow, derives objections to the thetic theory. I take the following remarks to suggest the Bold Argument.

...it is impossible any thing should be by will only, that is, without a nature or entity, or that the nature and essence of any thing should be arbitrary.

And since a thing cannot be made any thing by mere will without a being or nature, every thing must be necessarily and immutably determined by its own nature, and the nature of things be that which it is, and nothing else. For though the will and power of God have an absolute, infinite and unlimited command upon the existences of all created things to make them to be, or not to be at pleasure; yet when things exist, they are what they are, this or that, absolutely or relatively, not by will or arbitrary command, but by the necessity of their own nature. There is no such thing as an arbitrarious essence, mode or relation, that may be made indifferently any thing at pleasure; for an arbitrarious essence is a being without a nature, a contradiction and therefore a nonentity. Wherefore the natures of justice and injustice cannot be arbitrarious things, that may be applicable by will indifferently to any actions or dispositions whatsoever. For the modes of all subsistent beings, and the relations of things to one another, are immutably and necessarily what they are, and not arbitrary, being not by will but by nature.

Now the necessary consequence of that which we have hitherto said is this, That it is so far from being true, that all moral good and evil, just and unjust are mere arbitrary and factitious things, that are created wholly by will; that (if we should speak properly) we must needs say that nothing is morally good or evil, just or unjust by mere will without nature, because every thing is what it is by nature, and not by will.[15]

The line of thought goes something like this. How are we to picture the alleged imposition of an essence (i.e. a property?) on a thing by an act of will? Either the act changes the nature of the thing, or the essence is 'attached' to the thing without there being any such change. But either kind of occurrence seems metaphysically impossible. The natures of things are immutable. And there is no such thing as an 'arbitrarious' essence that can be imposed upon any of a wide variety of natures at will.

This attack on the thetic theory seems to me unpersuasive. Thetic theorists want to say that moral properties are metaphysically (or in their 'logic') similar to the property of *being illegal*. If this latter property isn't 'thetical' (because no property is), we have, somehow, gotten the wrong concept of what it is to be thetical. By hypothesis, a 'thetical' property is one that is metaphysically (or 'logically') similar to illegality; and it is certainly possible for something to be illegal.[16]

Suppose it is illegal to park on the north side of High Street. Given this supposition, there is a deed-type (parking on the north side of High) such that deeds of that type are illegal. Parking on the north side of High has been made illegal by an act of will (the decision of the relevant authorities). Of course there is nothing in the nature of parking there which, in itself, makes the behavior illegal. To put the point in the Cudworthian way, being illegal is not part of that nature. In fact, parking on the north side of High seems to be *legally indifferent* in nature.

The property of being illegal has a nature of its own. Deeds that are illegal have been forbidden by some relevant and legitimate legislative body. But, given this, how can deeds that are by nature legally indifferent be illegal? Imagine some mixed-up philosopher reasoning as follows:

(1) Parking on the north side of High naturally and immutably has a certain nature, N.
(2) Being a neutral matter so far as legality is concerned (i.e. not being either legal or illegal by nature) is part of N.
(3) If being a neutral matter so far as legality is concerned is part of N, then parking on the north side of High is naturally and immutably a neutral matter so far as legality is concerned.
(4) Hence, parking on the north side of High is naturally and immutably a neutral matter so far as legality is concerned.
(5) Hence, it is impossible to make parking on the north side of High illegal (e.g. by an act of will).

Conclusion (4) can't be true, or, at least, can't be true in a sense that would permit conclusion (5) to be drawn from it. Parking on the north side of High is not, by nature, either legal or illegal. Nothing can change that. But it does not follow that parking on the north side of High cannot be made illegal by an appropriate act of will. If we want to speak Cudworthian, our claim should be that the immutable natures of some kinds of deeds allow them to be made legal, or illegal, as the proper authorities see fit. Such deeds might be said to be neutral by nature so far as legality and illegality are concerned. But illegality is thetical in that it can, by an appropriate act of will, be made a property of a deed-type that is tolerant in this way. Thus, for example, parking on the north side of High is now illegal. Parking there now has the nature that goes with that property (that is to say, parking there is a violation of duly enacted ordinance). This is a contingent and mutable matter. There have been, and perhaps will be, times when parking on the north side of High is not illegal and is not forbidden by any legitimate legislative body.

The bold line of attack depends upon bad reasoning that pushes us towards the mistaken idea that there are no thetical properties. But *illegality* is thetical.

To return to our proper topic, moral-status properties are, at least sometimes, in a sense, thetical. Don't we all know perfectly well that particular acts of some morally indifferent type can be made morally wrong by a prior act of will? If I have promised to meet someone for late breakfast at the Pancake House, and no insurmountable obstacle, or overriding obligation, has intervened, I should go there. My promise (based on an act of will) has made my staying home morally reprehensible. Here is another example. Suppose the local government has legitimately ordered me to prune certain trees on my land. In that case, if nothing prevents my doing so, I am obliged to prune those trees. Aren't these genuine examples of thetical obligations? Cudworth more or less admits as much.

> ...that common distinction betwixt things, φυσει and θεσει' things naturally and positively good and evil', or (as others express it) betwixt things that are therefore commanded because they are good and just, and things that are therefore good and just, because they are commanded, stands in need of a right explication, that we be not led into a mistake thereby, as if the obligation to do these thetical and positive things did arise wholly from will without nature; whereas it is not the mere will and pleasure of him that commandeth, that obligeth to do positive things commanded, but the intellectual nature of him that is commanded. Wherefore the difference of these things lies wholly in this, That there are some things which the intellectual nature obligeth to per se, 'of itself,' and directly, absolutely and perpetually, and these things are called φυσει 'naturally good and evil;' other things there are which the same intellectual nature obligeth to by accident only, and hypothetically, upon condition of some voluntary action either of our own or some other person's, by means whereof those things which were in their own nature indifferent, falling under something that is absolutely good or evil, and thereby acquiring a new relation to the intellectual nature, do for the time become *debita* or *illicita*, 'such things as ought to be done or omitted,' being made such not by will but by nature. As for example, to keep faith and perform covenants, is that which natural justice obligeth to absolutely; therefore, *ex hypothesi*, 'upon the supposition' that any one maketh a promise, which is a voluntary act of his own, to do something which he was not before obliged to by natural justice, upon the intervention of this voluntary act of his own, that indifferent thing promised falling now under something absolutely good, and becoming the matter of promise and covenant, standeth for the present in a new relation to the rational nature of the promiser, and becometh for the time a thing which ought to be done by him, or which he is obliged to do.[17]

Cudworth thus explicates the 'common distinction' between deeds that are, in some sense, 'thetically' good, or obligatory, and deeds which are good by nature. Suppose, as yet another example, that God commands us to abstain from eating apples from the Tree of Knowledge of Good and Evil. And suppose we have a moral obligation to obey his commands. The result would be that it is now morally good to abstain from eating apples from this tree, and morally wrong to eat them. How are we to understand these consequences of the command? If God had not prohibited eating apples from this tree, our eating them, or not eating them, would have been a morally indifferent matter. Has the command changed the nature of the deed-type? Cudworth would, quite properly, deny this. Eating apples from the Tree of Knowledge of Good and Evil is still, in its nature, a morally indifferent matter —neither morally good nor morally bad. Nothing can change this fact. But eating those apples has been given an additional, *accidental*, property. God's command has brought it about that deeds of this type now have the additional 'nature' of being acts forbidden by God; and it is, immutably and by nature, morally wrong to do anything he has forbidden. Thus an act-type which is immutably in its own nature something morally indifferent *can* (for now) be made morally wrong by an act of will.

Going to the Pancake House for late breakfast is, in it's own nature, another morally indifferent deed. But this is the 'matter' of a promise—that is to say, it is what I have promised to do. I am obliged to do it simply because of that promise. The additional, accidental, property of its being the fulfillment of my promise makes it obligatory for me. If I had not made that promise, but instead had pledged never to go to the Pancake House again, my trip there would be morally wrong.

Exposition and Assessment of the Essentialist Argument

In the essentialist argument as I have stated it we are left in the dark as to whether the 'D' under discussion is a particular deed-token, or a deed-type. (For the sake of simplicity, I more or less disregard dispositions.) Nevertheless, as we have just seen, it is fairly clear that deeds of a certain type (e.g. eating apples from a certain tree) can be made morally right or morally wrong by a command or promise. And, if this is so, it is possible for the moral status of some deed-types to be accidental and temporary rather than essential. Hence, it seems to me that the more promising interpretation of the argument deals with the essential features of particular deed-tokens.

'Moral essentialism', as I call it, has two components. The first is that each particular deed-token has a nature by virtue of which it belongs to a certain natural class of deeds. The nature of an individual deed-token is essential to it and is thus 'immutable'. The second component is the claim that the moral status of each particular deed-token is part of its nature, and is thus one of its essential features. Here is an analogous set of claims: Plants and animals belong to natural kinds. Each individual plant or animal has certain characteristic features (e.g. its DNA structure) by virtue of which it belongs to its kind. Having these features, and thus belonging to this kind, is an essential property of the individual plant or animal. Hence, for example, each individual oak-tree is essentially an oak; each frog essentially a frog.[18]

It is easy to make the mistake of thinking that moral essentialism is incompatible with the thetic theory. Given moral essentialism, and given that some unjust deed has been done, it seems to follow that there is something (namely, that deed-token) that is naturally, and immutably, unjust. And, of course, by hypothesis, it is true that nothing could make, or have made, that particular deed-token just, or morally indifferent. Nevertheless, the thetic theory is not strictly incompatible with moral essentialism.

Consider the following situation. Suppose that Judge Albert Snide has condemned Reggie Boot to jail for six months (on a trumped-up charge) simply because he (Snide) strongly dislikes people with little, close-set, eyes. (Boot has eyes of this sort.) Snide is quite aware that his judgment is based upon his peculiar personal bias.

Most people will admit that Snide's deed is genuinely unjust. How would Cudworth analyze the situation? I take it he would claim that the deed must belong to at least one general type such that, necessarily, all deeds of that type are morally wrong and unjust. It's a necessary truth that condemning people to imprisonment out of dislike for their appearance is unjust. In addition, Cudworth might say that this individual deed-token is essentially unjust. Nothing we, or God, could have done, or could now do, would make this deed just, or morally permissible.

By way of contrast, Hobbes seems to subscribe to the empiricist theory of necessity.[19] According to this view, all necessary truths spring from definitions, or verbal conventions. Hence, I suppose, his view would be that Snide's deed is unjust, and necessarily so, *under some descriptions*, but not under others. We have set up our legal system in such a way that it is 'unjust' (by definition) to condemn someone to prison for personal (legally irrelevant) reasons. On the other hand, *condemning someone to prison* (simpliciter) is not, as such, either 'just' or 'unjust'. If someone says that Snide's deed is 'naturally and immutably unjust', the charitable reading of the claim (from a Hobbesian point of view) would be that the deed falls under some general description such that by virtue of our present legal system, and our present set of definitions, it is a necessary truth that it is 'unjust' to do deeds of the type described.

How are essentialist claims supposed to help Cudworth's cause? Suppose we grant that being unjust is an essential feature of Judge Snide's deed. It follows that nothing could make, or could have made, that particular deed just, or morally permissible. But clearly it does not follow that the unjustness of the deed is *natural* as opposed to '*thetical*'. Pretend (1) that God had decided that this general sort of behavior is morally permissible, and (2) that God's decision is enough to make it so. Given moral essentialism, it would follow that Snide could not have done the actual individual deed he did in fact do. Of course he could have condemned Boot to prison for the same absurd reason; but the resultant deed would not have been morally wrong. Hence (under present assumptions) it would have been a numerically distinct deed-token.

I take it, then, that moral essentialism is not, in itself, strictly incompatible with a thetic theory of morality. A thetic theorist could, in principle, accept moral essentialism, and yet persist in the view that what makes Snide's actual deed unjust and morally wrong is nothing more than a certain prior act of will—perhaps a decision made by God. (I do not mean to suggest that a thetic theorist, or anyone else, for that matter, would do well to accept such a view.) The supposed fact that nothing could make, or could have made, Snide's actual deed morally acceptable does not permit us to conclude that the moral wrongness of Snide's deed does not derive from an act of will.

There is a closely related point to be made in regard to the 'nature' by virtue of which Snide's deed is unjust. Cudworth would claim (1) that the deed cannot be unjust unless it has the nature that is the necessary companion of unjustness. And it is not altogether absurd to think he would add (2) that the nature that accompanies the moral status of a particular deed-token is an essential feature of that deed-token. Let's pretend that both (1) and (2) are true. Thetic theorists of the theological sort would still be free to claim that the 'nature' in question is nothing other than *being a deed of a sort forbidden by God*. If this is an essential feature of Snide's deed, then, if deeds of this sort had *not* been forbidden, Snide could not have done this individual deed. Nevertheless, he might well have done a deed indistinguishable from it.

Suppose a certain dog, Rover, has the property of having been the over-all winner at a dog-show. Of course he has this property by virtue of having a certain 'nature'; but the 'nature' in question is, I take it, nothing other than the property of having been picked out as 'best dog' by the judges at the show. If Rover lacked this 'nature', he would not have been the over-all winner. But it does not follow that having been the over-all winner was not just a matter of will (as distinct from nature). The 'nature' in question here *is* a matter of will.

In effect, I am saying that the essentialist argument against the thetic theory is a non-sequitor. Suppose it is part of the essence of a particular deed-token, D, that D is unjust. It follows that D necessarily has the 'nature' linked to the property of being unjust, and that no act of will could make D just, or morally indifferent; but it does *not* follow that the final explanation of D's wrongness isn't thetical.

Of course Cudworth thinks the nature immutably linked to the property of being unjust is *not* thetical. But this is what is at issue. He cannot use this (undefended) assumption in an attack on the thetic theory.

Can one coherently hold moral essentialism while at the same time admitting that the present moral status of some deed-type is thetical? I don't see any incoherence here. Cudworth is clearly committed to the view that deeds of a type such that some acts of that type are morally indifferent, or permissible, can, in some sense, be made morally impermissible by certain acts of will. Where this is the case, we seem to have examples of deeds that have been made morally impermissible by an act of will. This may generate the impression that an act-token can have an accidental, non-essential, moral status. Nevertheless, this temptation should be resisted. Moral essentialism is compatible with the observation that a deed-type (e.g. going to the Pancake House for late breakfast) can include morally obligatory, morally neutral, and morally forbidden, instances. We say a deed of this type has been rendered obligatory by a prior promise. But this does not mean that some particular deed-token was transformed from being morally neutral to being morally obligatory.[20]

My obligation to go the Pancake House is, in some sense, 'thetical'. Nevertheless, being done in compliance with a promise, and thus being obligatory, could be viewed as an essential feature of my actual visit to the Pancake House. If there had been no such promise, 'this' would have been a numerically distinct deed.

A flat-out admission that the moral status of a certain deed-token, or deed-type, is basically thetical would be incompatible with the bold claim that *nothing* is thetical. Cudworth seems to be trying to maintain the over-all coherence of his view when he tells us that the moral status generated by legitimate commands and promises is not *strictly* thetical.

....if we would speak yet more accurately and precisely, we might rather say, that no positive commands whatsoever do make any thing morally good and evil, just and unjust, which nature had not made such before. For indifferent things commanded, considered materially in themselves, remain still what they were before in their own nature, that is, indifferent, because as Aristotle speaks, το φυσει ακινητον 'will cannot change nature.' And those things that are φυσει αδιαφορα 'by nature indifferent,' must need be as immutably so, as those things that are φυσει δικαια or αισχρα, 'by nature just or unjust, honest or shameful.' But all the moral goodness, justice, and virtue, that is exercised in obeying positive commands, and doing such things as are θεσει, 'positive' only, and to be done for no other cause but because they are commanded, or in respect to political order, consisteth not in the materiality of the actions themselves, but in that formality of yielding obedience to the commands of lawful authority in them. Just as when a man covenanteth or promiseth to do an indifferent thing which by natural justice he was not bound to do, the virtue of doing it consisteth not in the materiality of the action promised, but in the formality of keeping faith and performing covenants. Wherefore, in positive commands, the will of the commander doth not create any new moral entity, but only diversely modifies and determines that general duty or obligation of natural justice to obey lawful authority and keep oaths and covenants, as our own will in promising doth but produce several modifications of keeping faith. And therefore there are no new δικαια, *justa* or *debita*, 'things just or due' made by either of them, besides what was always φυσει, 'by nature' such to keep our own promises, and obey the lawful commands of others.[21]

There is an important point being made. A command, or promise, cannot create the general obligation to obey legitimate commands, or to fulfill one's promises. One might even say it cannot create the obligatoriness that is conferred upon the thing commanded, or promised. Rather, the prior, indeterminate, obligation to do whatever is legitimately commanded, or promised, is 'modified', and made 'determinate'—shaped, or focused, as it were, into a specific obligation. Nevertheless, Cudworth seems to deny, or at least forget, another, equally important, point. A legitimate command, or promise, *can* make the performance of a deed of a certain kind (which, in its own nature is morally indifferent) morally right and good, or morally wrong and evil. *Nature* did not make my going to the Pancake House morally obligatory. My promise made it so. It is absurd to insist that, strictly speaking, my obligation is not to go to the Pancake House, but to fulfill my promise.

The essentialist argument—that is to say the argument based upon moral essentialism—has a questionable premise (namely, premise (2)). Why should the thetic theorist grant that the moral status of every particular deed-token is part of that token's essential nature? Worse yet, the argument is, at best, a subtle non-sequitor. Given moral essentialism, it may yet be the case that all moral status properties are thetical.

Exposition and Assessment of the Disjunctive Argument

The raw materials of the argument (if not the thing itself) can be found in the following remarks:

...it is so far from being true, that all moral good and evil, just and unjust (if they be any thing) are made by mere will and arbitrary commands (as many conceive) that it is not possible than any command of God or man should oblige otherwise than by virtue of that which is φυσει δικαιον⫿ 'naturally just.' And though particular promises and commands be made by will, yet it is not will but nature that obligeth to the doing of things promised and commanded, or makes them *debita*, 'such things as ought to be done.' For mere will cannot change the moral nature of actions, nor the nature of intellectual beings. And therefore, if there were no natural justice, that is, if the rational or intellectual nature in itself were indetermined and unobliged to any thing, and so destitute of all morality, it were not possible that any thing should be made morally good or evil, *debitum* or *illicitum*, 'obligatory or unlawful,' or that any moral obligation should be begotten by any will or command whatsoever.[22]

Cudworth is a Platonist. On his view, in the absence of overriding obligations and insurmountable obstacles, it is naturally and immutably right and good to fulfill one's promises. This alleged *non*-thetical fact is taken to be the underlying source of the particular, thetical, obligation. Cudworth stresses that a command, or a promise, could not generate a moral obligation in the absence of this underlying source. Thetical moral obligation cannot be brought into existence *ex nihilo*, by a mere command, promise, convention, practice, or whatever. On his view, thetical moral obligation presupposes non-thetical, 'natural' moral obligation.

Here is the heart of the Disjunctive Argument. Suppose that at least one genuinely unjust deed has been done. That deed must either be 'materially' unjust by its own nature, or thetically ('formally') unjust (i.e. unjust by virtue of some prior act of will). On the first supposition, we have found a class of deeds that are naturally and immutably unjust—God himself could not make deeds of this sort just. On the second supposition, there was a prior act of will, W, such that, *given* W, a deed of type D is unjust. But then we have found a naturally good deed-type, namely acting out of obedience to, or in compliance with, W. Going to the Pancake House for breakfast, or staying home, are, in themselves, morally indifferent options. But, given my promise to be there, I have a moral obligation to go. Staying home has been made morally wrong, and going made morally right, by the act of promising (together with the general fact that one ought to keep one's promises). The rightness and wrongness of these alternatives is thus thetical. But, Cudworth claims, the moral obligation to keep one's promises is *not* thetical. If it is morally right to keep them, and morally wrong to disregard them, then neither God nor man could make it otherwise. Hence, underlying the thetical rightness and wrongness here, we find a class of actions such that, necessarily, if an action belongs to that class, it is an action that is (prima facie) morally right (or wrong). The up-shot thus appears to be that given a deed it would be morally right or morally wrong to do, there must be a deed-type that is naturally and immutably right, or naturally and immutably wrong. Hence, given that some deeds have genuine moral status, it cannot be the case that all such status is thetical.

Cudworth apparently thinks his opponents are committed to the following two claims: (a) that moral-status terms (e.g. 'moral goodness' and so on) designate genuine, irreducible, properties; and (b) that given any class of deeds definable in non-moral terms, the moral status of deeds belonging to that class is a *contingent* matter dependent upon some act of will. These views do seem to be incompatible, and the Disjunctive line of thought shows us the danger. But this does not constitute a refutation of the Thetic theory. Thetic theorists need not (and should not) endorse (a). There is one well-known, and important, passage in which Cudworth himself offers such theorists a (reductive) alternative.

> ... it is a thing which we shall very easily demonstrate, That moral good and evil, just and unjust, honest and dishonest (if they be not mere names without any signification, or names for nothing else, but willed and commanded, but have a reality in respect of the persons obliged to do and avoid them), cannot possibly be arbitrary things, made by will without nature; because it is universally true, that things are what they are, not by will but by nature.[23]

I take this to say, among other things, that we have *three* options: (1) we can hold that moral goodness, and so on, are *bogus* properties—like 'containing phlogiston' and 'being haunted'. This is the 'eliminativist' view; or (2) we can accept thetic *reductionism* in regard to such properties, or (3) we can admit that these properties are genuine, and at least conceptually distinct from the 'natures' to which they are necessarily wedded.

Cudworth does not worry much about options (1) and (2). As I have said, he apparently assumes that he and most of his opponents agree in accepting (3). But the disjunctive line of thought might well be taken to show that thetic theorists should reject (3). Hence, perhaps, they should defend option (2).

This result is not surprising. Clear-headed thetic theorists do advocate a reductive account of moral properties such as 'right' and 'wrong'. Unfortunately, it is all too easy even for thetic theorists to slide, inadvertently, into non-naturalistic, non-reductive, moral claims, and this may well confuse us. William Paley, for example, plainly intends to defend a reductive thetic line:

> Now, because moral *obligation* depends ... upon the will of God; *right*, which is correlative to it, must depend upon the same. Right therefore signifies *consistency with the will of God.*[24]

But, naturally enough, he is inclined to think that what God does is morally right. He sees, or nearly sees, the potential vacuity, or incoherence, here; but it is not clear that he escapes unscathed.

We have wandered into the neighborhood of one form of the so-called 'naturalistic fallacy'. This might better be called the 'Reductive, Non-Reductive Waffle', or 'the Reductivist's drift towards Platonism'.

Back to the disjunctive argument. Of course thetic theorists will not grant that some deeds are naturally and immutably morally good, or whatever. On their view, if D has a moral status, it must have that status by virtue of some act of will. The burden of the argument thus falls on (3):

(3) If D has a particular moral status by virtue of an act of will, then it must, under these circumstances, be naturally and immutably morally good to conform to this will in these circumstances and thus... the thetic theory is false.

Thetic theorists must deny this. But the proper escape route seems obvious. They must hold that it is *not* 'morally good' to comply with the will which grounds 'morality'. God does not command us to obey his commands. Nor is there a human convention to the effect that we ought to comply with human conventions. Either the search for the grounds of moral obligation simply ends in human or divine acts of will, or the ultimate source of moral obligation isn't moral at all, but, say, *prudential.*

As we have seen, Paley is wonderfully clear and candid on this point. Moral obligation, like all other obligation, is grounded in self-interest. According to Paley's version of the thetic theory, a person, J, is *obliged* to do x if, and only if, J is urged to do x "... by a violent motive resulting from the command of another."[25]

Thus Paley would say that (3) is false. Thetical moral obligations do *not* require natural, and immutable, *moral* backing.

Cudworth, of course, utterly rejects the Divine Command theory.

> Did obligation to the things of natural justice, as many suppose, arise from the will and positive command of God, only by reason of punishments threatened, and rewards promised; the consequence of this would be, that no man was good and just, but only by accident, and for the sake of something else; whereas the goodness of justice or righteousness is intrinsic to the thing itself, and this is that which obligeth, (and not any thing foreign to it) it being a different species of good from that of appetite and private utility, which every man may dispense withal.[26]

NOTES

1. *The Shorter Oxford English Dictionary* defines 'thetic' as "characterized by laying down or setting forth; involving positive statement". 'Thetical' is said to mean "of the nature of or involving direct or positive statement; laid down positively or absolutely; dogmatic; arbitrary." J. A. Passmore calls the sort of theories Cudworth has in mind 'legislative'. See his, "The Moral Philosophy of Cudworth", *The Australasian Journal of Psychology and Philosophy*, Vol. XX, No. 3, Dec. 1942, pp. 161- 83. "His (Cudworth's) real enemy is a legislative ethics, whatever form it takes." p. 171. But Cudworth would, I think, include in the group he means to be attacking, theories that ground ethics and morals in human *institutions, customs* and *practices*, but do not require explicit human or divine *legislation*. The terms 'thetical' and 'thesei' are used a good number of times in the *Treatise* to designate the relevant cluster of theories.

2. Aristippus presumably held that his own immediate pleasure was good, and his pain bad, not absolutely, but *relative to himself*. I don't think we should say this makes good and bad *thetical*. Aristippus would, of course, insist that *moral* goodness and badness, like justice and injustice, are grounded in nothing more than human convention. An outline of Aristippus' epistemology can be found in Sextus Empiricus, *Against the Logicians*, The Loeb Classical Library, Vol. II, pp. 102–109.

3. Ralph Cudworth, *A Treatise concerning Eternal and Immutable Morality*, added to *The True Intellectual System of the Universe*, Printed for Thomas Tegg, London, 1845, Vol. III, p. 522. The quotation is from the analytical table of contents for Book I. I am not entirely confident that this table of contents is the work of Cudworth himself. *The True Intellectual System.* came out in English in 1678, and in Latin in 1733..

4. Ibid. Book I, Ch. 1, p. 525.

5. Hobbes, *Leviathan*, Edited by Michael Oakeshott, Basil Blackwell, Oxford, 1955, Part 1, Chap. 13, p. 83.

6. Ibid.

7. Cudworth, op. cit., p. 529.

8. Ibid.

9. See ibid. Book I, Ch.3.

10 . Ibid. Book I, Ch. 1, p. 530.

11. Ibid.

12. Ibid. Book II, Ch. 1, sec. 1, p. 540.

13. Ibid. Book IV, Ch. 6., sec., 3, p. 640.

14. Ibid. sec. 1, p. 531.

15. Ibid, secs. 1-3, pp. 531-532.

16. Another example would be the property of *having been prescribed*. A certain drug is made to have this property, with respect to a certain patient, by a particular Doctor. She (the doctor) does it by making the relevant decision, and informing the relevant people as to what she has decided.

17. Cudworth, A *Treatise Concerning Eternal and Immutable Morality*, Book 1, Chap. 2, sec. 4. Op. cit. pp. 533-534.

18. On this view, it is impossible for a frog to be transformed into a prince, or visa versa. Presumably, such a metamorphosis would destroy the original creature. I am not at all sure this doctrine is true. Suppose the transformation proceeds very slowly.

19. Hobbes says, for example, "...in every *necessary* proposition, the predicate is either equivalent to the subject, as in this, *man is a rational living creature*; or part of an equivalent name, as in this, *man is a living creature*, for the name *rational–living–creature* or *man*, is componded of these two, *rational* and *living-creature*.", *Concerning Body*, part I, ch. 3, par.10. I quote from the Molesworth edition, London: John Bohn, 1839, Vol. I, p. 38.

20. There are various elements conducive to confusion at this point. Here is one. Suppose a promise, or command, has made it obligatory that Jones now do a deed of kind K. We should not conclude that there is a deed-token of kind K, such that J is now obliged to perform that particular one. The proper conclusion would be that J is now obliged to perform a deed-token (any one he pleases) of type K.

21. Cudworth, Op. cit. Chap. 2, sec. 5; p. 535.

22. Ibid., sec. 6.,

23. Ibid., Book I, ch. 2, sec. 1,. pp. 530-531.

24. *The Works of William Paley*, Vol. II, *Moral and Political Philosophy*, printed by J. Vincent, Oxford, England, 1838, Book II, chap. 9, p. 55.

25. Paley, Op. cit. Chap. 2, p. 38.

26. Ralph Cudworth, *The True Intellectual System of the Universe*, London, printed for Thomas Tegg, London, 1845, Chap. 5, sec. 5, p. 512.

I n *Utilitarianism,* Mill suggests that Kant sometimes employs something like the Utilitarian principle. Mill expresses Kant's 'first principle' as: "So act that the rule on which thou actest would admit of being adopted as a law by all rational beings."(*Utilitarianism,* Ch. 1, par. 4) He then writes:

> But when he begins to deduce from this precept any of the actual duties of morality, he fails, almost grotesquely, to show that there would be any contradiction, any logical (not to say physical) impossibility, in the adoption by all rational beings of the most outrageously immoral rules of conduct. All he shows is that the *consequences* of their universal adoption would be such as no one would choose to incur.

This is plainly compatible with an admission that there are *some* immoral maxims that *cannot* (as a matter of logic or physics) be made universal laws. All Mill needs to make his point is that in regard to *some* immoral maxims Kant is forced to fall back on the fact that universal compliance with them would produce widespread, if not universal, misery. We 'cannot' will such a maxim to be a universal law *because we want to be happy,* not because the idea of universal compliance with it is incoherent.

I assume that Mill has Kant's 'Formula of Universal Law' in mind. But, if so, he is misrepresenting it in a fairly obvious, but natural, way. The proposed test requires us to be able to *will* that the maxim be a universal law. In the *Groundwork of the Metaphysics of Morals,* Kant sketches two cases in which a bad maxim *could* be made a universal law, but there would be a 'contradiction in the will' of anyone who tried to *will* it as a universal law. Let's look at the cases.

The Unhelpful Man

Consider an unhelpful, selfish, man who governs himself by the maxim: "Let each be as happy as heaven wills or as he can make himself; I shall take nothing from him nor even envy him; only I do not care to contribute anything to his welfare or to his assistance in need."
Kant says, in effect, that there is no contradiction in the idea of this being a universal law of nature; but then adds:

> ... it is still impossible to *will* that such a principle hold everywhere as a law of nature. For, a will that decided this would conflict with itself, since many cases could occur in which one would need the love and sympathy of others and in which, by such a law of nature arisen from his own will, he would rob himself of all hope of the assistance he wishes for himself. (GMM 4:423)

Clearly Kant is talking about the consequences that would follow if the maxim in question were to be a universal law. We sometimes need love and sympathy from others and need their help. If this maxim were a universal law, we would seldom if ever get the love, sympathy, and help, we need. I take it we want these things because we (quite properly) want to avoid misery, pain, loneliness, and so on, i.e. we want to be happy.

> ...the natural end that all human beings have is their own happiness. (GMM 4:430)

As I understand it, a human will that willed the maxim in question as a universal law would conflict with itself in that it wills a state of affairs in which she (the willer) would often not get the love, etc. she needs and also now (naturally) wills that she get these things when she needs them.

Strictly speaking, Kant is not assessing the morality of an act by means of its consequences. His claim is not even that the unhelpful man is acting immorally because the consequences of universal compliance with the relevant maxim would be very unpleasant (for all of us).

Nevertheless, as I see it, those unpleasant consequences *do* enter into the demonstration that the unhelpful man is acting immorally. Mill is right to that extent.

It may be difficult to believe that Kant thinks we all necessarily will our own happiness. Nevertheless, this idea is plainly in the text:

> There is, however, *one* end that can be presupposed as actual in the case of all rational beings.., and therefore one purpose that they not merely *could* have but that we can safely presuppose that all actually *do have* by a natural necessity, and that purpose is happiness. The hypothetical imperative that represents the practical necessity of an action as a means to the promotion of happiness is *assertoric*. It may be set forth not merely as necessary to some uncertain merely possible purpose but to a purpose that can be presupposed surely and a priori in the case of every human being, because it belongs to his essence. (GMM 4:415)

The Talented Man

Consider the talented man who prefers not to develop his talents (GMM 4:423). In trying to will his maxim as a universal law he bumps into the fact that "as a rational being he necessarily wills that all the capacities in him be developed, since they serve him and are given to him for all sorts of possible purposes."

(Notice Kant's assumption that an individual's talents are given him for a purpose—presumably by a wise and benevolent God. Without this assumption, one might suppose that, by chance, one had, say, at least one talent one didn't really need, and didn't have time to develop.)

How, in this case, does the man's will 'contradict itself'? I take it he is, in effect, trying to will both that his talents not be developed and, at the same time, to will that they be developed. As a rational being he necessarily wills that all his talents be developed (?) and as a lazy pleasure seeker he tries to will that they not be developed.

So, allegedly, there is contradiction in his will, and his maxim is morally unacceptable.

Absurd Consequences

My impression is that Kant is in trouble.

Surely a virtuous person can will to sacrifice her own happiness, or the development of (some of) her own talents, in the service of others? But how can this comply with the Universal Law test? Given that as a rational being she necessarily wills that her talents be developed, and necessarily wants to be happy, there must be a contradiction in her attempt to will her virtuous, self-sacrificial, maxim.

(I am assuming that she doesn't believe in a God who will reward her after death, and doesn't believe in Karma, or whatever. Perhaps she is a skeptic about these things. She wills her sacrifice whether or not there is a God, or whatever.)

As we have seen, Kant holds that rational creatures necessarily will their own happiness and necessarily will that all their talents and capacities be developed. Consider a morally heroic young woman who is about to sacrifice her life in order to save five innocent children. Her maxim is something like: "If I can save several innocent young lives by doing so, I will sacrifice my own life (even if there is no God, or whatever.)."

In it's universal form it would be something like: "If one can save many innocent young lives by doing so, one must sacrifice one's own life (whether or not there is a God or whatever)."

Here is a possible case, in probabilistic form: The woman is alone on the seashore in an isolated region. She sees a raft with five children on it drifting out to sea. They are screaming for help. She is a fairly good swimmer; but she knows that she has a serious heart condition. If she tries to save the children, e.g. by swimming out and back to rescue each one, there is a very good chance that the struggle will kill her. Nevertheless she plunges into the water.

The Universal Law test says: Act only according to that maxim by which you can at the same time will that it should become a universal law.

Can the maxim of the morally heroic young woman pass this test? My suggestion is that (under our suppositions) it cannot. This is because her attempt to will the universalization of her maxim generates a contradiction in her will. As a rational creature she wills to be happy (now and in the future) and to have a chance to develop all her talents. (She has musical ability and had hoped to take piano lessons. She had intended to learn Latin; and so on). But, given universal compliance with her maxim, she could, conceivably, find herself in a situation roughly like the one she is actually in—one requiring heroic self-sacrifice. Hence, to will the universalization of her maxim requires her to will and not will the sacrifice. That is to say, her heroic maxim violates the Universal Law test. Hence, presumably, it would be *morally wrong* for her to save the five children.

I am suggesting that this sort of case generates exactly the same sort of 'contradiction in the will' that is (allegedly) generated by the unhelpful man's maxim and the talented man's maxim. I conclude that the Universal Law test, as Kant uses it, yields morally absurd results.

In a discussion of the first formulation of the categorical imperative, John Rawls raises a similar objection:

> ..it rejects all maxims leading to any form of the precept of mutual aid. The reason is that any such precept will sometimes enjoin us to help others when they are in need. But situations may arise in any associated adjusted social world in which we very much want not to help others, unless the precept involved is quite trivial. Our circumstances may be such that doing so is extremely inconvenient, given our current plans. ...by a law originating from our own will, we would have prevented ourselves from doing what we very much want..[1]

One might say that Kant's procedure is yielding the correct result in regard to the heroic woman, since we have no moral duty to be heroic. But the situation is worse than that. Kant's procedure yields the outrageous conclusion that what the heroic woman is doing is *morally wrong*.

Was Kant a Realist?

Kant is *not* a realist in regard to some property, M, if he holds that, for every entity, e, such that e has property M, the fact that e has M is *constituted*, at least in part, by our representing e as having M, or, perhaps, by our obligation to represent e as having M.

For instance, suppose that, on Kant's view, our 'being intrinsically valuable' is constituted by our valuing ourselves and each other as ends, or, perhaps, by our *obligation* to value ourselves and each other in this way. This would *not* be realism in regard to our value. (It might still be realism in regard to our having this obligation. That is to say, Kant might yet hold that our *having* this obligation is not constituted by our *taking ourselves* to have this obligation, or by our *imposing* this obligation on ourselves.)

On the other hand, suppose Kant thinks that we are intrinsically valuable because we are creatures that have moral obligations. Hence we are valuable, *whether or not we value each other and ourselves*. In that case, he is a realist in this regard.

I do not know how Kant stands on this matter. Sometimes he does seem to imply that intrinsic value is conferred on a thing by it's being valued.[2]

Now consider the property of *being accountable*. According to Kant, this is a property we all have. Is it our holding ourselves accountable that constitutes our accountability? In so far as this question makes sense, I don't think it expresses Kant's view. According to Kant we are accountable because we have (Kantian) free will. We have noumenal freedom to establish in ourselves a 'fundamental maxim' that directs, or tends to direct, our policy in regard to happiness and virtue.[3] Even if we choose not to exercise this freedom—choose, by default, to be happiness seeking machines—the choice is ours; and, on Kant's view, we could, in principle, still choose otherwise. Our accountability is an essential feature of our nature. It is not a feature of something we construct, or a matter of how we choose to view ourselves.

I don't see how Kant could be anything but a *realist* in regard to accountability. Furthermore, this looks like an *irreducibly moral* property.

If this is correct, then, as I understand it, Kant is not a full-scale 'Kantian constructionist' in Rawls' sense of the term. Rawls says things like the following:

> The parties in the original position do not agree on what the moral facts are, as if there already were such facts. It is not that, being situated impartially, they have a clear and undistorted view of a prior and independent moral order. Rather (for constructivism), there is no such order, and therefore no such facts apart from the procedure of construction as a whole; the facts are identified by the principles that result.[4]

And:

> We have arrived at the idea that objectivity is not given by 'the point of view of the universe,' to use Sidgwick's phrase. Objectivity is to be understood by reference to a suitably constructed social point of view, an example of which is the framework provided by the procedure of the original position.[5]

NOTES

1. John Rawls, *Lectures on the History of Moral Philosophy*, Edited by Barbara Herman, Harvard University Press, Cambridge, Mass. 2000, p. 173. Here Rawls also provides a modification of the categorical imperative procedure (or, perhaps, an alternative to it) which, he thinks, might do the job.

2. For instance: "...if the world consisted of mere lifeless, or even in part of living but irrational beings, its existence would have no worth, because in it there would be no Being who would have the least concept of what worth is." [*Critique of Judgment*, section 87, towards the beginning.]

3. See, for instance, Kant's *Religion within the Boundaries of Mere Reason*, 6:31-32.

4. Rawls "Kantian Constructivism in Moral Theory" in *John Rawls: Collected papers*, Edited by Samuel Freeman, Harvard University Press, Cambridge, Massachusetts, 1999, p. 354.

5. Ibid. p. 356.

APPENDIX D   MILL

In this note I comment on two features of Mill's ethical theory: (1) Mill's metaethics, and (2) Mill's moral psychology.

Mill's Metaethics

It is fairly clear that Mill does not want to be a Platonist. He certainly rejects the 'intuitionism' of his day.[1]

In his paper "Professor Sedgwick's Discourse on the Studies of the University of Cambridge" Mill discusses, among other things, Sedgwick's attack on Paley, and, more specifically, Sedgwick's claim that Paley denies the existence of the 'moral sense' in man.[2] There is, Mill says, no dispute in regard to our having moral feelings and making moral judgments. That we have such feelings and make such judgments is obvious.

> But there are two theories respecting the origin of these phenomena, which have divided philosophers from the earliest ages of philosophy. One is, that the distinction between right and wrong is an ultimate and inexplicable fact; that we perceive this distinction, as we perceive the distinction of colors, by a peculiar faculty; and that the pleasures and pains, the desires and aversions, consequent upon this perception, are all ultimate facts in our nature; as much so as the pleasures and pains, or the desires and aversions, of which sweet or bitter tastes, pleasing or grating sounds, are the object. This is called the theory of the moral sense—or of moral instincts—or of eternal and immutable morality—or of intuitive principles of morality—or by many other names, to the differences between which, those who adopt the theory often attach great importance, but which, for our present purpose, may all be considered as equivalent.

> The other theory is, that the ideas of right and wrong, and the feelings which attach themselves to those ideas, are not ultimate facts, but may be explained and accounted for; are not the result of any peculiar law of our nature, but of the same laws on which all our other complex ideas and feelings depend: that the distinction between moral and immoral acts is not a peculiar and inscrutable property in the acts themselves, which we perceive by a sense, as we perceive colors by our sight; but flows from the ordinary properties of those actions, for the recognition of which we need no other faculty than our intellects and our bodily senses. And the particular property in actions, which constitutes them moral or immoral, in the opinion of those who hold this theory (all of them, at least, who need here be noticed), is the influence of those actions, and of the dispositions from which they emanate, upon human happiness."[3]

Mill goes on to commit himself clearly and unequivocally to the second approach. He is an empiricist—and, perhaps, a reductive naturalist realist. The 'immorality' of an immoral deed just is, or is constituted by, its tendency to produce pain and to spring from a disposition which tends to generate such actions. There is nothing 'queer,' or Platonistic, here.

Mill apparently takes belief in a peculiar kind of perception as a distinctive feature of the sort of theory he rejects. In fact he seems to regard this as the central issue: Do we perceive right and wrong by means of a special sense, or do we recognize right and wrong by means of our intellect and our ordinary senses?

I do not regard this as the central issue. I think that intuitionism, or at least Platonism, is compatible with a denial of any special moral sense: see Chapter Nineteen.

Given these remarks from the paper on Sedgwick's Discourse, Mill's exposition in *Utilitarianism* seems unclear, or even, perhaps, misleading. There we are told that the general happiness provides the one and only appropriate criterion of right and wrong. Actions are morally right to the extent that they tend to promote the general happiness, wrong to the extent that they tend to promote general pain.[4] Sidgwick (the Platonist) would, of course, agree. But Sidgwick takes the claim to state an absolute, irreducible, moral fact. This, apparently, is *not* Mill's view.

Perhaps Mill's claim is partly sociological and historical, and partly a suggestion in regard to social engineering.[5] On careful study of the various kinds of behavior, the various traits of character, the various practices, and laws, that have been called 'good', 'virtuous', 'just', and so on in various human societies at different times, we see a wide variety—in fact an apparent hodge-podge. What, if anything, holds these things together? Here is an hypothesis: x is called 'good' (or whatever) in society S, at time t, because, roughly, x is beneficial to S at time t. It serves S's purposes. It is conducive to the happiness of the members of S (or, at least, of some dominant group within S). It is *'expedient'* there and then to them.[6] Presumably, it is this which, in fact, we have been talking about in assessing actual, or possible, systems of 'virtues', moral codes, and so on. We have been judging these things on the basis of how well they serve the interests, the happiness, of the members of the group that adopts, or maintains, that system.

This view is available to a reductive realist, and, for that matter, to a disenchanter. A particular system of ethics, we are told, is a product of conscious, or unconscious, social engineering. At it's best, it is designed to maximize something the members of the society, or group, very much want. If, someday we encounter a society whose members are only, in the last analysis, interested in maximizing the amount of mayonnaise there is in the world, then it makes sense for their 'folk ethics' to be designed in such a way as to maximize the production and storage of mayonnaise. A 'virtue,' among these people, will presumably be a trait conducive to this end.

I have argued that bad behavior is sometimes conducive to our happiness and the long-term satisfaction of our desires. Presumably the same thing applies to social groups. A society, or a sub-culture, of happiness seekers may find itself in a situation in which a nasty policy towards some outsiders would be profitable. Perhaps, then, a well-designed 'folk-ethics' for such a group should encourage this sort of behavior and provide painful internal sanctions for those who do not comply.

Suppose that rationality evolved simultaneously in two species of animals one of which was the primary predator of the other—sheep and wolves, as it were. Now both groups are developing systems of ethics. Couldn't it be the case that the 'wolves' would be happier, and, in some sense, better off, if they occasionally permitted themselves to hunt and kill 'sheep', rather than treating them with the respect the 'sheep' might think themselves to deserve?

Mill's actual view seems to be that our ethical system should be designed in such a way as to maximize happiness taking *everyone* into account, all human beings, all rational beings, and even, "..so far as the nature of things admits, the whole sentient creation."[7] He may think, mistakenly, that compliance with such a system must maximally serve the interest of all the subgroups among these creatures. On the other hand, he might, surreptitiously, be relying on an irreducible Platonistic moral intuition concerning fairness, justice, or the objective, absolute, value of pleasure as opposed to pain.

Mill's Moral Psychology

In Chapter Two, paragraph 19, of *Utilitarianism*, Mill considers the claim that his kind of ethics is too exacting - demands too much of us. Thus, for instance, some critics say that it is absurd to require ".... that people shall always act from the inducement of promoting the general interest of society." According to Mill, these critics confuse (1) the rule of action with (2) the motive of action. "It is the business of ethics to tell us what are our duties, or by what test we may know them; but no system of ethics requires that the sole motive of all we do shall be a feeling of duty; on the contrary, ninety-nine hundredths of all our actions are done from other motives, and rightly so done if the rule of duty does not condemn them."

In a footnote to this paragraph, Mill stresses another distinction. *Motive* must not be confused with *Intention*. "The morality of the action depends entirely upon the intention—that is, upon what the agent *wills to do*. But the motive, that is, the feeling which makes him will so to do, if it makes no difference in the act, makes none in the morality: though it makes a great difference in our moral estimation of the agent, especially if it indicates a good or bad habitual *disposition*—a bent of character from which useful, or from which hurtful actions are likely to arise."

These quotes from *Utilitarianism* give us some idea of an important aspect of Mill's theory that, I think, is not much stressed in that work, and is easily overlooked. There is more about motives elsewhere. Here is a significant passage from his "Remarks on Bentham's Philosophy":

> That the actions of sentient beings are wholly determined by pleasure and pain, is the fundamental principle from which he [Bentham] starts; and thereupon Mr. Bentham creates a *motive*, and an *interest*, corresponding to each pleasure or pain, and affirms that our actions are determined by our *interests*, by the *preponderant* interest, by the *balance* of motives. Now if this only means what was before asserted, that our actions are determined by pleasure and pain, that simple and unambiguous mode of stating the proposition is preferable. But under cover of the obscurer phrase a meaning creeps in, both to the author's mind and the reader's, which goes much farther, and is entirely false: that all our acts are determined by pains and pleasures *in prospect*, pains and pleasures to which we look forward as the *consequences* of our acts. This, as a universal truth, can in no way be maintained. The pain or pleasure which determines our conduct is as frequently one which *precedes* the moment of action as one which follows it. A man *may*, it is true, be deterred, in circumstances of temptation, from perpetrating a crime, by his dread of the punishment, or of the remorse, which he fears he may have to endure *after* the guilty act; and in that case we may say with some kind of propriety, that his conduct is swayed by the balance of motives; or, if you will, of interests. But the case *may* be, and is to the full as likely to be, that he recoils from the very thought of committing the act; the idea of placing himself in such a situation is so painful, that he cannot dwell upon it long enough to have even the physical power of perpetrating the crime. His conduct is determined by pain; but by a pain which precedes the act, not by one which is expected to follow it. Not only *may* this be so, but unless it be so, the man is not really virtuous. The fear of pain *consequent* upon the act, cannot arise, unless there be *deliberation*; and the man as well as "the woman who deliberates," is in imminent danger of being lost.[8]

Note (1) Mill does *not* think that a good person's motive in doing what is right is, typically, the hope of generating pleasure and minimizing pain (taking everyone into consideration). Often, there is little, or no, thought of the consequences, and this is as it should be. (2) Mill's theory of moral psychology (unlike that of Helvetius and Bentham) is not egoistic psychological hedonism. Or, at least, that's not his view if EPH is the theory that our behavior is always ultimately determined by our desire to maximize our future pleasure and minimize our future pain. (3) His moral psychology enables him to explain self-sacrifice. In effect, his good, but tempted, man is a sort of self-sacrificer. He presumably sees perfectly well that the bad deed he is contemplating would almost certainly yield him a greater surplus of pleasure over pain (taking the long view) than would his abstention from it. Nevertheless, he is, so to speak, frozen into abstention by the pain he feels (now) in contemplating what he must do to gain that surplus.

Does the moral wrongness of the contemplated deed play any real role here? Mill doesn't say so. What seems to matter is the social conditioning which has brought it about that thought of the deed produces a painful blockage. Even if the deed in question had, in fact, been perfectly harmless—the violation of an absurd taboo—and the man had seen it as such, he might have felt the same sort of inhibition.

NOTES

1. See, for instance, Mill's *Utilitarianism*, Chapter I, paragraph 3 and 4.

2. The person referred to here is Adam Sedgwick, not Henry Sidgwick.

3 John Stuart Mill, *Essays on Ethics, Religion and Society, Collected Works of John Stuart Mill*, Volume X, University of Toronto Press, 1969, p. 51.

4. See *Utilitarianism*, Chapter II, paragraph 2. This is, perhaps, only a rough first approximation of the theory - there may be further complications. Perhaps, strictly speaking, an act is morally wrong – we have a moral obligation not to do it—if, and only if, optimal social engineering would provide internal (and, perhaps, external) sanctions (punishments) for acts of that type. (The degree of excellence of the social engineering is, of course, measured by its success in maximizing the general happiness.) This is a reading of Mill defended by David Lyons in his *Rights, Welfare, and Mill's Moral Theory*, Oxford University Press, Oxford, 1994. Note the counterfactual 'would.' This could be taken as an indication of a slide towards, if not a plunge into, Platonism. It seems to make the theory rest upon the moral claim that our actual, present day, behavior ought to comply with the moral rules that would constitute the folk ethics of an optimally designed society (even if our own actual society is far from optimal). But why should we do this? Do we somehow just 'see' that this is the right way to proceed?

5. This is, roughly, how I read Helvetius. An ethical system is, and should be, designed to serve the interest of some actual group, society, or nation.

6. Mill often uses this term in *Utilitarianism*. See especially Chapter Five.

7. See *Utilitarianism*, Chapter II, par. 10.

8. This is from the *Collected Works of John Stuart Mill*, Volume X, *Essays on Ethics, Religion and Society*, Ed. by J. M. Robson, University of Toronto Press, Routledge & Kegan Paul, 1969, pp. 12–13.

Key Terms

Disenchantment Theories (moral)

These theories, in effect, include the claim that 'morality' (i.e. *genuine* morality) is a kind of hoax. We are swindled into believing that there are absolute, objective, moral rules, standards, values, and so on.

Our assumption has been that there are just two relevant kinds of Disenchantment theories:

Thin Rationalism:

This is the view that 'thin', instrumental, reason provides us with the right, rationally defensible, standards and procedures for decision making. On this basis we can decide when it makes sense to comply with our local 'folk ethics', and when it doesn't. Thin Rationalism includes the claim that the ultimate normative principles of 'thin' reason are absolute and objective. In other words, it includes Realism in regard to the principles of 'thin' practical reason. In principle, this Realism could be reductive, but I have no clear idea as to what such a theory might look like. Consequently, I have assumed that thin rationalists are realists, but not reductionists, in regard to practical rationality. That is to say, I have assumed that they are Platonists in this regard.

Total Disenchantment:

Disenchanters of this sort reject Realism in regard morality and in regard to practical reason in general. They 'disenchant' even prudential norms.

Dualism (of practical reason)

Anselm held that there are two basic 'wills' in us. One is a will for 'justice' (moral rightness), and the other is a will for happiness. Somehow, over the years, this dualism got transmuted into the claim that practical reason is divided into

(1) *Conscience* and

(2) *Self-love* [as in the work of Bishop Butler].

In Sidgwick (the last of the great dualists) this was a dualism between two general, rational, strategies for the conduct of life. So far as he could see, this constituted an irresolvable dilemma (unless there is a God). If both are equally defensible in the court of reason, then neither one is, in itself, whole-heartedly endorsed by reason.

Full scale Morality

By this I mean the sort of morality that, in some situations, requires sacrifice of one's own happiness, or even one's life. I also assume that it is, in general, quite demanding. Full-scale moral systems reject the idea of supererogatory deeds. In full-scale morality, *nothing* is 'above and beyond' the call of duty.

Genuine Morality

This is the realm that Platonists accept as objective and real, but disenchanters reject as illusion. It is the domain in dispute between these two meta-ethical theories. The idea that people everywhere 'count,' or have 'rights,' belongs to this disputed domain.

Naturalism

(1) The world view according to which the only *real* individuals, properties, relations, events, and so on are those of the types mentioned in the laws and explanations offered by genuine areas of science—physics, chemistry, biology, and the like, or *'reducible to'* such individuals, properties, and so on.

(2) The doctrine that philosophy in general, and epistemology in particular, is, or should be, 'scientific', and, in fact, a chapter of natural science. [See W. V. Quines' "Epistemology Naturalized", in *Ontological Relativity & Other essays*, Columbia University Press, New York, 1969.]

(3) [In ethics] the theory that all legitimate moral and ethical properties, relations, etc. can be 'reduced to' non-moral, non-ethical, (scientific?) properties, relations, etc.

Platonism

For the most part, in this book, the term is used to refer to theories of morality that take at least some basic moral properties to be real—not mind-dependent—and to be irreducible to non-moral properties. The idea is that morality is 'autonomous.' It is, perhaps, useful to divide Platonism into (at least) two kinds:

(1) *Intuitionism*

Intuitionists are Platonists who hold, in addition, that there are at least *two* distinct self-evident, irreducible, fundamental moral principles. Butler (at least in his later years) and Ross are examples.

(2) *Non-intuitionistic Platonism*

This, obviously, includes any Platonistic moral theory that rejects intuitionism.

Possibility

(1) *Epistemic possibility* (*sense A*): A proposition, P, is epistemically possible relative to someone, S, at time t, if and only if, for all S knows at t, P is true.

Epistemic possibility in this sense does **not** imply **metaphysical** possibility.

There are, presumably, lots of falsehoods about other planets in distant galaxies that might be true for all any of us now know. These falsehoods are 'epistemically' possible (relative to us) in sense A.

(2) *Epistemic possibility* (*sense B*): A proposition, P, is epistemically possible (relative to us) in this sense if and only if, it is not true that we can know a priori that not P.

(3) *Metaphysical* possibility is, by hypothesis, not epistemic. All metaphysically possible worlds (ways things could be) are *epistemically* possible in sense B. But it doesn't go the other way around. There are epistemically possible worlds (in this sense) that are not metaphysically possible. Metaphysically possible worlds are those epistemically possible (sense B) worlds that satisfy all the constraints imposed by brute metaphysical facts.

(4) The realm of **physical** possibility is delineated by the laws of physics that govern the actual world. *Physically* possible worlds (i.e. naturally possible worlds) are the metaphysically possible worlds that obey those laws.

Rationalism (in Ethics)

(1) The view that the Ethical-Moral *rightness* of an action, or policy, is the same thing as *its reasonableness*, its *rationality*. 'The *right* is the *Rational*.' According to this theory, when we ask whether or not Walter did the right thing we are asking whether or not Walter's deed 'makes sense' all things considered.

(2) The view that rationality requires agent-neutral reasons for action, and that these, in turn impose morality, or at least its core—the duties we owe one another—upon us.

(3) The view that through the exercise of reason we can work out what is morally right and what is wrong. Inexplicable insight is not needed, nor is this, basically, a matter of natural human *feelings*, '*moral sense*', or social practice.

> (Note that (3) does not entail (1) or (2). It is quite possible to accept (3) but deny (1) and (2). For instance, one might do so on the grounds that reason allows us to work out both what is in our own long term interest and what is morally right, and, furthermore, equally recommends both the prudent pattern of life and the moral, and thus does not insist on either one—or, if you prefer, insists on both.)

Realism [In regard to ethics/morals]

The doctrine that there are some objective moral/ethical truths which are not, so to speak, *made* 'truths' by our taking them to be true, or by our eventually, after long consideration, taking them to be true (Idealism, Pragmatism), or by our practices, conventions, or whatever.

> (Note: if there are true moral assertions, and all such assertions can be analyzed into ('reduced to') biological, or psychological, claims that are objective and scientifically acceptable, the result is a *naturalistic* form of moral realism. Similarly, if all those assertions can be analyzed into objective theological claims, as in the Divine Command theory, then the result is a *supernaturalistic* form of realism.)

Reason*s* [some kinds of]:

Suppose that J's reason for doing D, gives J good reason to do D (that is, provides sufficient prima facie justification for J's doing D). This reason is said to be *agent-relative* if, and only if, for every rational agent, R, having this reason for doing D would give R prima facie justification for doing D. The reason is said to be *agent-neutral* if, and only if, for every rational agent, R, knowledge of J's reason for doing D gives R prima facie justification for aiding and abetting J in doing D, or perhaps, doing D on J's behalf. In addition, I have suggested that we should say that a reason is *strictly agent-relative* if it is agent-relative, but not agent-neutral.

Super-naturalism

The view that there are rational, or at least sentient, entities by nature forever inaccessible to scientific investigation or comprehension; or that some of the 'basic' physical events in our universe are, or were, directly caused by non-physical mental events, and are thus miraculous. Alternatively: the doctrine that some such exalted property as truth, wickedness, or holiness, has direct 'basic' effects, might also count as 'supernaturalism'.

INDEX